THE LIVING GOD OF
NOWHERE AND NOTHING

Books by Nels F. S. Ferré
Published by The Westminster Press

The Living God of Nowhere and Nothing
A Theology for Christian Education

THE LIVING GOD OF
NOWHERE AND NOTHING

by

NELS F. S. FERRÉ

THE WESTMINSTER PRESS
PHILADELPHIA

LIBRARY OF CONGRESS CATALOG CARD NO. 67–18727

PUBLISHED BY THE WESTMINSTER PRESS®
PHILADELPHIA, PENNSYLVANIA

PRINTED IN THE UNITED STATES OF AMERICA

To Vaughan Dabney

With thanks for his unflagging
friendship, generous support and
loyal expectation for over three
decades.

Contents

vii

THE LIVING GOD OF
NOWHERE AND NOTHING

Preface

THE LIVING GOD OF NOWHERE AND NOTHING speaks to our main modern questions: the death of God, Christological humanism, the new hermeneutic, the new morality, the turn to social ethics, and whether the Christian faith has any permanent message. Each chapter as well as the Appendix centers respectively on one of these critical issues.

I am with the 'death of God' theologians completely in their rejection of the Western tradition of substance. They are right in maintaining that God cannot be worshipped or legitimately conceived either as the Supreme Being or the Cosmic Personality. To do so is to forfeit God's being infinite; it is in effect to make God a 'thing' with external relations, a Being among other beings. The theologians who espouse process philosophy have likewise seen this danger and avoid it, but they do so at the expense of an adequate understanding of God who as Ultimate Concern and as the Source of Significance is both the Ground and Goal of life. The living God of the Bible can no longer be understood in traditionalistic terms, because the so-called Christian doctrines presuppose a false framework. Thus I both accept and reject the 'death of God' theology; accept with alacrity its wrecking of the false Western metaphysics that has carried the Christian faith, but reject its negative and tentative conclusions, showing instead that a new day has dawned for the Christian faith in which we can live, think and worship with honesty.

In place of either substance or process I have presented the concept of God as Love and Personal Spirit, not only for devotion but also as the fundamental category of thought, the 'field-encompassing field' with maximum facility to constitute the final framework for both thought and life. I have already written hundreds of pages supporting the thought of this chapter in the Systematic, to which my position as Scholar-in-Residence at Parsons College enables me to devote full time.

1

The second chapter, the A. S. Peake Memorial Lecture which I gave in Britain in the summer of 1966, deals with Christology. Usually the choice is between an outmoded two-substance doctrine and the new Christological humanism that rejects the dimension of transcendence. With a new, more adequate framework, arising from within the Christian faith itself, the whole question is revolutionized. We simply cannot keep on the old debate about the deity and the humanity of Christ in substance terms. I welcome attempts to rework Christology in terms of process philosophy in spite of the weaknesses inherent in that philosophy. What substance, process and personalistic modes of thinking stand for, however, are fulfilled one and all in the ampler power for identity and distinction within the framework of God as Spirit, to which I am now devoting much time in redefining the meaning of such topics as eternity and time, God's presence and absence, uniqueness and finality. The present chapter, while not specifically dealing with the categories, cannot be grasped apart from the sense of the new perspective that underlies the whole discussion. During my recent lecturing at British universities, for instance, I observed that in the matter of Christology the problems invariably boiled down to the fact that substance thinking was assumed. I foresee a total, constructive revolution in Christological formulation and in theological adequacy for both proclamation and life as soon as we begin radically to think in terms of the New Testament categories as themselves the framework for all thought.

The interpretation of the Bible is crucial for the Christian faith. For one thing, we have to go beyond the liberal-fundamentalist debate; we also have to declare outdated all attempts to deal with the Bible as isolated from general thought and from the professions of the other world religions. The orthodox claim that the Bible is truth from God must stand, but so must the liberal insistence on openness to all truth in secular knowledge. We cannot avoid the question either in terms of existential versus propositional truth or in terms of linguistic analysis as opposed to metaphysics. Both approaches have some truth, but are basically dodges or makeshifts. I have tried to discuss the question in terms of a postliberal, post-neo-orthodox seriousness that will deal with both the internal and the external problems of the Bible. We have to live in a new day that is open to all truth; the Bible understood from within its own central reality and message is both definitive as God's revelation and yet ever open to all truth that God is publishing in his ever fresh editions of needed truth for each generation and for all the world.

The new reformation in morals has the Christian community both agog and adrift. Can we live by rules and regulations? Can we live without them? Is Christian conduct a matter of objective or subjective directives? Or both? In this chapter I point to the master model for Christian conduct that is at the same time adequately directive and yet creatively flexible. We have more than a rudder; we have also a motor. Both meaning and motivation find fulfilment. A critic who read this chapter was disgusted because I mentioned such trivial matters as smoking and drinking, and is there not now a new freedom even in sex? My answer is that these questions are personally real to millions of people, and they simply cannot be dismissed as of no importance even to the most sophisticated. I hope that I have dealt a deathblow, as far as writing can, to all moralisms and offered the full freedom of the Gospel, but that the writing is responsible as well as releasing.

The title of the chapter on the church and communism really should read simply 'Christ-community.' I felt that this word was too pious and fought it until my very last redrafting, for I am here dealing with all the secular questions of nation, race and war. Fortunately, it is now possible to discuss these questions with some degree of constructive response. I abhor totalitarianism and deplore Marxism as misleading ideology, but we cannot dismiss worldwide communism in those terms. The drive behind communism is the drive to full freedom for all and for full participation in the potential economy of eventual abundance. Teilhard de Chardin is right: we must get the drive to totalization from one side in the cold war without the by-product of totalitarianism; and the drive to complexification from the other side without individualism. This chapter will make many 'see red', but the red they ought to see is the full Christian impact on all of life. Can the atonement mean less than that for the modern world?

3

This is a radical stand for all social aspects of life, but a radically Christian one. It advocates full democracy for all life and for all peoples. We must dare a new creative day not only for nation and for race, but also for property. I give no full blueprints but I do offer a mood and definitive directives from within the implications of the Christian faith itself. Hence, Christ-community!

The Appendix gives a straight answer to a topic assigned me by the American Theological Society—What is permanent in the Christian faith? Some will say that by maintaining that the Christian faith has a permanent *Gestalt* as surely as do Marxism and Freudianism, I am excluding those who no longer believe in God or in Incarnation. I simply state a historical fact as to the nature of the faith. I do not judge the intention of those who reject both God and Incarnation, or God as Spirit, Love and personal Purpose in Jesus Christ, the Incarnate Universal Word, nor do I insist that, if they make even the human Jesus as the Christ central to their thought, they have no right as honest thinkers to call themselves Christian. I do maintain, however, that historically the Christian faith cannot be distorted at will or reduced to any mere good intention without words losing their meaning and faith its force.

In the past I have written for three groups. Some books, like *The Christian Understanding of God,* have been for scholars; others for ministers, like *Searchlights on Contemporary Theology;* and others for laymen, such as *Strengthening the Spiritual Life.* I seem called to cover the full scope of need. But THE LIVING GOD OF NOWHERE AND NOTHING is addressed, like Bishop Robinson's *Honest to God,* to all three groups, although laymen will have to dig through (or skip over!) the first chapter, which, because of its philosophical content, had to be written in a different dimension. Numberless people are willing, I believe, to spend some time and effort on this central theological problem of our day.

The first four chapters were given as the John Willson Lectures at West Texas State University. Seeing the vast auditorium filled with students for the four days, with some even standing, proved to me that modern students care and want not only debunking but something to stand for and to live

4

by. The material was given also as the John Lectures at Memphis Theological Seminary, Memphis, Tennessee, at the national ministers' gathering of the Cumberland Presbyterian Church. Again it formed the substance of the Southwestern Lectures, at Southwestern University in Georgetown, Texas. The A. S. Peake Memorial Lectures, to which I have already attributed Chapter II, are held at the Annual Conference of the British Methodist Church. My students at Andover Newton will recognize how I developed some of this material in my classes there. To all the persons connected with these lectures my deep and continued thanks.

Most of the book is in print for the first time, with the following exceptions: Part of Chapter I appeared in *Theology Today;* part of Chapter V in the *Journal of Religious Thought* of Howard University, Washington, D.C., where the substance of the material was given in two lectures at their annual Pastors' Convocation. The Appendix has been published in *Interpretation* and I am glad to include it here for the wider reading public.

Since I set out to write this book a radical change has come into my life with the generous invitation of Parsons College to become Scholar-in-Residence, a position which will enable me to devote nearly full time to creative scholarship. I have been for so long a part of Andover Newton Theological School that I had thought nothing in the world could induce me to move, but President Millard Roberts' promise to support fully my undertaking to provide, under God, a theology for a universal faith won me for this exceptional opportunity.

It gives me peculiar pleasure to publish with The Westminster Press. For many years I have been connected with them in minor capacities but now to publish a second volume with them concentrates my indebtedness.

My wife again has assisted me in every way. She has patiently read and typed several drafts with a watchful eye for clarity and ease of style. I have long ago given up trying to say how much I owe her! I am grateful to Myrna Marie Read for typing the final draft. To all who have helped me, to Parsons College, and especially to God for the privilege of serving him, I am continually thankful.

N. F. S. F.

Chapter I

God without Theism

MIXED drinks can cause malaise; a far more serious malady results from mixed theological perspectives. The modern age suffers from such a mixture, resulting in confusion, sappage of meaning and enervated motivation. We are not sure of God, that he is, who he is, and what he wills. Nor should we be, in the light of the inconsistencies we have been accepting in his place, and in the face of the guilt of our wicked and frivolous days. Our day is doomed. We cannot keep disintegrating and not perish. Yet disintegrate we must until we find the faith that holds us steady by its truth and ready for its living.

I hail the radical revolt against God that is dragging to destruction the false ideas of God that have been embedded in our main Christian tradition. It is not God but the sacred cows we have put in his place that are being sacrificed. Therefore, even more boldly and confidently, I await the coming of a new and better day in Christian theology. In order to present a clear and convincing view of God and what that view involves for faith, I shall at the outset analyse traditional doctrines of God in an attempt to show that the living God must go beyond them all to provide the full focus for a consistent Christian standpoint. A focal centre of this nature, however, is so dynamic, touching all life with vibrant movement, that to live and look from it can no more be standing still than can an astronaut on a space platform. Upon reaching it we find that our very resting moves with the space-speed of God. I believe that only such a view of God and such a follow-through in life and thought of what this view involves can supply both the courage and the resources for a new creative day.

The traditional ideas of God may be roughly grouped under four headings: theism, deism, pantheism and atheism. Any discussion of the nature of God necessarily depends upon the terms used. Many misunderstandings arise simply from dearth of analysis, indefiniteness of terms and a general lack of communication that, while sometimes purposeful, is often the result of carelessness.

I am going to reject 'theism' as an unchristian term, but in order to do so I must first assign definite meaning to the term. In fairness to numerous theists I observe that they are using the word in a wider sense than I. I also admit that a good deal of historical usage is on their side. Throughout its history, however, 'theism' has been so often connected with a certain philosophy (albeit one not necessary to it) that it has become difficult to think of one without the other. Because of this nearly constant association, while granting that others have a right to use 'theism' in a broader sense, I want to dissociate myself from the term.

The philosophy that has become so closely and constantly associated with theism as to make it nearly impossible to use the term without using the philosophy is, of course, substance philosophy. In this view, which I shall consider more fully later, reality consists of discrete, or separate substances, or things such as sun and stars, rocks and trees; these are real in themselves, just being there, needing no explanation in terms of anything else. Simple or compound, static or dynamic, these things are basically what they are in themselves. On this basis God would be the supreme instance of substance, the supreme Being. The Christian faith, however, cannot hold that there is a supreme Being in the sense of substance. In this sense the Christian must reject theism. To make clear the reason for rejection let us first discuss the other choices among the previously mentioned traditional ideas of God.

I

1. Deism holds God to be a separate, self-sufficient Being who has created the world, but has since left it alone. If such a god enters the world or works in it he must necessarily interfere in the world's now self-sufficient workings. He must intrude as an alien power. Such an understanding of God has never been a real option for the Christian faith, with its view of Incarnation and Providence. There have been periods, like the Enlightenment, when such a conception has had enormous appeal and

much acceptance. Even today, some thinkers would like to believe that they can still be considered to hold a Christian position if they declare that somehow God may be responsible for the original hydrogen molecules, which are presupposed by prominent modern views of creation, but that there is no need to resort to God for any explanation apart from his having provided, so to speak, the start of our cosmic process. Such a view of God, however, is only an accommodation to scientism. Christian faith thus rejects deism.

2. Pantheism is the position that God is the spirit of the whole universe. He is no separate being, creating or coming into the world. He is the soul of the world. He is the world bethinking itself. He is the process directing itself. The pronoun 'he', to be sure, in spite of common usage, is meaningless, for in pantheism God is not a personal being distinct from the world or the process, but the inner directedness of the world or the process itself. The world has, so to speak, its mental aspect, even its evaluational capacity, not as separate from the world but as a function of its own total being. This view of God is nature creating, shall we say, so that we can even speak of 'God or nature'.

Pantheism cannot, of course, be nailed down to one limited understanding. Like all other views of the whole it is a mood and a method as well as an ontology or a theory of being. Whitehead and Tillich have both told me at times that they would prefer, in contradistinction from theism, to be called pantheists. In our latest talk in 1965, however, Tillich disclaimed the term, calling pantheism a 'swear word'. Pantheism can be a high and holy view of God. It does not have to approach the caricatures of it that charge that the god of pantheism is equally manure and a rose, or equally good and evil. The process can even be alive, seeking to further and to enhance existence from within its dimension of depth. Nevertheless pantheism is not a Christian position, lacking as it does, God the creator, a doctrine of personal providence, and capacity for Incarnation.

A variation of this view is 'panentheism', which tries to understand God as within the total process and yet as somehow distinct from it. At times Tillich, for instance, has preferred this view. But on the assumptions of substance philosophy (that is, of any thinking that makes being ultimate) God either is or is not a separate being. If he is, the view is theism. Panentheism's assumption, when viewed in the light of substance philosophy, that God could be a distinct being and yet work from within the world, is, as we shall see, simply theism.

If God is not genuinely a separate being, on the other hand, but merely the logical presupposition for existence or whatever necessity obtains within it, or possibly some ultimate meaning without existence in ultimate terms, panentheism becomes by and large an empty and meaningless term. It no longer has theism in it! When substance philosophy is presupposed, panentheism, in fact, is a misnomer. Unless God is in the world in some sense, we have deism. If God is more, and therefore other than the world and yet in it, we have theism. Panentheism as a term merely confuses and beclouds the issue. In one sense the Christian faith, by definition in terms of its primitive or essential claim, is theistic. The reason I nevertheless disown the term theism, as will become increasingly clear, is its close, almost inseparable connection with substance philosophy, which has arbitrarily defined God in its own terms. Substance philosophy, posing under the name of a theology of being, alone provides modern critics with the right to deny the existence of God. On their presuppositions these critics have the right to claim that for honest, competently trained modern man God is dead. But only, as we shall see, on their presuppositions! Panentheism, however, in this context is a red herring.

3. It remains to discuss the classical view of atheism. Technically atheism merely rejects theism. It is a-theism. If theism stands for God as a general category, to be an atheist is simply to deny entirely the reality of God. If, however, theism stands for a particular view of God, namely that God is the supreme Being, a person can call himself an atheist and still believe in God. Much confusion comes from this indefinite use of the term theism. Some reject theism and call themselves religious atheists simply because they do not believe that God is a *static* being, but that as the Ground of Being he is, rather, *dynamic* being. They are merely radically revolting against the traditional association of theism with substance philosophy in a narrow sense.

Many claim, however, that no one can be an atheist because God is whatever for us is ultimate, and that all of us inescapably have such an ultimate. To live is unavoidably to have some unprovable presupposition; a presupposition obviously cannot be proved. Therefore, they aver, no one living can be an atheist. Notice that they are using the term 'theist' in the general rather than in the particular sense, not only beyond the identification of theism with substance philosophy but also beyond any definitely specifiable or distinguishable reality of God. The many definitions of theism result in, on the one hand, both honest confusion and plain lack of analysis, and, on the other, dishonest avoidance of the question of God altogether a hiding behind the ambiguities of definition. Crooked thinking is like a zigzag rail fence that seems forever trying to be on both sides at once! Too facilely the use of the term keeps shifting to fit the company or the argument.

To make our definition clear and precise, I repeat that the term 'theism' has become so associated with substance philosophy as to be no longer practically available for general constructive usage. If by espousing theism one means merely that one is neither a deist, a pantheist, nor a general denier of God in some such sense as humanism or naturalism, as a Christian one obviously has to be a theist. Definitionally there is no other choice. The Christian faith as an historic entity stands or falls with its worship of the living God who is more and other than the ordinary world and who is yet naturally present in it and working through it. But the term 'theism' has taken on the very substance of the philosophy that bears that name. For this reason I hold that the Christian faith is not theistic in the common use of the term with all its natural associations.

The only reason that the charge can be made that God is not a being, or even the supreme Being (for in such case he would be *a* being among other beings) is simply that being has itself been made into an ultimate category in terms of substance. God is, of course, not a finite object among other finite objects, God is certainly not a thing among things. God obviously cannot be objectified without being made finite. God can never be considered as a concrete entity. Defining God in terms of some such philosophical ultimate as being gives us in a final sense two ultimates: God and being. Mathematics may allow many infinities but two infinite beings cannot exist. There cannot be two infinite realms in terms of substance. The choice, therefore, is either to make philosophy in this sense ultimate, with an ultimate ontology or a doctrine of being as such, in which case the living God of the New Testament, the Spirit of Love, cannot be ultimate (and then theology cannot be a subject dealing with ultimates); or to make theology ultimate, saying then that God is God, the inevitable tautology of the definition of the ultimate, in which case we much define being in terms of God, not God in terms of being. The living God is ultimately *not* Being, but self-revealed as Spirit, Love and Father. We cannot have it both ways.

To call God the supreme Being, therefore, is either an impossible dualism or a mistake. It is to define the ultimate God in terms of another or a second ultimate. Either we mean simply that being has to be defined ultimately or supremely in terms of God (in which case we should not classify him by definition in terms of being) or else we define God in terms of some independent realm of being, i.e. substance (in which case he is not God but only the supreme instance of some philosophical rather than theological ultimate). If God is Love ultimately, he cannot ultimately *be* being. It is right to say that God *is*. We cannot avoid discussion of being in this merely analytical sense. But then, who or what God is, is left open. To say that God is being, however, is either to say superfluously that God is *is* or that God is substance, a category of being in its own right. Then the question of being is no longer merely analytical but a matter of content. I reject the theism that defines God in terms of being. In this sense God is not the supreme Being. God is God who cannot be defined in terms of any category that would permit him to be finite. God cannot be defined except in terms of himself. (For more sustained analysis of this topic the reader may wish to consult *Reason in Religion* or *The Christian Understanding of God*.)

This kind of substance philosophy has bedevilled the history of theology. Christian theology has languished long in the dungeon of Greek philosophy. Thus imprisoned it has starved and withered into impotence. One marvels that the Christian faith has managed to live in spite of being shackled to the wall of substance thinking. Only for illustration, we can mention how theologians have worried about God's relation to the world. If he is absolute, they have pondered, he cannot be relative, for to be relative is to have relations. Therefore God, being ultimate and not relative, cannot have real relations to the world, or at best his relating himself to the world is a dark and deep secret called paradox. All such paradoxes or denials add up to no more than wrong and superficial thinking, an attempt to think the Christian faith within a framework that cannot possibly fit it. What fun, for instance, such a keen critic of theism as Ronald Hepburn has with such thinking in his *Christianity and Paradox*.

In the same way, Tillich dismisses theism in the sense that God cannot be 'a' god because, if he were, the supreme being would be conditioned either as outside the world by being related to it, or, as inside the world, by being confined and made relative by it. With regard to the kind of theism that is based on substance philosophy, Tillich is right in his analysis; but with regard to the Christian faith that espouses the living God in terms of Spirit who is both more and other than the world but who is yet also in control of it and working within it, he takes the wrong path. He dismisses not only theism but the living personal God. And many a student, minister or university professor does not know the difference, sometimes because they have not been informed and sometimes because they prefer not to know.

In the name of the theism of the Christian faith a multitude of similar problems have been approached from the point of view of substance philosophy. The resulting formulations are poison for Christian thinkers to swallow. For instance, God is supposed to be unchangeable or unable to suffer. That there is some truth in such assertions is undeniable, for practically all falsehoods are part-truths, distorted out of context or parts made into wholes; but the unvarnished fact is that all such problems (as to whether God changes or suffers) dissolve when the Christian faith is seen from within its own truth. They are pseudo-problems springing from our attempt to couch the Christian faith in terms of an alien philosophy. The simplest way out now, therefore, is an outright rejection of theism for what it has become in the history of Christian faith.

Theism has also been accused of using comparative language

for God, whereas God cannot be in a class with anything else or be compared to anything else. On the basis of theism as substance philosophy this charge is correct, for then God is the unique being among other beings who can be known only externally. But we have no way of knowing anything that is totally different from all else. The finite as such cannot contain the infinite; the finite as such is not capable of the infinite. If our language is couched in terms of things we know, we cannot proceed to know God in such terms, for by definition he is qualitatively different. If, on the contrary, we try to define him in no terms that we know, we are left with no knowledge of him as well. No knowledge leaves us in agnosticism; and faith can have neither substance nor language for its life. Along such lines we are forced to a *via negativa* which, however consistently we walk in it, leads us nowhere. When the Christian faith is understood from within its own presuppositions, however, there is no such dilemma between what is technically called univocal or equivocal language.

Under substance philosophy, too, revelation becomes impossible. In so far as revelation comes through experience and words of our understanding, it cannot be proved to be from God. If, however, revelation comes as God in human form, all we can be sure of knowing is the human form, for what is above the human is unique, alien, ungraspable. Even so, whatever God in human form is supposed to have done cannot be demonstrated to be a revelation of God but is no more than an assertion that deeds of the same kind as ours, which we can therefore understand, were done in an exceptional way. Since, however, strictly speaking, comparisons are impossible in the case of God, we can claim such deeds to be revelation only by an arbitrary faith which either cannot or does not dare to analyse its own presuppositions.

Enough! If theism is defined in terms of substance philosophy we cannot use comparative human language; yet without such language and comparison we can have neither knowledge of God nor an authentic way of communicating knowledge of him. If God is a self-sufficient, unique supreme Being, some unique supernatural substance, he obviously cannot be known in terms of anything human or natural, but we know nothing else. Because of substance philosophy, Aristotle, himself the

14

formulator of substance philosophy *par excellence*, long ago rejected the basic approach of theism. How tragic that Christian thinkers, by taking for granted this kind of Greek philosophy, set up the impossible problems of Christian theism. God is not the supreme Being of the Christian faith. God is, rather, the living God, the all-pervasive, all-relating Spirit, in terms of and in relation to whom all else must ultimately be understood, and understood, at that, in terms of internal as well as of external relations.

There should be little need to stress that substance philosophy occasioned spatial thinking. God, if not 'up there', was 'out there'. Somehow God had to be localized. If God is a being, he is somewhere. Theism assumed spatialization by its very way of thinking. But the living God, as Jesus pointed out, is Spirit, and Spirit dwells neither on mountain-tops nor in temples. The steeples of substance philosophy can crumble and fall and yet the bells of the Spirit can ring on. God does not dwell in temples made by hands. In one sense the Christian claim is obvious. But it is altogether obvious? Do we not subtly assume the theism of substance philosophy? Surely, we think, God is 'somewhere'. If we say merely that he is equally 'everywhere', we are spatial pantheists. Or, to say that God is 'nowhere' is for most people equivalent to saying that he does not exist; and to say that he does not 'exist' is the same as saying that there is no God!

The living God of the Christian faith, however, is precisely nowhere. The living God is the God of the spatial nowhere. But then how can anything at all be 'there' if it is nowhere at all? That is the point. God is not anything. He is precisely no thing. Therefore he exists nowhere. But if he is nowhere and nothing, how can he be the living God? If he is not in heaven, at least must he not be a condition of the human heart? Is he not in our imagination, if not in our legitimate thinking of reality? No; we must change our way of looking at the problem.

God is no thing, in this sense, literally nothing; and he is no where, in this sense, nowhere. All things exist in God even as all time is in God; thus God is never in space or in time. Space and time are adjectival to God's work. Things, persons, relations, times stand out from God as creations of his love for his own purposes. Is not God, then, at least the centre, at least some dynamic substance from which all things and times come, and to which they are related and kept in being? Only if time and space are in some way real in themselves can such be the case. But both space and time, are adjectival both to God and to his activity; they have no being except for his purposes. They come for his temporary and limited purposes 'out of' the womb of the unlimited, unbounded, unlocalized, non-temporal reality of God. Space and time become dimensions of what is objectified, aspects of what is 'reified', or made into events. Space and time themselves appear as time-and-space-bounded events 'from out of' the creative womb of God, the invisible, unlocalized, non-temporal Spirit.

To say even this much, however, is to drag God into that which is bounded in terms of our negative definitions. The world of things and time is actual, but not real. It is for God's purpose, but not *as* God's purpose. The conditions of eternal Spirit are unimaginable except through God's love for us in this kind of existence. We can imagine through sound and colour, through space and time, and thus come to know through Incarnation a conclusive Life in time and space, the Spirit of Love on whom we can depend. God is faithful. We can trust him as unconditional or all-conditional Love. We can try to imagine God as the Source not only of all significance but also of all being; but when we say that God is *in* the world or *with* us, we use our own mode of understanding, speak under our objectified conditions. By so doing we really make ourselves central and define God in terms of creation. We make real and normative what we ourselves know and can partially control.

The opposite is true: God as Spirit, the Infinite, is nothing and nowhere, no event in space-time; and precisely therefore he is the Living God of eternity. He forgives us not only our unwitting arrogance but our human limitation when we rob him of final reality by using such language as 'the God who inhabits eternity'. Even biblical writers had to use such language, comparable to 'The sun rose'. There is no eternity to dwell in! Eternity is adjectival to God, *God's time*. God is continually creating eternity. God is continually creating being. God is continually creating space. They come to be because he is the living God, and they exist only for his love as the constituents of a temporarily objectified, pedagogical process for our sake. Through lack of language, therefore, we say they come *from* him. But God, being nothing and nowhere, cannot be the supreme Being. Unable, therefore, to be a theist in the traditional sense, I choose, rather, the living God of the Christian faith.

II

The god of process, moreover, is no more God than the god who is supreme being. Disgusted with the contradictions and pseudo-problems of a theism based on substance philosophy, many, especially among our younger thinkers in the United States, are turning to process philosophy as a vehicle for Christian theology. Two originating prophets of process philosophy stand out today: Alfred North Whitehead and Pierre Teilhard de Chardin. Without going into the systems of either in detail we can garner their main harvests.

Whereas Whitehead's philosophy is mostly process, with some 'Christian' modification, Teilhard maintained a definitely Christian background that always amplifies and deepens his process thinking. Process theologians either take what they like of his thought and leave the rest, or, as Teilhard himself does, remain closer to Christianity itself. In the case of Whitehead, some like his thought unretouched because they really mean to develop straight process theology; others try to say that he could have meant, or at least that his system allows for, something far closer to the Christian faith than he intended. Such claims, as I know from personal conversations with him as well as from his writings, are mostly in the nature of wishful thinking. He himself had considered and deliberately discarded near-Christian choices.

Process philosophy is a direct protest against substance philosophy. In reality, it holds, there are no substances which need only themselves in order to exist. There is nothing that simply is. A tennis ball, for instance, can lie on a table. It seems to be an independent entity. But at the bottom of the ocean it would be crushed and no longer be a ball. Thus a ball depends on the pressures of gravitation and simply is not as it is. Everything, rather, is interdependent.

In science we may speak of seven dimensions which describe

the way things interact and are interrelated according to our best present knowledge. Not only do we have the dimension of time-space, or the dimensions of time beyond the usual three dimensions, but we also have gravitational, magnetic and electrical fields in which things (I almost said 'lie'!) 'are' and 'exist' since nothing is inert and merely passive, for all things are interdependent and interacting. Some, I believe rightly, would add mind and spirit as dimensions inherently characterizing reality. In Whitehead's thought, in any case, all things are mutually immanent. They both include all else (except for certain possibilities or 'eternal objects') and in turn are included by all else, that is by all other things, or 'events', 'actual entities', or 'occasions of experience'.

God himself, as the mind and lure for satisfaction of the whole process, is also an actual entity. He himself is 'an accident of creation'. God is as much created as creating. The drive to creativity in all things is fundamental to the process. This drive is 'the category of categories', even more general than God. It is, so to speak, prior to God and drives him. God envisages all possibilities for the total process and for each actual entity in it. His job is to direct the total process with a view to achieving both the greatest possible total harmony and also the fullest possible creative satisfaction for each actual entity or occasion of experience in the process. These possibilities are not real in themselves, but neither are they merely the creation of God. They are, rather, most consistently part of the creative process, and as such neither independently real nor dependently deficient, but interdependently both real and deficient. This ideal aspect of reality can be abstracted from process for analysis, but is or has no abstract reality.

In process philosophy the thoughts create the thinker as much as the thinker the thoughts. There are no real, abiding selves, but each self is a locus of actual entities or occasions of experience. Reality comes in drops of experience. In one sense, these drops alone are real and all things are to be explained in terms of them; but this 'ontological principle' has to do only with the resulting satisfactions that the drops of experience finally feel, and not with their process of becoming, which is explainable only in terms of the interaction and interdependence of the total process.

The point is that in process philosophy there is no self-sufficient being. There is no eminent reality, no permanently real as opposed to deficient being. There is no eternal being. There is no Being as Such or In Itself. There is no eternal Ground or Goal of cosmic process, for reality itself is process in one of its basic aspects. The reality of satisfaction is only momentary. God is almost entirely the reality of the total process in becoming and of the total satisfaction in being, felt moment by moment, but preserved beyond all moments within the resultant satisfaction of his eternal vision, or 'envisagement', which as objectively eternal, provides the concrete possibilities for all future guiding of the process. Thus there is no eternal being beyond process but only an eternal being ever becoming in and of process, the personal, conscious God who is 'the sufferer who understands' and the companion of all our choices. For all intents and purposes we can say that God is supposed to serve the purposes of eternal being in classical Western thought, although he is constantly created as well as creative. God alone is eternal in any sense of reality, but he has no eternal purpose for either history or man.

The fundamental distinction between theism as the philosophy of substance and the theism of cosmic process is that in the former, God is the supreme Being, the self-sufficient, needing nothing else in order to exist, whereas in the latter, God is created as well as creative, as much dependent upon the world, in fact, as the world is dependent upon him. In the former God can give man of his own eternal life, whereas in the latter God alone, by the very analysis of what is, can be eternal. What is at stake in process philosophy is whether God is more than the process with final power over it and whether God can give man eternal life, or life beyond death. Since I originally undertook the writing of this book, John Cobb, in *A Christian Natural Theology*, has argued with real competence for the consistency of personal immortality or eternal life with Whitehead's philosophy. He is right. The possibility is philosophically open. Whitehead himself admitted as much to me in personal conversation; but it is open basically only because Whitehead's thinking was modified by Christian impulses. The case for personal immortality or eternal life in the writings of Pierre Teilhard de Chardin, as in *The Phenomenon of Man* and *The*

Future of Man is as in the writings of Whitehead, an admixture of Christian thought.

In order to escape substance philosophy, do we need to land in the inadequacies of process philosophy? Is there not a way of truth which possesses in itself the truths of process philosophy without its limitations? For most modern thinkers, of course, the ultimacy of God as well as the reality of the resurrection have in any case lost most of their meaning; therefore many have been willing to settle for process thinking. I believe, however, that the living God of the Christian faith, the Spirit who is Love, has all the capacities that both these philosophies afford, without their deficiencies. For this reason I am confident that when the Christian faith is rightly understood we shall see it reborn to a new vigour.

Process thinking in its deepest impulse is rather Buddhist than Christian. Buddhism at its original heart teaches the total interdependence of all things. Nothing is real, in the eminent sense; everything is relative. Nothing is eternal, claims Buddhism. No god, no thing, nothing at all. Everything is flux in form, a suffering, deficient, transient flux that is mistakenly thought permanent and real. Buddhism has a strong doctrine of change in order and order in change. It has no real order of being and no order of real becoming. Nothing is, and nothing ever really becomes. Without substantive being nothing can really become, or come to be. Everything is change, suffering, impermanence. To recognize this truth is to be free from the tyranny of objectification, of absolutizing or eternalizing. Then false desires wither and die, at least with the death of the body, the semblance of permanence. No wonder that Whitehead knowingly claimed to be nearer Buddhism than Christianity. We need today to face and to converse with other religions. Process philosophy can be a good bridge; but man cannot live forever on a bridge, and there is no solid ground on the other side. Non-being as an ultimate is hard to stand on! Even ultimate agnosticism is an unlivable land.

Process thinking will not do for an ultimate. Nothing in process is ultimate. Are we then hankering for theism based on substance philosophy? Such theism has an ultimate and a strong doctrine of being. True; but it has no real doctrine of becoming and no real doctrine of non-being. We do not want substance thinking merely in order to escape the deficiencies of process philosophy. Process thinking, on the other hand, has no real ultimate, no permanent reality that explains and directs all else. Cosmic process at least falls far short of the Eternal Purpose of the Christian faith.

Whitehead's system gives no real explanation for continuity. The vision dies, the drop disperses, the satisfaction breaks. Can what is dead, what is less, what is mere drive create what is more and better? The overlapping of occasions through relativity is mostly a neat trick of legerdemain. This aspect of process thinking is covered over with words without the power of reality. Description is made to do for explanation. If we choose to make God into a non-temporal vision and power of continuity not participating in the process as such, we no longer have process philosophy. In such a case we have reality beyond process or some doctrine of being above process. If this is so, we can claim also an eternal Purpose for human history and eternal life for human beings. But in order to obtain such gains we have gone beyond process philosophy as such into, or at least towards, the Christian faith.

Process philosophy could have a doctrine of being if only it would mature into a theology of Spirit as permanent reality and ever directing purpose. It does have a doctrine of becoming; but its doctrine of becoming could itself be strengthened by a fuller conception of being in terms of creative Spirit. Spirit is far more than merely dynamic being or merely structured and evaluative becoming. Spirit also has ample capacity for a real and fulfilling meaning and function of non-being. At this point the Christian faith can really meet with the East and provide what both Hinduism and Buddhism lack.

As far as I know, no Eastern religion has developed creative Spirit, the Spirit of Love, in such a way as to understand this Spirit as capable of remaining self-same yet creating that which is 'other than'; able both to give such 'other than' genuine self-being and to remain equally both present and absent, 'with and in' it; having besides the power to communicate with what is 'other than' (as we shall observe later in the chapter), and at the same time affording to the 'other than' both private and public reality. Technically, co-ordinate predication, attributing seemingly contradictory predicates to the same subject, is in the case of Spirit a contrapletal relation wherein the attribution is guilty of no logical excluded middle but rather uses distinctive predicates in different senses because of the nature of Spirit as 'subject'. ('Contrapletal' means a complementary relationship of seeming opposites, like night and day or summer and winter, in a larger unity that includes both.) Even Christian thought has never adequately explored the metaphysical meanings and mysteries of Love. Yet in the Christian faith Love is exactly this creative and communicating reality that affords understanding of the personal, of being, becoming and non-being in terms of Spirit beyond any present seeing. To explore these contrapletal regions is a central task for generations ahead, with possibilities as ample and as expanding as the creative reality of God.

Process thinking receives much acceptance because it seems to provide meaning for existence and direction for life without the necessity of facing up to the overwhelming problems of eternity. Cosmic time seems enough for us. Why bother with more? Can man even begin to understand the eternal God? What can eternal life mean for finite human beings? Can we even want it? Such humility, on the one hand, and evasion of the total problem, on the other, are the real reasons for the attraction of process theology for many. Because of this evasion, however, process theology, humble and inviting though it be, can never deal deeply with the problem of evil.

Let me try, therefore, to indicate suggestively why Christianity, the religion of the Spirit, stands or falls according to its conviction that God is the living Spirit of Love. Our choice need not be limited to either the theism of substance philosophy or the God of process philosophy, both of whose ultimates are either contradictory or deficient. A more adequate ultimate than either is available: one that will make us want to face eternity as our due, for which we are made, and to confront eternal life not as a problem but as a power.

III

Christianity is the religion of the Spirit. When everything is understood spiritually, when the category of Spirit is taken with full seriousness, ultimates are no longer 'things' or processes.

Up to now my suggestive proposals have been stated in largely negative terms. Let me try to restate them more positively in the attempt to draw together into focus the claims I have scattered throughout the previous two sections.

What can it possibly mean that God is nothing and nowhere? Is Spirit merely a way of saying that we know God only negatively, in terms of what he is not? We say: God is not substance; God is not a bounded personality; God is not an aspect, however high, of process. Staying with negatives, however, denies us the right to make any claim to knowledge. *Via negativa* is the way of agnosticism. In effect it denies that we can know God. Therefore on to our positive task!

To say that God is not being, even Being itself, can mean that we refuse ontology, or any abstract theory of being or of reality, precisely because we know God himself to be ultimate. God is not defined in terms other than himself. Reality is defined in terms of God, not God in terms of reality. Being is defined in terms of God, not God in terms of being. God is Spirit; God is personal Life (our Father); God is Love. These three New Testament categories, Spirit, Life and Love, are primary descriptions of God, permanent distinctions within the unity of the ultimate Reality, God. We shall see that they better describe and explain what we know than does any other category. God cannot even be personality in the sense of our knowledge of personality. We do not define God in terms of personality, but we define the personal in terms of God who is also Spirit and Love. In the same way, God is not to be understood in terms of process, but process itself is to be understood in terms of God. God is not reducible to a part of cosmic process but cosmic process expresses the eternal Purpose, the purpose of One who is eternal. In no way, however, do we abolish or minimize these secondary realities like being, personality and process; rather, we complete them by placing them within their fulfilling relationships.

What does such a reversal of usual definitions involve? Surely we must not be content with words without filling them with content. Spirit, we say, is 'everywhere' without being 'anything'. Is Spirit then void? Is God literally 'nothing', not only in the sense of being no thing, or not objectified existence, but as being the category of non-being, whether as the denial

of particulars (*me on*) or as the denial of everything (*ouk on*)?
How can I say that God is everywhere precisely because he is
nothing? Have I not said before that God is nowhere? Are
nowhere and everywhere the same? For God *ultimately*, yes.
The God of nowhere is everywhere. The God of nothing 'up-
holds' everything. Such statements are true because all 'wheres'
are finite creations generated from the God who is prior to and
beyond all space. Even such expressions as 'prior to' and 'beyond' are inadequate because they make finite existence
determinative for our definitions. The Creative entity, the
Spirit who is Love, creates a pedagogical medium for pedagogical purposes. Spirit is not spatialized nor subject to spatialization. Neither are finite spirits as spirits, but they have being
under the conditions of creations.

God ultimately is nothing and nowhere, but finite spirits in
creation are something and somewhere for the sake of learning.
They *are* spirits but *have* being. They are given bodies under the
conditions of physical existence in order to become real through
choices. Finite spirits can learn indirectly from their choices by
observing and having to live the consequences. Thus they can
learn in freedom. They can learn indirectly from the results of
their own choices, and more, from the sum total of society's
choices. They can learn in the medium of space and time.
Space relates spirits to other spirits in the process of learning,
extensively or co-ordinately. Space makes it possible to live
with or alongside others to learn with and from them. Time
relates incarnate spirits to the results of the past as the process
brings to fruition the consequences of choices. Thus we learn
together in space and time. Each person becomes an individual,
a finite person, through this space-time learning. Furthermore
all learn of each other as they must share the consequences of
each other's choices. Thus people have to become responsible
not only as selves but also with and for others. We are wrapped
up together in a common bundle of life where yet each life
counts. Spirits thus grow in self-knowledge and in responsible
interdependence. Space-time is only a pedagogical medium in
which finite spirits may grow and become real as authentic
beings. Finite spirits are partially but importantly free from
the infinite Spirit. God is not personally but effectively present
within and by the order of creation.

The God of nowhere and nothing is thus everywhere and responsible for everything. Out of the indescribable 'depths' of Spirit comes creation in time and space. God there deals out such responsibility as is commensurate with our freedom. He puts us in control of our choices. Since he is, according to our modes of thinking, nowhere and nothing, he can withdraw in such respects as further our freedom. His presence can become only indirect in the sustaining of the created order and in the ripening of the consequences of our choices. He can thus teach us both through our own natures and through the kind of nature he made for us in which to choose and to reap consequences. The Creative Spirit who is Love can thus be personally absent from us in order to allow our freedom to become real and our choices to become responsible.

God can do so because he is not primarily a personality who has to be either present or not present. God can do so because he is not a substance, stuff, force or energy, that has to be there or else not there. God can do so because he is not a constant factor in process that either is there or else is lacking. No logic of excluded middle based on substance thinking hinders God. This kind of co-ordinate predication is indispensably contrapletal. In order to understand the claim that God can be both absent and present at the same time we have to understand the nature of Spirit. The nature of Spirit, in one dimension, is to be eternal, indestructible, ultimate reality. In Spirit, therefore, we have the eternal reality which characterizes philosophies of substance or personalistic philosophies, but which is lacking in process philosophies. But Spirit, in the other dimension, in quite another sense, has the capacity to be present in and with creation as is needed, under whatever conditions call for Spirit, because Spirit is the reality that can be at the same time nowhere and everywhere. Observe, Spirit can be present or absent *in different senses*. God does not have to be *personally* present in order to be effectively present in other sense. God as Spirit is both One and yet capable of such intentional personally presenting or absenting himself, for our companionship or for our cherished and needed privacy even from him. Because God as Spirit is transpersonal, he can withdraw as personal Spirit while yet remaining present as sustaining and directing Spirit.

Spirit is also the reality of creativity, causing to be what previously was not, as something real, new, having self-being. With respect to such created being of whatever kind, Spirit is not present as its self-being. Creation, for its purposes, is therefore real. Distinctions are real within the identity of the one Spirit. There can be different kinds of self-being and God can be absent especially with regard to personal self-being, allowing men privacy and freedom. With respect to such freedom, God 'there' is nowhere. His thereness is only according to the needs in question as supportive of the conditions for freedom. God is no single, 'solid' entity, but Reality inherently characterized by diversive competence. The God who in himself or as Spirit is nowhere, beyond spatialization, can thus be both present and absent at the same time. With God, presence and absence are not contradictory but contrapletal; with him what ordinarily seem to be mutually exclusive differences are actually co-ordinate predicates. The Spirit is capable of being with the new of creation, sustaining it and directing it in such a way that apart from such co-existence the finite, the created, could not be, while also becoming absent in such measure as is needed.

Thus Spirit both is nothing and nowhere and yet is sustainingly with all being and everywhere as needed. Spirit is not subject to spatialization nor bounded by time, yet generates both space and time for the purposes of creation and development of the finite. The finite is genuine and real as finite, but is never apart from its inmost relation to the creative reality that sustains and directs it. The invisible and eternal is thus never objectified or temporal, and yet is responsible for all creations and times. The Spirit creates the finite, persons and events in time and space, but is never finite in terms of time and space. The truth of such affirmations is what it means to say that God does not 'exist'. That God does not exist does not mean that he is not. On the contrary, God does not exist because he alone pre-eminently, or eternally, *is*. God as such cannot become objectified. Even God in Incarnation is never God limited to space and time, but rather the unlimited present in the limited, God in man.

God is the God of nowhere and nothing because he is the living God. He is the eternal Spirit who is Love. He is the

Ground of Being and the Goal of Being. But the Ground and Goal of Being is no Being-itself, but only the Ground and Goal of creation. It is he in whom we live and move and have our being. Ground and goal are of God because being is of God. God is, and creates all forms of finite being. God is, and communicates with all forms of finite being. Finite beings in the human category are first of all not beings but spirits. They *have* being because they *are* spirits. Persons are spirits who have finite being. Their finite being, in one sense, places them in the category of vegetables and animals. Like them, they are living creatures with finite being.

Persons alone are finite spirits. Spirit as such cannot be limited. God is Spirit. Ultimately there is no other Spirit. Human beings are limited by being, even by being persons. As created beings, they are limited like vegetables and animals. They are limited also by being finite personalities. All personalities are finite and limited. Indeed, every aspect of process, cosmic or not, is also limited. Human beings are limited as created, that is as objectified for a pedagogical purpose. God teaches these persons through their kind of being, their kind of existence, their kind of environment.

God in himself as Love, however, is not limited. God as Love is Spirit. As such he can limit his power, that is, his control. He can limit his freedom to act. He can limit his presence, and as personal for pedagogical purposes be the God of nowhere. But he cannot limit himself as Spirit and as Love. Love and Spirit in themselves have no being and therefore are nowhere and nothing, and as such everywhere and all-relating. God as the unconditional Love is thus also Love under all conditions, whether present or absent. God can limit only his personal presence and power. Similarly, human beings cannot be limited as spirits. As such they are inalienably part of God, even though distinctively real. Even to say that they are 'part of' God is to use limited space language and thus to limit them as spirit. In learning to become real through space-time man appropriates the reality, the wisdom, the goodness of God. Man learns to understand himself as spirit. To learn in space and time is to become free through responsible choosing, through responsible living.

God creates beings and persons. God creates personal beings.

But God breathes his own Spirit into them. Man is of Spirit. Spirit is; Spirit can never be created. Deepest down, man is spirit, spirit as the depth of man in his capacity for God because he is of God. God's image in man is the hidden directions of potentiality which is no mere possibility for creation but inner necessity for eventual appropriation. Man can most deeply become only in relation to what he most deeply is. Freedom is the fullest possible expression of one's nature. Through freedom of choice man attains freedom of life. Through freedom of contrary choice man is destined to find freedom as participation in God's life, man's deepest fulfilment. To find such freedom of life is to enter into creation as pedagogical process. Man must develop according to his nature, learn to understand himself as the spirit God breathed into him when he created him also as a physical being, a finite self. All finite learning, therefore, is becoming real by learning to know oneself as becoming in relation to what one really is. All finite learning in the pedagogical process of space-time is the appropriation of God. He eternally is. He eternally shares.

To be God is to be the Spirit of Love. To be God is to give. It is to give Love. God gives of himself; he shares himself. The method and message of God's love are that we are made not only for him but from him; we must learn to become in him even as we are of him. To be man is to learn to know God and his purpose for man. The more man learns this secret the more he becomes man. All external learning is for the sake of finally coming to know oneself as one is and can be. Man comes to know himself as made for love; that is to say, man comes to know himself by learning to know the other. Man learns to become man in community. Man becomes man by learning to communicate. To live in community and fully to communicate is to love. Only love finds full community and learns fully to communicate. But God himself is Love. God is Spirit. God is the Spirit of Love. Only by learning to know oneself as most deeply not only made for Love, but made in Love and ultimately made by Love, can man ever learn the lesson of life, and learning this lesson, find life's freedom.

Creation is for such learning. All the sufferings of Love alone can make Love real. Only suffering Love can win suffering man. Only by suffering can man come to himself in the far country and return to the waiting Father. To become real, the self must be set on self. Being set on self brings fear and frustration. Fear and frustration, in turn, bind and distort freedom. They reduce man. But they can make him willing to seek and to find the freedom that Love alone can bring. The self that finds freedom in Love has found not only community and communication. He has found himself. He has found God. He has found and been found by the final meaning of life. God creates in Love eternally, enjoying creation, suffering in creation, and finding increase of joy in the ever deeper meaning of Love. Man's learning is in time. Man's learning that he is of God is the enriching of God by the increase of Love. Spirit shares Love, suffering Love, for the sake of fulfilment of the Love that is freedom and joy. Creation is for the Cross that ends victoriously in the reality of Resurrection. Eternity is God's living of Love. Our eternity means our participation in that eternal life.

Spirit is the category of self-transcendence. Only spirit can go beyond self as self. Self-transcendence alone brings genuine freedom from self and others. The self transcends as spirit not only his body, and not only his mind, but his very self. He finds the freedom of the Spirit. He finds the reality of God. Such a self is free in God, and, therefore, while completely for and with others in their deepest reality and purposings, quite free from them in their partial limitations or their misdirected drives or desires. To be free is to know God, to be spirit in Spirit, to reach the goal of selfhood which is ever fulfilled by being transcended. No one can be free in any full sense who is a stranger to the reality of Spirit. How Jesus drove home this truth to Nicodemus!

We think of quantity, moreover, as basic to reality because we think in terms of space and time. Some have gone so far as to play, and more than play, with the idea that those things alone are real which can be quantified. Quantification, in one sense, reduces metaphysics to mathematics, or reality to measurability. Method determines metaphysics. But the living God of nowhere and nothing is the reality of quality. He is the reality of Love. He is the Reality of Spirit. He is the invisible, eternal reality out of whom all things come, in whom all creation lies, and to whom all finite spirits return. They have no reality save of God; and only by appropriating their reality as eternally of God can they find fulfilment. Spirits can be considered in the plural only partly for purposes of communication. They are not to be considered as substantive parts since they are not quantity. Spirits at the depths of reality always partake of the essential unity of Spirit. They are in deepest reality one, as God is one. But Spirit is not undifferentiated unity, but Love. The reality of Love is a unity of Spirit, far more than 'one flesh'; but Love intrinsically is and has relations. Unity is always rich in diversity without any final rupture. There is distinction without division.

Spirits, however, are eternal and unlimited. Man cannot be limited in spirit or as spirit. Truly to be in the Spirit is to be one with God. Finite existence diversifies and divides. Spirits seek Spirit; man seeks God. God is not quantity of creation, but quality for creation. Quality, that is to say, can be ascribed to God intrinsically, but quantity cannot. The 'why' of being logically precedes the 'how'. God can, so to speak, be qualified as faithful Love but never quantified as objective existence. We cannot see quality apart from quantity because it is not a thing. We can only see quantities, and quality as adjectival. The reason for this is that we think of quality as a kind of existence, a kind of being. God, however, is not being, but being is of God. Quantity, in this sense, is *of* quality. Purpose precedes being as substance. Spirit is invisible, eternal reality that creates or objectifies quantifiable existence. We can 'see' God only as a kind of life; love is quality of Spirit but Spirit is no substance.

Analogously we cannot see energy as such. We cannot see electricity as such. We can see objectified forms of these realities. Energy is capacity for work, but function never defines nature itself. Energy can come in visible or invisible form. Electricity is not limited to the objectified form of light or power. Even so God is not limited by distance. God is not imprisoned within time. He can create and be present in some form with space and time, but God is not his creation. He is not the quantified forms of his creation.

The tendency of Western thought throughout its history has been to shrink the significance of meaning. Science has increasingly reduced explanation to a matter of how. Final causes have simply been dropped as unimportant. When they have been used, they have been used more as description than as explanation. This shrinkage is fatal to both thought and life. To accept the 'how' as adequate for explanation is to neglect the purpose of both life and knowledge. It is to become descriptive rather than prescriptive. It is to accept the past creation rather than creative reality. It is to make the body, the physical, of primary importance rather than life itself which is spirit. We are now about to experience a change in the approach to knowledge so basic that as it took centuries to drift into the inadequacies of scientism based on quantity, so it will take centuries creatively to re-establish the centrality of the full meaning of quality. We shall go on from the how to the why, from the outer garments of life to its inner meaning and significance. But re-establishment is not enough. We must incorporate the lessons of the how and come out with a far fuller why. We must never underestimate or undermine man's critical understandings in terms of how. Our knowledge of quantity will help us to understand quality better. The history of science has not been futile.

God, the creative Spirit who is unconditional Love, is the quality of reality that creates every quantity of visible relations. God is ever the womb of quantities. They come from him, exist in him, and are made for his purposes. Quantities can cease to be when God's purpose is done because he is the God of nothing. Where there is no need for time, such time can cease, for God is the God of the never as well as of the ever. All time is the creation of God as adjectival to his purpose. Whatever is characterized intrinsically by finite time can cease to exist, return to non-being. With no thing and no time there is no-where and nothing. Neither God nor finite spirits need the now and the there, except as they need to grow in the in-directions of God's pedagogy through the process of creation. When finite spirits learn their lesson they know that finitude is of being and of person, not of Spirit. They are then eternally more than they can ever know in time. Eternal life is meaning fulfilled within the eternal Mystery of Spirit.

Theism has always been mixed up with theories of being, with theories of personality, with theories of process. God is the living God beyond all these, so far beyond that language in their terms, however much or little, misrepresents his reality. God is the living Spirit, the eternal, the unconditional Love who is the Ground and Goal of all creation. Therefore we look only pedagogically at things which are seen, for 'things which are seen are temporal but things which are not seen are eternal'. Instead of the myopic sight of theism I choose the full vision of the living, invisible God, the eternal Spirit who is unconditional Love.

Spirit is man's most adequate ultimate. God as Spirit is unconditional Love. Spirit is self-being, explaining all else. The Eternal Purpose 'behind' cosmic process is Spirit, focused by Love. Not some unknowable and superfluous Being-itself, deifying substance philosophy; not some Personality, with only external relations to the world; not some aspect of cosmic process, however refined; but the living God who is unconditional Love—the Eternal Spirit—is our wisdom and truth, our help and hope, our direction and destiny. God is not the supreme Being of theism but the living God of the Christian faith.

In the mood of the unimaginably Good and Great, the living God of nowhere and nothing, we can now turn to re-examine the separate items of faith that are especially involved in our ever expanding understanding of God. Our first subject is Incarnation, the presence of the Illimitable within the limits of human finitude, of the Eternal Spirit within not only personal spirit but personal being.

Chapter II

The Myth or the Gospel

MY mother and my sister, both conservative Christians, used to argue continually about Jesus. My sister contended that Jesus simply was God and that was the end of it. My mother, however, with equal fervour insisted that Jesus was not God but the Son of God. My sister granted, of course, that Jesus had humanity, but she fairly shouted that what really mattered about Jesus was the saving fact that in him God had truly come to us, spoken to us, died for us, and risen from death for us, winning once for all his final victory over death and over all of man's principal enemies. To stress the humanity of Jesus, she feared, might in fact psychologically belittle the central reality of his deity. Not so, said Mother, refusing to yield one fraction of feeling in her own devotion to the deity of Jesus; for her, the meaning, the relevance and the power of God's mighty Christ deed depended inevitably upon Jesus' being fully human as well as fully divine.

My own conviction takes sides with my mother's position. Indeed, I believe that the final line of demarcation between myth and Gospel goes precisely between the two confessions: Jesus is God and Jesus is the Son of God. The former position is basically theogony; the latter is Incarnation. That Jesus is God is a half-truth which may not be lost from the fullness of revelation without forfeiting the Gospel itself. But when this half-truth is used, however subtly and even subconsciously, to deny the contrapletal fact that Jesus was also truly man, it turns into a dangerous and even disastrous untruth. My present task is to do my utmost to show the difference between the two confessions and to indicate what is at stake in our choice between them. Before starting my analysis, however, let me make as emphatic as I can my own testimony from both life and thought that I believe in Jesus Christ as the definitive Son of God. Unless 'God was in Christ reconciling the world unto himself' in a historically factual way, without all cavil or equivocation, I know no Gospel for mankind. Both my life and my theology are founded on the fact that we have seen 'the glory of God in the face of Jesus Christ'.

Let me also speak plainly about the meaning of myth. I do not believe that Incarnation is myth. I believe, rather, that Incarnation is the historic fact that in Jesus God 'became man'. The meaning and the significance of that confession I shall try to elucidate as we go on. My acceptance of the presupposition that in Jesus we have a reliable index to the nature and the will of God should not be taken, nevertheless, to mean that I am therefore rejecting myth *in toto* as a theological means of communication. Myth, as Mircea Eliade has ably brought out, stands for the fact that ultimate origins cannot be explained in terms of any reasoned development of what we know. Myth, rather, stands for the reality of the sacred as alone capable of accounting for the miracle of becoming so that things seen were made from what is not seen (cf. Heb 11³). Eliade's studies, for me, unearth the most profound meaning of primitive myths and the reason for them. In the beginning God!

Thus even the mythical treatment of Jesus as God, apart from his humanity or with an emasculated human nature, aims at least at insisting that the meaning and the reality of the life and teachings of Jesus are not to be explained in human terms. Honest and informed modern man often tries to get at the real Jesus, or at the true Christ, by demythologizing the Gospel. Here again a laudable intention may bring a disastrous result. Many such attempts end by removing the reality of the eternal God from the life of Jesus, exhibiting him instead as our best example of an authentic human being. Theology is turned into anthropology. The Gospel is externalized out of its eternal reality and significance. Whatever the words, we are left with a human figure impotent to save in the classical dimensions of the Christian faith. My aim here, however, is not to attack myth *qua* myth nor to do battle with demythologizing in general. In the right way and in the right place, as any competent scholar should know, we have to demythologize. I aim, rather, to show that we are not left with the bare choice: Jesus was God or Jesus was not God. I believe that the most robust biblical position on this point within the full context of the New Testament, after all needed demythologizing is done, amounts to the confession: Jesus is the Son of God. The New

Testament never poses the illegitimate question as to whether Jesus was God or not God, but gives us instead the throbbing heart of the Gospel: in this man, Jesus of Nazareth, we encounter the reality, the will and the work of God.

My understanding of John Wesley's preaching of the Gospel is that however central he made the full Gospel of Christ, as he did in an almost incomparable way, he also fell victim to the myth. His writings are replete with illustrative instances. Perhaps, too, myth is by far the most potent channel for communicating revelation. Maybe the love of God which surpasses knowledge cannot be formulated in terms of the meanings of ordinary language. It may be that the language of faith has to be logically odd. I am often impressed by the truth of such assertions, especially as it is dramatized in the zeal of evangelical groups. The biblical message may have to depend basically on parable and story, on recalling God's mighty acts in history, and primarily on reciting the 'old, old story of Jesus and his love'. Theology may be neither the mood nor the method for conveying the sacred truth of God's self-disclosure. Often I ponder the question whether, in the light of the concrete results, Bible study and the prayer meeting may not be God's primary vehicles for his people to discover ever afresh the saving truth and power of the Gospel.

The hope of my life, however, is that I may be given the grace to portray the understanding of the Gospel as it burns in my heart and glows in my mind. After all, St Paul recommended the use of the understanding in its proper place. The tongues of rapture he held to be for private edification; the tongues of understanding, for public communication. I am not endeavouring to share with you any personal experience of ecstasy; I am, rather, trying to express how overwhelmingly true I have found the Gospel both for faith and for reason, both for the rapture of the Spirit and for the understanding of ordinary life and knowledge. If my strictures on the abuse of the Gospel—for it is an abuse whenever the half-truth that Jesus is God is used to obscure the fact and full significance of the Incarnation—become structures of criticism that block you from sharing with me the joy and challenge of the Gospel, I shall have failed both you and my own purpose.

My aim in this chapter is explicitly to show the reality and the meaning of the life of Jesus as basic to our knowing God, ourselves and, indeed, all creation. In order, however, to carry through this determination to make central the full meaning of the Incarnation, I must first make quite clear the nature of the untruth, which is only a half-truth used in the wrong way. I must also uncover how destructive of the Gospel this manner of the myth can be. I invite you, then, to wrestle with me through both negative conflict and positive victory as I elucidate the confession that Jesus is the Son of God.

John Wesley, I believe, most deeply intended the Gospel rather than the myth. I am convinced that no theologian of first rank ever came closer to the original depth-meaning and reality of the New Testament than did he. For many years I have yearned to call attention to the centrality of Christ in Wesley's thinking, his emphasis on Christ as the Incarnate Love of God, 'all loves excelling'. Particularly important to me is the Wesley doctrine of sanctification as in *Plain Account*, which unites Christ intrinsically with the Christian. The presence of Christ in the believer through the power of the Holy Spirit, the passing through conversion to Christ from prevenient to enabling grace, the taking seriously the biblical goal 'to present every man perfect in Christ', are emphases that lie at the very heart of the Christian faith.

In truth, the Gospel has to do with both theology and anthropology, both with the eternal Word made flesh in Jesus and with all those to whom he gave power to become sons of God, who were born 'not of blood, nor of the will of the flesh nor of the will of man, but of God'. The New English Bible renders Apostle Paul's famous passage in the third chapter of Galatians: 'Through faith you are all sons of God in union with Christ Jesus.' Indeed, John Wesley's sterling doctrine of justification by faith, accepting the majestic stress in the Letter to the Romans, is fulfilled as in the New Testament itself by his equal insistence on the fact that of Christ's fullness we have all received 'grace for grace'. Thus the love of God as depicted in John Wesley comprises intrinsically the full gamut of the New Testament promises.

There is also an almost unique wholeness in Wesley's understanding of the Gospel since, according to the way he taught the fruit of faith, Galatians 3, I Corinthians 13 and Romans 12 fit flexibly into the fuller context with the Kingdom ethics of the Synoptic Gospels, particularly of the Sermon on the Mount. There is no artificial estrangement between the Gospel of Jesus and the Gospel about Jesus. The love of God reigns supreme throughout God's work in Christ and his teachings through Christ. Even the social implications of the Gospel are brought out with a naturalness that make them part and parcel of the whole Gospel without usurping the place of the Gospel itself. This fullness of Wesley's theology refuses to make even Romans 13 a stumbling block, but transforms it instead into the open road of the royal law of love which fulfils the intention of all law.

It would be exciting to devote an entire book to the special subject of Wesley and the Love of God, showing concretely the fullness of his Gospel both as a theologian and as a preacher. Here, however, I must relinquish this tantalizing topic in favour of framing a systematic analysis both of the dangers of the myth that Jesus is God, inasmuch as the affirming of the half-truth in effect denies the full truth of the Incarnation, and of the power of the full Gospel that 'God was in Christ reconciling the world unto himself'. My intention is to show how God's purpose in Christ is that we all may come 'to mature manhood, even the measure of the stature of the fullness of Christ'. I have noticed how readily the newer translations of almost all the Bible verses relevant to our topic nibble away at their central meaning; but the main purpose of Christ's coming according to the New Testament is clear, namely that Christ might in us be 'the hope of glory', that we might be 'raised with Christ', and become 'joint heirs with him'. Boundless promises beyond belief, for the doubter sheer human presumption, but such exactly is the full teaching of the New Testament Gospel which John Wesley, more than any other first-rank theologian, dared to accept as reliable revelation from God for both faith and life.

I

First, then, we shall examine the dangers of the myth, and thereupon proceed to proclaim the power of the Gospel. I have agonized over the negative nature of exposing the abuse of the Gospel, but I believe such exposure is necessary in order the more sharply to highlight the true nature of the full Gospel of the Incarnation.

Jesus is not God but the Son of God. The eternal Son, God's outgoing Word in creation and redemption, became fulfillingly present in a human being, Jesus of Nazareth, who thereby in one genuine personality became the Godman. Chalcedon is right: Jesus was truly God, truly man, without division and without confusion, in one authentic personality. When God finally fulfils a human being, man thereby becomes not less but more human, while the all-important partner, obviously, in that dynamic unity of personality is the eternal Word, the divine Logos. The eternal Son might even be more clearly seen for who he is if we define the Holy Trinity in terms of the three basic definitions of God in the New Testament: God is 'Our Father', God is Love and God is Spirit. The Father comes to the world as Son, the Incarnate Love, working in the world and especially in the Christian community as Spirit. Jesus himself acknowledged that he of himself could do nothing apart from the Father who was in him and worked in him. Sophisticated scholarship would like to keep God the Father out of the world, maintaining that God can come only as Son or as Spirit. But the unity of God cannot be thus sundered. The Father is in the Son and in the Spirit. The Athanasian Creed untiringly stresses that there is 'one Godhead of the Father and of the Son and of the Holy Spirit'; 'they are not three Gods but one God'. The eternal Son became Incarnate in Jesus as the Christ.

God the Son, whom we know as Incarnate Love, is eternal. 'In the beginning was the Word and the Word was with God and the Word was God.' Many people, however, confuse the eternal Son with the historic Jesus. We tend to forget that the Athanasian Creed, for instance, speaks of the Son as God, 'begotten before the ages of the substance of the Father' while the human Jesus is, of course, a man born in the world. The 'only begotten' thus refers to the God part, so to speak, of Jesus as the Christ, and not to the human part of Jesus' personality. The Godman is therefore as God, the eternal Son, from eternity, while as a human being he is born into history and grown there. The 'only begotten' is a relation in God's eternal nature, not an historic event. This fact all the major creeds of the early Church emphasize. Therefore the dominant, decisive reality of the historic personality of Jesus, the Son of God, is eternal, but his humanity is not. Nevertheless the creeds cause confusion when

38

they use the term Jesus Christ in connection with the Son's being 'begotten before all ages', as in the Nicene Creed, for Jesus Christ as an historic personality refers to the Godman who was not thus begotten in eternity. Jesus Christ consists of the Son of God and the full humanity of Jesus, and only the former is begotten in eternity as a relation in God himself. Such confusion, which comes easily, can underlie the calling Jesus God rather than the Son of God.

To consider the New Testament itself: an original manuscript of the Gospel of John reads for chapter 1[18] 'the only begotten God' instead of our usual reading 'the only begotten Son'. The two versions mean the same, but well-meaning readers think of the historic Jesus when they read of 'the only begotten Son'. As a matter of fact, many think of the historic Jesus with no distinction between the eternal Son and the historic humanity when they read that 'God so loved the world that he gave his only begotten Son that whosoever believeth in him should not perish but have everlasting life'. Even worse, some think that 'only begotten' refers to the human personality and to his being conceived by the Holy Spirit and born of Mary! The human personality came to be in a manner common to all men, as Jesus grew 'in wisdom and in stature, and in favour with God and man', in a specific place and time, in Palestine at the beginning of our era.

The New Testament, in fact, is most sparing in calling Jesus God except for exclamations, as when Thomas recognized Jesus after the resurrection, or in the Book of Revelation (which had great difficulty in getting into the canon and is not even yet fully established in some Christian circles in the East). Jesus' own favourite title for himself was the Son of Man. For me, this term stands increasingly for human authenticity, the hallmark of Jesus' ministry. Any one who will take the trouble to read Vincent Taylor's *The Names of Jesus* or William Barclay's *Jesus As They Saw Him* will note how often the designations for Jesus, or his self-designations, are Son of Man, Messiah, Christ, the Son of God, perhaps even particularly when the scope of the whole New Testament is taken into account.

The unfortunate fact is that Christianity as generally conceived by preacher and pew alike has usually meant by 'the Son of God' not the eternally generated Son before all ages who indwelt or inspirited the human Jesus, thus effecting the Godman, not the eternal Word made flesh, not the Logos who in the beginning was with God and was God, but just plainly the son of Mary. Little or no distinction has been made between what Emil Brunner in *The Mediator* calls the eternal Person and the historic personality of Jesus. The eternal Son must be genuinely identified with the historic personality of Jesus as central to both the process of becoming of this personality and the final product, indeed, as central to both its reality and significance, without at the same time being equated outright with the historic personality or without any limiting of the eternal Son by the human being that Jesus truly was.

Please take note of the fact that I do not say the *human* personality of Jesus but rather the *historic* personality. By the presence and power of God in him, by the reality of Incarnation, Jesus, while being fully human, became more than an ordinary human personality. He became the historic Son of God by the presence of the eternal Son of God, and thereby made it possible for us to become sons of God and share of his fullness 'grace for grace'. Therefore I advisedly and emphatically use the term 'the historic personality' of Jesus who was the Godman, the human personality uniquely fulfilled in history by the real, organic presence of God.

Theologians have spoken of the hypostatic union which became unique in Jesus Christ, meaning thereby a miraculous togetherness of the divine and the human without division and confusion in one genuine personality. But such language is due to the assumptions of a false substance philosophy which precludes the natural union of the divine and the human. Such substance thinking, as we saw in the previous chapter, distorts and disturbs all theological problems which are posed in its terms. The fact is, rather, that God in the very beginning so made man for himself that the more man allows God to indwell or inspirit him while he also worships and relates himself rightly to the God who is transcendently beyond him, the more man becomes truly human.

Irenaeus, with both precision and depth, showed that Adam was only potentially man. Full manhood came first with Jesus Christ, who knew God to be universal Love and who lived this reality into human history. It is into such 'mature manhood' that all are invited to enter when they come to the full measure of the stature of Christ. No new translation of the Bible should be allowed from enfeebling theological contexts to reduce the key verses in the New Testament which undergird our sanctification. Christ must be 'formed in' us and we must 'present every man perfect in Christ'. The eternal Son came in Jesus Christ for all men!

The church, *nota bene*, fought valiantly for centuries to keep theologians, as well as the pressures of common piety, from minimizing the humanity of Jesus and to prevent all detractions from its genuineness. As long as they could, the Fathers warded off insistently the urgent but misdirected piety, which in turn affected the theologians, which wanted to subtract from Jesus what in the thought-world of those days amounted to a human ego or a human will. Indeed, the explicit reference to Jesus as the 'only Son', a phrase which is of course found already in the Bible, had an uphill even though an ever-winning battle. Observe, for instance, the vehemence and care with which Gregory Naziansus and Gregory of Nyssa fought Apollinaris in what seemed to them his attempt to remove the core of Jesus' human nature and make him instead of the Godman only God in human form; or recall with what fury Nestorius attacked the Alexandrians when they used the expression *theotokos* (mother of God) for Mary, on the grounds that such language undermined the acceptance of Christ's genuine human nature. Mary was not a tube for artificially transmitting the Son of God in a human body but the authentic human mother of an authentic human child. Jesus was born not as a freak or sport of supernature but as an ordinary, common child of our human race. Theodore of Mopsuestia's tireless witness to the full nature of the Godman portrays the truly human Jesus in whom God had come to visit and to save his people.

An ardent, though misdirected piety, mingled with an altogether natural fear-filled longing to evade the full relevance of the Gospel, increasingly distorted the Gospel, substituting the myth for the full reality, the half-truth of both devotion and evasion for the 'whole council of God' in the Incarnation. Admittedly, the mischief was done under the auspices more of worship than of theology. Devotion often wants to remove God far from us in order that he may seem the more 'real' to us.

41

We dread to accept anything in human history as authentically of God lest we become idolatrous and bow down to gods of our own making. God chose Incarnation, his actual coming to us, in order to stay with us. He came in Christ that the Holy Spirit might be available to us all. But in order for Jesus to mediate God to us we are tempted to put the whole of the historic personality on the side of God. Thus Jesus as God becomes more real to us than Jesus as the Son of God, a truly human being fulfilled in himself and fulfilled for us all.

The ardent piety of worship with a logic all its own, it sometimes seems, at the same time combined with an ambiguous dread of God's full revelation and its demands upon us, conspired in depth-slyness, below full conscious choice, to bypass historic and systematic criticism, and created its own theology to fit its own moods and needs. No human being or set of people can therefore be held responsible for the historic transformation of the Gospel into the myth. The development of the fuller understanding of the Gospel and the subtle reshaping of it walked hand in hand, even though not without tension. The history of thought moves from depth of need, and human need is always heavily conditioned by general attainment. Religion is no exception as it produces its thought-forms. The craving for the half-truth created the confession that Jesus is God as the central emphasis that shoved aside and made nearly impotent the full truth of the Gospel, namely that Jesus is the Son of God, the human being who became co-inhabited by the eternal Son and thus 'the pioneer and perfector of our faith'.

Even today many of us are still ambivalent concerning the finding and the re-establishing of the true Gospel. The myth seems both easier for worship and less demanding for life. But all over the world Christianity is now fighting for its life among the honest and the educated. The moment of truth for the Church is now upon us. In Sweden and on the Continent the Christian faith is hardly a viable option. We have felt some of this atmosphere in Britain and now it is increasingly observed even in the United States. However 'old hat' Bishop Robinson's *Honest to God* may now seem, no one can deny that once it struck a most sensitive nerve. People are concerned with the faith, but they cannot endure traditionalistic mythology. Those of us who believe that the Christian faith at its centre is true had better make a clean breast of our problems. Those of us, in any case, who live and think in the light of the Incarnation are under the most serious obligation to confess what we do *not* mean by the term. However much we may glow inwardly and however intellectually overcome we may be by the truth of the faith we confess, we must be sober and concerned to express to the outside world what we believe and why. If we begin by being truly honest with ourselves in facing our inner doubts we may receive the courage to be genuine in sharing even our misgivings with others. Faith can live only by the truth that both grasps and holds us.

We have theological problems, for instance, with the hymns we sing; we do, that is, if we have been awakened to the distinction between the myth and the Gospel. What, for instance, do we intend by the affirmation 'Jesus shall reign where'er the sun doth its successive journeys run'? To some, this use of Jesus seems merely convenient shorthand, substituting the historic personality for the eternal Word, but to others such use of the historic name amounts to sheer blasphemy, putting a human being in the place of God. Are Jesus and God simply the same? What, then, of the human personality born of Mary, who in all things was like us except for being victorious over sin? If Christ is in *me* the hope of glory, if for *me* to live is Christ, if the Spirit of Christ be truly in *me*, if the Son of God form the inmost core of *my* new being, *my* new creaturehood, dare I say, with whatever poetic licence, that I shall reign over all times and places? Indeed, I am joint heir with Christ and all things are ours for we are Christ's and Christ is God's.

All these expressions are biblical and true, but are such ascriptions what come to mind when we sing, 'Jesus shall reign'? To be sure, the problem goes deep into human hearts as well as into historic realities. I suggest that neither those who fasten on the divine side nor those who focus on the human side of the historic Godman are right, for the Godman represents God and man in conclusive fulfilment which is the very power that shall win the ultimate victory. Nevertheless the use of the name, Jesus, is theologically inexact and therefore theologically illegitimate. Jesus must not lose his humanity, his full relevance for us, by being equated outright with God and only with God, even in the most devoted moods of worship. Thus we are troubled. Is it possible merely to ignore such mythology, such use of myth as half-truth, and yet suffer no anxiety for how the Gospel, the full truth of Incarnation, fares in the hot fires of worship? Do we need to be literal minded, after all?

I am reminded of a well known Methodist bishop who told me in a jocular mood of informal confidence that often during services of worship he had to keep his fingers crossed in order to remain honest. The outside world, however, observing such attitudes, calls us hypocrites, and not without real justification. The bishop, of course, felt understandably that we are all prisoners of liturgy. We cannot help participating in the on-going worship of the congregation, mostly prescribed by the past, any more than we can escape being involved in a war which our country declares. Perhaps we believe in the meaning of the affirmations in general and would deny more truth by not participating than by lisping some things which we do not personally believe. The further question is, however, whether we protest what we believe is wrong and try to have the content of worship changed. Do we protest our misgivings, or do we simply ignore them and thereby help to increase the moral insensitivity of the world in general? The question is exceedingly complex and involved, but the least we can do is to admit that we do have genuine and searching problems.

To take an even more painful example, take a look at the glorious, rousing Methodist hymn 'Crown him Lord of all'. Is it Jesus who is Lord of all, or is it the Holy Trinity, the God who is Father, Love and Spirit, Creator and Redeemer, world without end? I believe with all my heart and with all my mind, and I hope with all my strength, that we meet God himself in Jesus Christ. I believe that Incarnation is basically a direct revelation of God as the personal Spirit who is Love. The life of God triumphed in the life of Jesus. To use technical language, I am one of the few theologians who believe that revelation at its centre is univocal, that is that revelation through Incarnation is reliably directive for both truth and life. In Jesus God fulfilled time, his eternal purpose for man. In Jesus God came to be understood in his inmost nature and purpose, and through Jesus God made a living way to himself, a reliable way for us to follow.

I also believe that God took on our sins, and our mortal

enemies of meaninglessness and death, showing us both of what to be forgiven and how to be brought to our true self by God's grace. God's presence in Jesus as Love made him both go to death and be put to death in order that we may know, not only the full nature of our guilt in our sinning against Love, but also the power for forgiveness which became accessible to mankind by the deathless love of Christ. I believe furthermore that God raised Jesus from the dead; in fact, that the Christian faith stands or falls not with historic details but with the reality of the resurrection: the final victory of love over sin and of life over death. In the deepest realities and affirmations, in spite of my difficulties with traditionalistic language, I am classically a confessor of the transcendent living God and of his triumphant being and working in Christ for our salvation, both in symbol and in summary.

I also believe with equal firmness the human side of the Gospel. I believe in the full humanity of Jesus, that he was one of us, an ordinary man in his original, essential make-up. Therefore the language of some hymns, however stirring and appealing, by being falsely one-sided often causes me genuine intellectual and moral problems. Is part of this pain attributable to my training as a technical theologian and my responsibility for the faith of the Church? It always gives me comfort to think that a theologian like Calvin would exult in being able, as he said, better to sing the creeds than to say them, because saying them made them seem more literal and wooden. Perhaps hymns as poetry are not subject to the strict requirements of theological truth. Perhaps many of us are too literal-minded in the first place, and that is really what is the matter. The question, however, concerns not so much our own private feelings as the fact that now the judgement has begun with the house of God and we are asked to use at least honest and dependable language. How can one 'let oneself go' in honest and committed worship if one feels that the full truth is not expressed? How much more difficult worship becomes when one realizes that the myth plays a decided part in obscuring the full reality and relevance of the Gospel.

Christmas brings the problem of theological honesty to a head. We know that Christmas signifies a fuller and more amazing truth than any pen can print or tongue can sing. We celebrate the birth into human history of Incarnate Love. But alas, for too many the celebration never comes off full-fledged and marvellous because their minds will not allow it. 'Newborn deity'? Was the eternal Son, who is begotten before all ages, ever born? Can God be born? Can God die? Or was Jesus born? Was not a human being born? Was it not Jesus who died? Did not the historic personality, and in particular the human personality, die? Celebrating faith created glorious myths to signify the miracle of God's birth into human history, not God's birth! Celebrating faith created numinous poems to carol at Christmas-time.

The literal minded miss the stars in the sky and the arduous trek of Wise Men. The literal minded choke on the carols that chime Love's miracle in coming to us. Many worshippers consequently feel deep within that to discuss Christmas in an ordinary mood and in our usual language would cause it to evaporate like faith in Santa Claus. They avoid raising, even to themselves, the issue of honesty in Christian worship, and attend Christmas pageants with a knowing look that betrays their ambivalence. How they long to believe! How what is high and holy and right and good is centred in the Christmas drama. They do not want it spoiled for them, but neither can they really believe it. They can neither accept nor let go what means the most of them, what they should want to be true.

Divided loyalty to the myth thus often keeps the Gospel from coming strong and clear through our worship. But need it be so? The early Church got along without any celebration of Christmas. The strong Puritan faith in Britain and the American colonies refused special holidays since all Christian worship celebrated the truth of Christmas and Easter. By returning to the Gospel can our faith become strong enough and real enough to make us historically honest and creatively celebrant? Why should not our 'Joy to the world, the Lord has come' really refer to the full Gospel that the eternal Father has come as Incarnate Love to offer us the 'miracle of Christmas'. Why do we value the frame more than the picture? Even though we mean merely to lean on symbols and myths, in fact they may prove disastrous if they affect not only the worshipper's own sense of reality but also the moral fabric of society.

We could go on to speak of the problematic nature of prayers to Jesus, with whatever strong precedents, even biblically, and to point out how many aspects of our common liturgies fail to distinguish between Jesus as God and Jesus as the Son of God, between the half-truth of the myth and the full truth of the Gospel. If we did so, we should have to discuss first the nature of Scripture as the sourcebook, not the textbook of truth, as we shall do in the next chapter. We should, indeed, have to query the prayer to Jesus by St Stephen as he looked up into heaven and saw Jesus standing on the right hand of God (and we might find ourselves caught in the literal problem why Jesus *sits* on the right hand of God according to the creeds while St Stephen saw him *standing* there!), and we should have to conclude that this incident is framed in mythological terms.

We should even have to explain why prayers to Jesus are not according to the full Gospel but only according to the half-truth of myth, even though in Philippians St Paul writes of every knee bowing to Jesus above, on and under the earth. Does he not really mean here the eternal Son, the Incarnate Love, the Word made flesh rather than the historic personality? Or is not the historic personality, the Godman, also legitimate if in that humanity is included all humanity potentially, the corporate reality of man as one personality 'in union with Christ Jesus'? Two realities are at stake in prayers to Jesus. We must not pray to man but to God, and we must not sunder the humanity of Jesus from our common humanity.

The point is already sufficiently made. There is no need for further elaboration. In this first section of our analysis I have illustrated what I mean by the myth rather than by the Gospel and how essential the true part of the myth is for revelation. We must never lose sight of the fact that what makes Jesus of final importance is the reality of the Incarnation, that God was truly present in him for man's salvation. I must go on, however, to point out not only how ardent but misdirected piety helped create the myth and substitute it for the full Gospel, but also how, as I have already hinted, fear-filled man longed to escape the burden and the responsibility of the full Gospel. Fear makes even the Gospel of God's love into law, the most demanding and therefore the most dreaded of all laws. Love both led Jesus to the Cross and made others drive him there. When I have treated this aspect of our analysis, I must go on to make clear, beyond the shadow of honest and informed doubt, that I am advocating nothing less than the true Gospel of the Christian faith, even the full truth of Incarnation, God's being in Christ reconciling the world unto himself.

II

Religion is subtle business. What in fact motivates us is often different from what we assume to give life meaning. In this way, we may even mean or consciously intend the Gospel, when, in fact, our depth-driven self is motivated by the half-truth that is omitted in the confession that Jesus is God. Thus we allow the half-truth that Jesus is God to turn motivationally into the un-truth that Jesus is not man. If Jesus' life is not generally and authentically human, his life is irrelevant to ours and we are enabled to escape the high and holy demands of the Gospel. We only cheat ourselves of the glory of the Gospel, of course, but in our depth-conscious we hide this fact in order to be able to enjoy our escape from the threat of the Gospel's demands. We therefore can very well worship Jesus as God in order to escape facing ourselves as men. I repeat, then, at the opening of this second section of our analysis, that the Gospel deals with the Word made flesh, God in full humanity, whereas the myth is not full Incarnation but rather theogony, God on earth in a human body rather than in an authentic human being. Theogony we can look at and wonder; Incarnation calls for acceptance and commitment. The myth offers us a magical salvation without real cost to us; the Gospel offers joy of forgiveness and change of life, the joy of being right with God in grace and faith. Fearful and sinful man dreads the Gospel as demanding what to him is an unreasonable sacrifice of the pleasures and profits of ordinary life.

Worshipping Jesus as God, of course, puts him conveniently out of our class. We crave to do so, for then we can be thankful for both his life and his work without their having direct relevance to our own lives. The myth never intimately involves us; it enables us to reason thus:

Jesus could be such a person; Jesus could do such deeds; Jesus could say such things. But that was Jesus. He was the

Son of God. That was God himself speaking. He is eternal, he knew everything, he could do anything. But surely it is presumptuous for us even to think that we can be in the same class. After all, we are not little Christs walking around; we are not God as he was. People who think that God is in them and working in them have messianic complexes. We modern men have psychiatrists to ward off the claims of those who speak directly for God.

We know exactly how to blunt the Gospel and how to make it unacceptable by appeal to modern thought forms. We have been going through a strange period of Christian thought which has prided itself upon radical secularity or complete absence of God in human affairs. What would John Wesley say if he could reappear in our day? What would Augustine say, not to mention Jesus himself? One of the strongest moods of the modern Church is to disclaim all comparison to Jesus. The refusal of the Gospel in favour of the myth is strong and steady. In the meantime the Church is confused, impotent, and even decaying.

We forget that God in Jesus must never be confused with the human personality. We forget that the eternally personal nature of the Infinite Spirit effected a historic personality, the Godman, but was never changed into a human being. Similarly, at the same time and to the same end, we ignore the fact that the same eternal Spirit alone can finally fulfil our lives. There is only one eternal Son of God, one Word, one Logos, who must light every one who comes into the world. He who became flesh in Jesus must become flesh in us and our hope of glory. We must all receive of his fullness 'grace for grace'. We fail to take with full seriousness the injunction that we not only should but can walk 'even as he walked'. We pay only lip service to Jesus' promise that we should do greater works than he because he had gone to his Father. We choose to suppress, and even repress, his open acknowledgement that the Father did the works in him, and the same Spirit should bear the same fruit in us.

In the guise of humility it is easy to forget or to ignore the fact that all of us are sons of God, who are born not 'of blood, nor of flesh, nor of the will of man, but of God'. Much of the reason for such forgetting or ignoring is a deep seated doubt, and even dread, that if these promises are truly for us also, the

Gospel cannot be true. If so, we have to be tested; God offers to test the Gospel in us, and we are rather certain that we shall fail that test. Therefore, in order to keep the Gospel at all, we resort to the untestable myth.

One of our most basic problems, moreover, is that the myth from its earliest inception became enmeshed with both biblical and systematic theology and thus gained the power of established truth. Indeed, those who promote the myth are usually praised for their 'high Christology'. A high Christology, however, is never a one-sided half-truth but rather the full truth of the Gospel, the glorious whole truth of the Incarnation! The more central and the more inclusive to all of life and to all men that Incarnation is understood to be, the higher the Christology. But our craving for myth is almost like the craving for narcotics. It perverts the interpretation, elevating the irrelevant but convenient half-truth as the high truth of our faith.

The myth never fits the human situation. Jesus is worshipped into irrelevance. He is put on the altar and kept there, as safe and attractive as the altar ornaments. The Gospel, on the contrary, is a shoe that fits. It fits the hand, too, tighter than a glove. The Gospel fits like a spiritual skin. The humanity of Jesus lets Jesus be one of us for all of us. The deity of Jesus lets Jesus be the Son of God who gives us the power also to become God's sons with him. The myth lets us off the hook. The Gospel impales us in the very middle of our sinful selves.

The Gospel shows up our fatal cancer. It declares our impotence to heal ourselves. The Gospel is so realistic and so unsentimental that it thrusts the X-ray pictures of ourselves unavoidably before our eyes. But in so doing it all-importantly reveals our condition to be operable. It offers us true hope and healing, encouraging us to face the full facts of our situation because it can meet those facts. The Gospel promises to overcome the disaster which it shows us.

Obtusely, however, most people prefer the myth as long as they can hang on to it. It seems pleasanter than the Gospel. The myth promises quack medicine, which the patient tries to convince himself will work. Jesus did what is needed for us, runs the myth, and all we have to do is to accept what he did. The damaging half-truth turns into a disastrous untruth.

Subtly we insinuate the word 'only' into our confessions; we have *only* to accept what Jesus did for us. We have *only* to confess his name and believe. We have *only* to make confession with our mouth. We have *only* to be assured that God for Jesus's sake will cure us forever. Thus we make grace cheap, salvation for us becomes 'free', and we labour to convince ourselves that the Gospel is really true. All the while we wonder at our Churches' impotence to stem the world's wickedness or to stay its destruction. The reason: we have falsified the Gospel by accepting the myth.

The Gospel, rather, demands that we enter into the same relationship to God which made Jesus' life become what it was. The Apostle Paul maintained that unless we have the Spirit of Christ we are none of his; and there is only one Spirit of Christ. We either have that Spirit or not. We must let the same mind be in us also which was even in Jesus Christ. It does us no good to translate the phrase 'among you' instead of 'in you'. The mind or the spirit cannot be shared unless it is had! We cannot put off these verses by slanted translations. They stare us stubbornly in the face. Without being textbook quotations, they are primary source material for the most basic Christian verities.

That mind which was in Christ Jesus haunts us and helps us. The way has been made for us by a lonely sufferer who walked there for us. But we have to walk the same way. The cross he bore for us of self-renunciation and or complete other-concern is for us to take up and to bear also; otherwise we cannot be his disciples. This glorious Gospel of release from self and of joy in faith in God and other-concern has the sure remedy for our lives and for the ills of the world, but we hold it off by accepting only a part, the half-truth that Jesus was God, while denying the rest, namely that the same God waits to save us and our world, only on the condition that we accept the full Gospel. For our sakes God has entered human life in Jesus as the Christ in order to make it possible for us to become right with him, to have our lives fulfilled, and to help heal the sickness of the world. We detonate the explosive power of that Gospel by refusing to carry it through to its full point of contact. We worship the power line of salvation, but do not dare to connect it to our own lives.

Not only, however, do we worship Jesus as God in order not

to have to face ourselves as men. We also worship Jesus as God instead of as Son of God in order not to have to face God himself. We tend to make God himself unknowable and inaccessible. Jesus often takes the place of God, for we say we cannot know God, but we can know Jesus. In this way Jesus becomes a go-between rather than a mediator. He becomes a wall that keeps God out, rather than a door through whom we can go to find God our Father. He becomes a roof to shelter us from God, rather than a skylight to reveal him.

Accordingly, we abuse Scripture to the same effect. As we shall see in the next chapter, we fail to use the Bible as a source-book with Christ, the universal Love, as the pattern for interpretation and the model for living. Thus, for instance, the passage that claims that no one comes to the Father except through the Son is made into an exclusivistic in-group position of defence. The Son is made into a historic personage of limited dimensions rather than the Eternal Son who reveals the only true God, Father, Spirit and Love. Only those who see and accept that universal Love of the Father for all men know and can accept the right relation with God and men, which alone is salvation. If this passage is taken in any other manner, it belies the Gospel at its heart and reveals the hardening of the spiritual arteries of the early Church.

The eternal Son alone can show us the Father, for the Son as the Incarnate Love of God is unconditionally the only way to the Father. Truth is the way to life as Love has prepared it. There is no other eternal Life. There is no other Father of life. Therefore the Johannine witness, as a whole, organically connects God who is Life, God who is Spirit, God who is Love, with the Son who thus reveals him.

How far avoidance of the true God has gone! The founder of an important conservative Christian youth organization wrote me that despite his uncertainty that Paul Tillich taught the living, personal God of the New Testament, nevertheless that question was of secondary importance since Tillich believed Jesus to be the Christ. In the United States, at least, many agree with the outstanding Baptist minister who assured me that faith in God is far less important than faith in Christ as Saviour. Van Buren's *The Secular Meaning of the Gospel* has at least been indicative of a strong trend among sophisticated theologians and preachers. This book was fittingly reviewed in *The Christian Century* under the caption 'There is no God and Jesus is his Son'. Indeed the myth has, for many, replaced God. The living God who acts in history, who matters to man's meaning and destiny, has become a theological option. Even though at first such was mostly subconsciously the case, now the infection has come to the surface and the purulence is exposed.

I realize, of course, that our situation is far from simple. Old ideas of God have to die and new thought forms must come to birth. For those who are unsure of God, the best approach to an understanding that is both honest and real to them as a Christian confession is to start with Jesus Christ as the most saving truth they know. As they develop this confession to an ultimate, can they fail finally to arrive far from the Christian view of God? Can we wonder at the concrete need of these thinkers to hold on to something that is genuinely Christian? Can we not, indeed, feel a good deal of sympathy for them? Thus what sounds preposterous, to believe in Christ as Saviour without believing in God, may even have a certain attraction. The God these seekers find may be the greater God, the Father of our Lord Jesus Christ, unfettered from much hampering theological development and illumined by new thought forms that better accord with modern knowledge.

It is up to those of us, in any case, who are committed both to truth and to our Christian heritage—and who care within the total responsibility of the needs of people and of the world—to make the Gospel come vibrantly alive for our day and for the years to come. We must honestly acknowledge that modern scepticism is due not only to modern knowledge but also to the fact that we have anaesthetized the Gospel by substituting the half-truth of theogony for the whole truth of the Incarnation, that we have complacently or evasively proclaimed Jesus to be God instead of insisting on the fuller truth that he is the Son of God, normative to both theology and anthropology, the truth of both God and man. We have made him unique, but uniquely inaccessible rather than explanatory. We have worshipped him as uniquely God rather than as the one who finally brings God and man together into the fulfilment of creation.

The myth is magically irrelevant and externally saving; the

Gospel is totally relevant and concretely saving. The myth sounds great by removing God from man in actual fact, even when he is claimed to come into history; the Gospel tells us that God has come to save us and stands now at our door in judgement for salvation, that we might repent and reform, and find the only righteousness in him that can finally satisfy life and remake our world. But precisely that note makes men fear God and flee him in proportion to their dread. It seems easier, too, to escape him by distorting rather than by denying the Gospel.

John Wesley started a flaming evangelism by insisting on a high doctrine of sanctification with regard both to personal life and to the Christian impact on society. That evangelism is exactly the import of this analysis. God must be proclaimed as great but also as near, and ready to enter our lives to be again the power of salvation. God longs to free the world for a new age. He needs the leaven of our accepting the full Gospel to enter the whole loaf. Can we for our own day not only recapture that radiance of the full truth of the Gospel but even go on to develop more fully and effectively 'the whole council of God'? I have a deep, throbbing conviction that the power of John Wesley's message was in making the Gospel of God's love in Christ exceptionally relevant to both personal life and civilization. In a new, critical day of modernity we may have to rework our doctrines of both Christ and God; but must they not aim at that power which John Wesley helped to release for the world? I believe we stand on the edge of a new era of Gospel preaching and Gospel power.

We may worship Jesus partly not to have to face ourselves; we may also worship him in order not to have to face God; but may we not also worship him as God rather than as Son of God in order not to have to face the real, historical Jesus? This Jesus may in fact be harder to find and to face than either ourselves or God! Is it not excruciatingly difficult to know clearly what Jesus was really like? It is far easier to encounter a theologized, yes, a mythologized Christ than to meet him who humbly preferred to be called the Son of Man. Far better it seems to ponder some eternal Christ, or even some Christ-figure from theologized history than to come into the presence of the genuine human Jesus who walked the gentle hills of Galilee and trudged the long, barren valleys of Judea. On an

Israel hillside I have myself meditated on the difficulty of coming to grips with the life through which I best see God. How can one be both completely honest with oneself and also unconditionally concerned to help people from within the ideas of Jesus which they already have?

Even piety hides Jesus from us. For example, a deeply Christian denominational executive of generally progressive convictions spoke of standing in a public garden where there was a compelling statue of Jesus. As he stood there he noted that casual strollers invariably stopped smoking when confronted by this sculpture. Reverence for this Son of God made every person be at his Sunday best. In the presence of God in human flesh all levity fell away; there could be no joking, no smoking, but only a longing to fall to one's knees in worship, or at the very least, in searching silence. As the speaker recounted this experience we were all moved by his magnificently reverent spirit and by his constraining testimony to the living Christ. Who would not be at his best facing God, particularly when facing God in human flesh, even through a compelling representation?

Yet Jesus of Nazareth historically was a man so real and so common that he thought nothing at all of human opinion and despised all false piety that removed God to some extraordinary realm of life. As I listened to the speaker, therefore, I was torn between on the one hand, my own deep appreciation and reverence for Jesus as the Son of God, which involved the renouncing of the ordinary, the profane, the secular for the beauty of holiness in the realm of the sacred, and, on the other hand, my carping, critical conscience which kept telling me that I was in fact betraying the meaning of the Incarnation. Jesus in historic dress ate with publicans and sinners; he even ate with unwashed hands; he associated with harlots and preferred their righteousness to that of the Pharisees who would be touched by no evil habit, who were altogether respectable, who would associate only with the righteous, who wanted always to be at their Sabbath best for God. No mingling for these righteous folk with the common lot of sinful men! Certainly no chance of finding them with the disreputable, with the openly unacceptable segment of society. Certainly no cigarettes or pubs for them (or whatever the equivalent may have been) in the presence of God. But to Jesus these pietists represented the dried crusts of respectability. If we dare trust the record as direct reporting rather than as imaginative creation, Jesus even called these best-of-all people 'sons of snakes'. Was relegating Jesus to a statue to be revered in a garden not rejecting the historic Jesus, the rough realist of human nature who seemingly specialized in shocking those who were at their Sabbath best for God?

A denomination known in the United States for puritanical leanings once asked me to present Jesus in modern dress to a nationwide assembly of college youth. (No smoking on the convention grounds!) The more I pondered the invitation the more uneasy I became. I had either to offend my sense of historic integrity by dressing him up according to their ideas of him or run the risk of hurting them by trying to be historically honest and imaginatively accurate. Unhappy about either choice, I demurred. But the denomination sent a distinguished committee a considerable distance to urge me not to be abstractly theological but actually to make Jesus 'come alive', as he would appear now if he were presented appropriately in the best light of what he was then. Make him live for our day! Make him concrete and effective! Make the young people actually encounter him!

Eventually I set out to do what they requested, but the more I imagined him in modern dress, the more he offended me first of all. God's manner of Incarnation was not to my liking. I began to realize how prim and moralistic I myself was, how shrunk up within my vital self. Jesus admitted that he came eating and drinking to the point that people called him a winebibber and a glutton. He consorted with the outcasts and the morally disreputable. Where would that put him today? In a pool room, in a pub, at the races, in a gambling joint, at a cocktail party?

One of my most interested and interesting theological students worries me because he claims that he enjoys spending ample time in bars, where he goes especially to talk with the call girls he meets. He tries to prevail on other students to join him, averring that there is something real, human, unpretentious and open in that kind of community. Frankly, I should be afraid to enter such places and timid in such company. I should much prefer to feel 'holy', kneeling before the out-stretched and blessing arms of Thorwaldsen's Christ or some other such representation of him.

Jesus did consort with the untouchables, however, with sinners, with tax collectors, with publicans and harlots. In his presence externals became secondary and the concerns of the heart primary. I hold that the purity of Christ was no external righteousness, but a walking before God wherever he was the most needed and the most readily received, with complete concern for God's will and for human welfare. Therefore, in preparing for my address on Jesus in modern dress, I struggled to be honest with the historic Jesus and also to present a figure that was God's universal love and righteousness for the world. My presentation caused a major explosion, not so much among the college youth nor the committee that had invited me, as with the Bible-loving Fundamentalist wing of the denomination. As a consequence we held a small meeting to review the results. There the leaders of the conservative moralists, with a dignity and realism I shall always remember and respect, told me that although I was unmistakably correct historically, such a Jesus could not be presented to our day without leading people astray.

Do we, then, want the real Jesus? Or do we want to create a more effective Incarnation for our own day? Who can really depict the historic Jesus in modern dress? What shocking offence could touch sharply enough the nerve of the pillars of society to cause his death? The people who rejected him out-right were, we must remember, the 'best' people of Jesus' day, the most respected, the most balanced, the most envied and emulated for their righteousness. Should you and I, today, see God in such a strange, offensive, radical figure? Would the Son of God today be recognized in some beatnik, in some odd outsider, no matter how much he believed in God and how kindly he acted towards those who needed him? Should we ourselves not be outraged if he called into question, yes, seemed to undermine, the very foundations of what to us are definitely the ways of God and the good of society?

In any case, we need to examine ourselves closely to see whether we are making Jesus God rather than the Son of Man, God's presence and power in a genuine human being, in order

57

not to have to face the real historical figure who still is offensive to us. Jesus seems to have cared for nothing except God's will for those who needed him most and were most open to his friendship. He seems to have felt that religion makes men hide from God, seals them off from their fellow men, and dries up the juices of human kindness within them. He seems to have believed that the righteous tend to be concerned more with religious rules, like the observance of the Sabbath, than with human healing. Those of us who believe in spiritual disciplines and hanker for the security of some definite don'ts of pietism to prove our Christian correctness still most likely prefer the respectable myth that Jesus is God to the crushing relevance of the Incarnation, especially in its concrete form in the historic Jesus.

In our hearts we still cannot approve of the actual way God chose to fulfil his presence for his revelation and for our salvation. Many of us know in the depths of our heart that we cry, yes, clamour within, 'Give me the half-truth that Jesus is God, but please, Father, spare me the pain of the full truth of the way Thou didst actually become flesh in our human history.' Can it not be, however, that today's stress on radical secularism represents a deep, honest, human longing to sweep away our obfuscations and face the concrete Saviour of men, the eternal Son who condescended to come not just into our Sunday best, but into our weekday worst?

Since there is little place for technical scholarship in this brief work, I hesitate to point out how even some aspects of scholarship prefer the myth to the Gospel, the half-truth that Jesus is God to the full truth of the Incarnation. A bare suggestion to that effect will have to suffice. We who work in the field of scholarship, to be sure, know how far from dedicated we often are, how human are our strivings, and how guilty before God we feel for the clumsy way we handle his Word. We have strong reasons for using our scholarship to hide from God. For us, to accept as dominant, in the interpretation of the use of the Son of Man for Jesus, the heavenly being coming with the clouds is much easier than to bow before the Man of Men who lays bare the very drives of our life. Surely, the simpler and more likely original strand of interpretation, however, is the one which makes Jesus representative man in the sense that the

Sabbath was made for man, not man for the Sabbath. Such a rendering of Jesus had to withstand the growing pressures towards myth-making even within the early Church. So real and so solid was it that it resisted all mythologizing and stands there for us today strong and steady. For many scholars, however, it is easier to use the thought forms of the day, then and now, rather than the revolutionary simplicity of the one who broke those very forms.

A study of the way in which new translations of the Bible increasingly enforce 'orthodoxy' by the choice of theological contexts for exegesis would be illuminating. We are always bringing the Bible up to date, not only by the finding of new manuscripts but by the spectacles we use in reading what has been there from the beginning. Every age does so, of course. Yet consider the rock-ribbed primacy of the universal love of God which Jesus increasingly intended. Joachim Jeremias, for example, has even proposed that Jesus used the word 'Father' exclusively and eschatologically, not in the sense that God was by his intention in creation the Father of all men, but rather that Jesus alone had a right to call God Father and that all others may call him Father only by courtesy as we are invited into Jesus' company.

Thus what purports to be scholarship basically changes the inner core of the New Testament understanding of God as the personal Spirit, who is by nature unconditional and universal Love. To be sure, scholars have a right to differ. What is completely, almost compulsively, clear to one from the primary evidence may not appear equally compelling, nor even constraining, to other investigators. Nevertheless I am convinced that much scholarship, with whatever conscious intention, serves the purpose of removing the historic Jesus from us and substituting for him a God figure that lacks the reality and the relevance of the Incarnation.

Not only may piety and aspects of 'scholarship', furthermore, help us to evade the authentic Jesus as he actually was in human history, but professionalism also may help to hide him. By professionalism, I mean the total feeling or craving for the approval of the Christian in-group, the rewarding *status quo* (call it churchianity or nominal Christianity), which deals so often and so generally with the faith that it becomes almost banal, while at the same time the pressures from the *status quo* make it inexpedient to deviate from the general line. The relationship is exceedingly subtle and difficult to gauge. There is enough seeming independence to make the general approach appear vital. At the same time there is a line of 'correctness' that pays the theologian well to keep, and costs him much in professional reputation to leave.

Some scholars today are using the term 'ecumenical consensus' for the kind of stand and attitude that is correct. Conformism becomes subtly Christian! Even Christian conduct becomes contextualist. Ministers know without being told that for their maximum acceptance, and certainly for maximum approbation, they must recognize that certain subjects should not be threatened by discussion, while at the same time certain shibboleths should be used properly and frequently. On an airplane flight in which my seat mate happened to be the president of a theological seminary, I received a lengthy and illuminating lecture on what 'can' be said and what 'cannot'.

Not only the pulpit, but the pew as well, shares the same situation. As an author I get letters admitting that for years the letter-writer has held certain convictions or has entertained certain thoughts on theological subjects, but has never dared to utter them because he thought that he was not 'supposed' to have them. Thus laymen may even hear certain things from the pulpit and accept them as proper *from there*. The preacher is after all expected to hold these teachings and to proclaim them, but certainly they themselves do not believe them in the same way. In this way professionalism bedevils both preacher and worshipper. The subject above all which should not be threatened is the myth. Indeed, it is rather to be stressed as the central shibboleth. Yet deep down, numberless Christians cannot believe that Jesus actually was God himself walking on earth. They long instead for the true meaning and reality of the Gospel, the setting forth of the Incarnate Love of the Father in all its relevance for ordinary human life.

Such a situation, I am sure, is as old as the Church. The New Testament offers a radical understanding of God through a life that lived and taught God as the personal Spirit of Ultimate Concern. But the New Testament also reveals the beginning process of mythologizing the Gospel. The lines between myth and the Gospel are never clear. God chose to come in this obscure and questionable way. The Gospel came for faith, not for sight! Again in the history of the Church, as the Ecumenical Councils testify, there was determined effort to keep stressing the humanity of Christ as well as his deity. But from the earliest times, too, the ties between Christ and the Christian, between Jesus and all humanity, were increasingly cut. Rather than being the true relation between God and man, the God-man who became the Godman, to offer us also the power through his life and teachings to become sons of God with him, Jesus became deified outright and removed from his full humanity. Instead of allowing Jesus to stand between God and us as an effective bridge for us all to walk on, so to speak, we destroyed the bridge with the claim that Jesus came from the other side and returned to the other side, pulling up the bridge behind him.

Despite the fact that it is the humanity of Jesus that ensures the full reality and relevance of the Incarnation, the myth overcame Incarnation and frustrated its power. For nominal Christians the change was welcome. Professionalism flourishes under the reign of myth, whereas the full hope of the Gospel threatens it. My own most urgent problem, as far as I can dedicate my life and work to God, is how to floodlight the full Gospel that came with Jesus and how to make it clear and relevant for today. When that is done to the best of my ability, the harder part remains: to help motivate this meaning; to help make the true Christ wanted. How can we make the full Gospel not only relevant but appealing? The Gospel is not good news until it is winningly attractive.

So far most of my effort has been to elucidate the nominal Christian's fighting the true Gospel, his hiding behind the half-truths in order to escape the impact of the full revelation of God's love. I have suggested that he wants an irrelevant Christ to forgive his guilt and to provide his salvation, rather than the whole Christ to judge his total life and to remake him thoroughly according to the image of God which he bears deepest within him. Nominal Christians, we are told, comprise ninety per cent of those who confess the faith. But even these cannot be stereotyped as merely acculturated, as merely using the Gospel for other ends, for many of them love Jesus and want both to understand and to accept the will of God in a meaningful measure. I am persuaded that countless people are caught in a heritage of development that obscures for them the full meaning of the Gospel, and they have little time or occasion to question their faith. They mostly take it for granted, or quite naturally think within the framework which has been provided for them.

The fact remains, however, that whatever man thinks he wants and does want in some measure, unless he is thoroughly regenerated, unless he is what the Scripture calls 'born from above', he lives mostly in terms of his self-drives and protecting hopes and fears. His faith, therefore, reflects the fact that it is altogether natural and easy to join in the original sin which conveniently acquiesces in the *status quo* of previous and generally held interpretations. To deviate from one's heritage takes much competence, work and courageous concern. It is no easy matter in our day to find the all-demanding and all-liberating Gospel of the Incarnation. There can therefore be no total blame on any of us for what we now believe; but we should let ourselves be freshly confronted by the majesty and greatness of the full Gospel of Jesus Christ in all its relevance for man's total life and total civilization.

What, then, of those who are intrinsically religious? Professor Allport of Harvard University has conducted intensive and extensive studies to discover the ratio of intrinsic believers to nominal adherents to the faith. In so doing he found that approximately ten per cent of all Church members do not have ulterior motives for their believing but put the faith first in their lives regardless of other interests. Would these intrinsic Christians prefer the Gospel to the myth? Not necessarily. They may never have been shown the difference and therefore they may be deeply zealous in worshipping the myth, 'but not according to knowledge'. They may not understand what difference it makes whether one believes in the one or the other. They may simply love Jesus and mean to honour him. The best way they know to do so is in humility to remove him in his deity as far as possible from them in their sinfulness. Jesus is obviously in an important sense in a class by himself, and the easiest and most emphatic way to stress this difference is to worship him as God as no other human being ever may be worshipped.

These intrinsically religious believers feel the need, no doubt, for the highest possible Christology. Mistakenly they consider that the more different Jesus is from them *in all respects* the more likely he is to be God. They cannot see that no Christology can be higher than the one which finds God truly in Christ, but finds him so in an authentic human being who is one with all mankind. When the stupendous relevance of Jesus' life for the believer, and potentially for all men, breaks in on a person, he is almost numbed with the goodness and greatness of God, and exclaims with St Paul, 'O the depths of the riches both of the wisdom and the knowledge of God', as he sees in Jesus Christ the unspeakable gift of God's love.

Enough, then, of the myth! What matters far more to me is to share my understanding of the Gospel, both to explain it and to commend it. There is no need to repudiate the Christian faith (as some Christian leaders recommend) as unreal, as mythological, as antiquated. When rightly understood, the faith is as real as life and as relevant as breathing. It concerns the central meaning of life itself, not only to explain it but to bestow it, and not only to bestow it but to make a way for its effective appropriation. Away, then, with the myth that Jesus is God and up with the saving truth that Jesus is the Son of God; away with theogony and up with God's gracious Gospel of the Incarnation, that 'God was in Christ reconciling the world unto himself'.

III

Wolfhart Pannenberg in his *Grundzüge der Christologie* bemoans the difficulty of spanning the cleft between the Christ of dogma and the historical Jesus. Can we get them together without doing violence to truth, or must we choose between them, unless perchance we must reject them both as final guides to faith? Edmund Schlink is surely right in maintaining that the way from the New Testament to the climax of the great ecumenical creed, Chalcedon, is one way. Dogma has been developed over the centuries and is not to be found as such in the New Testament. Which, then, do we choose: dogma or the New Testament? Or do we hold, rather, that dogma is merely the development of what was already implicit in the New Testament?

We had better begin where God began, with the life and teachings of Jesus in concrete human history. If the objection is raised that our earliest writings are those of St Paul which have already theologized history, let us not take for granted that history and theology are necessarily opposite poles of interpretation. Instead, we want to understand the nature of the original basis for the faith and to what extent that basis was mythologized in its theological construction. History affords us a concrete life, Jesus Christ; theology deals with what is ultimate and universal. Our task, therefore, is to understand the historic basis of the faith and to see if the ultimate and universal its theologizing provides corresponds to the basis. There is no easy or simple way to do so, but no Christian theologian can legitimately take his stand until he has made up his own mind on the question through his most careful weighing of evidence both critically and creatively.

I shall then essay the task of stating the relation between the historical and the theological. My main contention is that the affirmation that Jesus is God is a myth while the confession that Jesus is the Son of God is sober truth. Somehow, then, Jesus as the Christ must be understood in terms of the Incarnate Word and of a true humanity in such a way that neither the presence of God in Christ nor the full humanity of Jesus, the historic person, is lost, even while Jesus is Son of God and Son of Man in one genuine personality, our Saviour. Such an interpretation of Jesus, too, must with all naturalness be related to previous human history and to all who succeed him. Irenaeus designated the relation of Jesus to previous history as his recapitulating the whole history of the human race. The New Testament renders the relation of Jesus to succeeding ages as his being 'the firstborn among many brethren' or the 'firstborn from the dead'. To put the matter differently: Jesus initiated a new age in human history by fulfilling the old. In him came the fullness of time, which is to say the fulfilling of God's purpose for man. God creates time in order that man might learn freely and lovingly to fill it with the kind of experiences for which God created him in the first place. In Jesus, God thus fulfilled time, and thereby prepared a way for us to follow and to find the authentic meaning of life.

The danger of using the historic life and teachings of Jesus as a point of departure is that we may never get to the fuller meaning which it took the Church centuries to clarify. The danger of starting with the dogma, on the other hand, is that we may never get to the concrete life, which is the only authentic basis of the faith. Let us attempt to avoid both dangers by beginning with the historic life and teachings and by moving along from there to the eternal meaning and power of the Incarnation. One problem will be that we have so long lived uncritically with the myth that it may seem more real and compelling than the Gospel. Another and deeper problem is whether faith *can* be stated with saving power in terms of truth, historic or theological, or whether man is chained to myth. If the latter is the case, I believe that Christianity is doomed, for man will now turn to new myths that are more in harmony with general knowledge, whether through a remythologizing of the Christian faith or by the abandonment of it. For myself, I find no faith more real either for truth or for life. Bear with me, then, as I try to begin the discussion of God's conclusive Incarnation in history where God began, with the concrete life and teachings of Jesus, before moving on to discuss the meaning of that life and teaching in its ultimate dimension and reality.

To present the life and teachings of Jesus concisely and accurately is no easy task. For our purposes, as far as the undertaking can be carried out at all (1) an impressionistic sketch of the quality of his life may best communicate to us what it did to his early followers. We can follow up such a picture of the historical life with (2) a suggestive portrayal of Jesus' central teaching concerning God, especially as his understanding of God bears upon his sonship. Finally we can try (3) to formulate the universal and ultimate meaning of our faith as it centres not in the myth but in the Gospel. It will be most important to start developing these three topics with a general 'feel' for his life as it comes out of the heart of the Gospels.

The life of Jesus could be trusted. Jesus hated sham; he spent his life unearthing hypocrisy. He wanted to give people more life. When Jesus saw people working under a load of pretence, when he saw them labouring under the burden of what others thought of them, when he understood that they were weighed down with narrow rules of the past, when he caught them imprisoned within confining loyalties of custom and class, of sect and nation, when he knew them oppressed by their religion, he suffered. He was too real not to care. He could be trusted to be concerned. He identified himself with what was truly human. The most sacred sabbath was only for man's good. Even the shewbread on the altar was for feeding the hungry if the need was urgent. Taking care of one's parents was more important than lavish gifts to the temple. A human being in need was a neighbour regardless of class, religion, or nation. The natural thing for a hungry man to do in passing through a field of grain was to pick it, crumble away the husks and eat the kernels. Healing took precedence over sabbath observance. Jesus shed externals and artificial rules in order to be real. The life of Jesus could be trusted because it was authentic.

Jesus cared for little children. He talked seriously to women in a day when such a thing was not done. He risked his reputation again and again by the simple and direct living of his common humanity. His was a generic manhood that drew disciples to him and held them with him. He rested when he was tired, with no sense of guilt in so doing, and helped people to understand life and religion when the time was right for doing so. He understood and accepted in patience a friend whom he felt he could not trust and who, indeed, cost him his life. He bore with another of his closest friends who tried to persuade him that he need not suffer, and who promised a loyalty Jesus knew he could not keep. Dying, Jesus thought of his mother, to do something for her. He did not blame those who were to kill him for carrying out their duty. He did not defend himself where he would not be understood. There is something so real about the life of Jesus that whatever comes through the records somehow speaks to us of a great, genuine human being. The more we read about Jesus in the Gospel records, with long pondering, having rid ourselves as best we can of all possible preconceptions, the more a genuine life comes through the pages. His experiences strike us as real beyond argument. Here is no constructed figure. Here is no concocted image. Our inmost and deepest selves know that he is right because he was right. A definite, generally unified, moving figure comes through the records. It is fascinating but not surprising to hear well-trained, critical non-Christians speak with utmost reverence, almost with sacred awe, of the kind of person Jesus must have been and how his teachings come right out of his life. Whatever details we can or cannot know, the depth-memory of the community affords us a generally reliable pattern of life.

Jesus was so authentic, in fact, that he knew men for what they were. When his adversaries tried to trap him by tricky questions he saw through not only the questions but the questioners as well. When men praised and flattered him he knew them better than they knew themselves and did not entrust himself to them. When they came to meet him with shouts of praise he had already set his face towards suffering. The quiet majesty of Jesus stems from the mystery of his being. The constraining dignity of his relating himself to friend and foe alike settles over the perceptive reader like the reality of the sun and the sky. No wonder the very ones who knew him best asked who he was. No wonder that those who observed him from the outside asked the same question.

For a long time it has not been fashionable in theological circles to touch the question of the historic personality of Jesus. After all, it is asked, how much can we know? And is not what we know only the human setting for the Christ of faith? But no! The historic personality was the human personality permeated, activated and consummated by the presence of God. Let us take up Wolfhart Pannenberg's challenge to make the connection between the historic person and the Christ of Christian confession. How could the one lead into the other, or how are they related?

We cannot address ourselves to this question without noticing the kind of life that impressed the disciples, that made them, even while he lived, ask who he was. To the claim that it was the Cross and the Resurrection that changed men's estimate of Jesus, the reply comes at once that Jesus went to death because of the man he was, nor could he be held by death because of the man he was. We must not leave out the manhood. However lacking may be our grasp of the historic figure, God himself used him without even the disciples understanding him while they walked with him. God started with the man. The man, the Messiah and the Son of God belong together. The God-man became the Godman in history; the final *product* which was the integrated historic Son of God became such through the concrete *process* of a human life.

That life did grow. Its growth was not staged but costingly real. When we read his exasperated, 'How I am straitened' (in the Authorized Version) we hardly feel the explosive depths of the anxiety and tensions which he faced in confronting that baptism of suffering through which he had to learn obedience. He grew weary and groaned in spirit. He grew angry and glared at the self-righteous. He complained that whatever he did people were not willing to listen. He had to struggle with temptations from beginning to end, wrestling with the Devil at the beginning of his ministry (whatever form the Devil took), and at the end wrestling with his own will as it balked at drinking the cup of suffering. Even on the Cross he felt himself forsaken by God. We need not blame the writers of the New Testament for these passages, for they help to present a real human being, not a smooth, sinless saint beyond temptation and beyond revolt; one who faced our full human task and who came through with consummate victory over sin. He may, indeed, as my colleague of years ago, Rabbi Joshua Loth Liebman, once claimed, have been too hard on the Pharisees, his real enemies. From our point of view he seems to have called them rather uncharitable names even when they at least seemed ready to listen to him.

We cannot know what happened in detail. Surely we cannot return to the consciousness of Jesus' school of thought. Jesus could have had blind spots both in what he liked and in what he lacked. Would he have been truly human if he had none? He was surely the victim of his own day as to the way he pictured or believed many things. For myself, I must admit that where the record seems to indicate defects of personality I find it easier, because of his character, maturity and depth of insight into the nature of God and man and his very understanding of the workings of love, to attribute these defects rather to the disciples, who continually failed to understand him while he lived and surely had no magic formula for depicting him correctly after his death. But we dare not leave out the possibility that he did have blind spots. At all costs we want the truth of genuine history, not the souped-up myths of 'orthodoxy'. Most dangerous is to refuse God's way of Incarnation, the way of full humanity with all its problems and without magic protection.

Does such a picture of Jesus spoil his life for us? Only if we worship a myth. Jesus knew life well enough to command the allegiance of disciples whose faith in him changed human history at its very centre. Jesus knew man well enough to make us feel uncovered in his presence. Jesus knew love well enough to cause its own inner meaning to come to its climax. The experience of God which Jesus had in his life was so real and so indefinitely expansive that I cannot see how even in principle it can be improved upon. The God he worshipped and lived with was the Father of whose faithfulness there is no end. He held, in other words, an indefinitely open-ended view of God wherein all possible new merely helps to fill in the ever expanding creations or deeds of his faithfulness.

At this point we had better turn from the life of Jesus to our second point, to his teachings about God, especially in so far as the nature of God revealed therein bears on the nature of Jesus' sonship. This latter question we have already touched upon in the foregoing chapter; nevertheless we do need to call it to mind in order to understand the power of Jesus as the Son of God not only in his living but also in his understanding of the kind of Son he was.

Jesus called God 'Father', as we have seen, from his earliest reported youthful appearing in the Temple to his dying on the Cross. He also taught his disciples to call God Father. Jesus' later followers, like St Paul, took over the usage. To be father in the best sense is to be dependable to provide for the children's every need. Jesus believed that God was ever faithful in his concern for all his children. No higher thought about God in principle, as we have already suggested, can come to anyone, now or to eternity. If thought is at all reliable, if truth is genuinely truth, if God is all-faithful and all-competent, one thing is certain: whatever we can learn about God throughout all eternity is only more of his faithfulness. Such a view of God, of course, provides incomparably more mystery than meaning, for who can know the endless eternities, and who can know what to us now is qualitatively quite beyond our ken? But whatever we shall ever come to know at any time and of whatever kind is only more unfolding of God's faithfulness.

Nor does the mystery ever end. The more meaning we come to know, the more we know how qualitatively different is God from man, the Infinite from the finite. Thus in calling God Father in the sense of ever-faithful and ever-competent care, Jesus gave us a quality of understanding God that is open-endedly final beyond all specific content or quantity of knowledge. The finality of faith is reliably directional. Just as the scientist is ever willing, if he is true to his best insights, to keep correcting his findings, assuming at the same time the importance of what he discovers and its indefinite expandibility, even so the man of true Christian faith builds on the kind of understanding of God that is reliable without being exhaustible.

Yet such a knowledge of God can never be a mere view; it must come out of the experience of a continuing relation with God. It comes like a child's understanding of his earthly father, through actual living with him. No wonder the disciples went straight to the heart of Jesus' understanding of God when they asked him to teach them to pray. They came to grasp the fact that they must themselves learn to know God in the way Jesus had done, by living with him, by walking with him in the many windings of the complicated road of life.

In the same way that he called him Father, Jesus interpreted God as the perfect Love who sent his rain on the just and on the unjust. God was the husbandman who rewarded the labourers in the vineyard according to their need beyond desert. Love fulfilled and surpassed justice. God was the Father who in love received back the impoverished and heartbroken son of shame. God was the Shepherd who sought even the hundredth sheep that was lost, even though the ninety nine were safe. This incredible, unconditional Love startled the people, undermined their sense of Justice, and upset their coveted merits as well as their ever improved defences before God. Not only was there no end to the faithfulness of the God whom Jesus knew as Father and Love, but also there was no limit to his outreach. The love of God was universal, unconditional and eternal.

It may be said, of course, that although Jesus had the best possible view of God, although there can never be a better one since whatever more may be learned of him is only more of the same Love, the objection can be raised that Jesus' view of God is precisely too good to be true. Nothing is too good to be thought of God. His goodness cannot be surpassed either actually or in imagination. Perhaps, indeed, the very opposite is the case: perhaps the superlative view Jesus had of God, forever qualitatively unsurpassable, is too true to seem good to most people! We want, we seem to need, a God who is more like ourselves. And keeping in mind the vastness of the world's evil, what a preposterous consummation in eternity there must be to justify such means.

Imagine actually believing that nothing God has ever made will ever be wasted, that God will not only put all things right, but will make out of the whole heap of human and natural tragedy a result so magnificent that in the experience of it whatever went into the making of it will seem sheer praise. Who can believe such a claim for God? If, however, we accepted Jesus' highest understanding of God as unconditional Love, the ever faithful Father, we should change within ourselves sufficiently to begin to grasp what can happen to us even now, how we can grow and change drastically, and how God can use even the evils in history and nature to make us real in ourselves and thus willing to become authentic in the fuller relation of our maturing in God. In *Evil and the Christian Faith* I have tried to pose all other choices and feel that I have shown the incomparable explanatory adequacy of the Christian faith. Jesus' view of God is not 'too good' in the light of the eternities of man's destiny—of that I am convinced—but it is too true for us to accept without allowing ourselves first to be radically remade. Nothing can be more demanding of us than the highest possible view of God. Such an understanding puts pressure on our lives and on the world to change radically for the better.

Another of Jesus' insights, we remember, was that God was Spirit and that only those who worship him in spirit and in truth can ever come to know him. Only those who are born of the Spirit, born from above, born of God, can understand God as Spirit. Only spirit can ever know Spirit, and then only by means of acceptance of the Spirit and living in the Spirit. Knowledge of God is a fruit of the Spirit. Only the indwelling Spirit can make God real in experience. Until man experiences God as Spirit he cannot have the content for knowing God. The experiences of Spirit and of Love are presuppositional for that filial relation to God which engenders authentic knowledge of his presence.

In our first chapter we found that God is no thing to be known by touch. God is no idea to be known by thought. Ideas indicate, but they do not convey reality. Intuitions hint at the directions and dimensions of spiritual interpenetration and personal encounter, but they cannot produce genuine experience. Faith depends upon the reliability of the reality of the Spirit and of the kind of knowledge in faith which the Spirit alone can supply. God is not even a personality to be known by a limited or localized meeting. God is Spirit and can be known only by Spirit in terms of Spirit. Jesus knew that even the learned and sympathetic Nicodemus had to be an outsider to spiritual realities until he became willing to be born of the Spirit. No arguments, no proofs, no analogies will suffice. Only the direct participation in the power and reality of the Spirit can afford us authentic knowledge of God. Jesus in this deep knowledge of God as Spirit joyfully thanked his Father that these things had been hid from the worldly wise and revealed only to babes, to the single-purposed believers in integrity and concern, in God as faithful and loving, who in himself was Spirit.

We have now looked at least impressionistically at the life of Jesus and have traced the centre of his teachings concerning God. We find that not only do we see life best in Jesus, and God best in Jesus (thus understanding through him both ourselves and ultimates) but we have also in the third place, the main approach to the Christian faith through Jesus. At the depths Jesus and the Christian faith are nearly synonymous terms. Please observe, there is nothing wrong about giving unequivocal allegiance to Jesus. The question is how we do so. Making Jesus God results in worshipping his humanity as God, and such allegiance without discrimination is either ignorant or idolatrous. When, however, we recognize that among all candidates for understanding God, Jesus is the supreme instance historically of God's inbreaking presence, we grasp that God is not to be seen abstractly as an idea or as a speculation of metaphysics, but concretely in a kind of life, in a kind of love, in a kind of spirit.

This is precisely what the Christian faith means by Incarnation, and Incarnation is central to the Christian faith both in understanding and in reality. The Christian faith stands or falls with its view of Christ, and Christ is not to be separated from Jesus. In Jesus we meet the eternal faithfulness of God, universal, unconditional and eternal. His life and teachings both point us to such a God. The Christian faith needs not to embrace a lower or thinner view of Christ or to seek a less exalted view of Jesus than the Incarnation, but rather to live the meaning of that event in our understanding, and through it both the nature of man and the purpose of all creation. Let us make a first attempt at a christological formulation that may, however brief, be foundational for the Christian faith.

According to the basic definitions of God in the New Testament, God is our Father, God is Love and God is Spirit. The Father is personal; therefore God is the personal Spirit who is Love. This God and no other became incarnate in Jesus Christ. God the Father created the world for the fostering of children. God's outgoingness by nature we can call Son in the singular and in the plural Spirit. It is one and the same God who in himself combines the one and the many, the unity of personal purpose and the multiplicity of its manifestation. From the beginning of human history God has worked to communicate his purpose in creation and to reveal himself for the final fulfilment of human life. Thus he has gradually prepared for being understood and accepted by man. This preparation found its fulfilment, the fullness of time, in Jesus. God offered his personal presence and power as the personal Spirit of Love, and Jesus came to understand and to accept this offer. Jesus thereby received fulfillingly into his own life the very nature of God both by his ever fuller encounter with God in prayer and his willing walking in God's way and also by the interpenetration of God's Spirit into the centre of his own personality.

The eternal Son of God thus became the shaping reality of Jesus' life, a life which became formed by that Son. The eternal Son formed the effective basis of the historic Son. He informed his life. Such forming within the freedom of the human personality enlarges the person in his freedom as his authentic nature grows. Jesus Christ, then, is a historic personality who is neither God nor man but both, within a genuine relationship of one human being. We may call this historic personality the

Godman. God and man are both present without being merged into one entity, in such a way that Jesus is neither God nor man but a new combination of both. A combination constitutes neither a mixture nor a compound. He is, rather, a new inter-relation and dynamic interworking of both God and man. He is truly human, but a human being for the first time truly fulfilled by God's purpose in creation, namely that man remains restless and unfree until he find his rest, freedom and fulfilment in his right relation to God. Therefore Jesus as the Christ is normative (or true) man, revealing the only final way in which all men also can find the meaning and the fulfilment of life. Only when the eternal Son of God becomes formed in us can we, too, become genuinely fulfilled according to God's eternal purpose in creation. In this full, critical and saving sense Jesus is the Son of God who gives us power to become sons of God and to partake of 'his fullness, grace for grace'.

Among Protestants, moreover, the work of Christ has been more stressed than his nature. The Reformers emphasized how God in Christ is known through his benefits. Increasingly, too, the modern age has turned subjective. We are not so directly concerned with the objectively existing God as we are with the Christ who came to us, and especially with the God and Christ who come to *us*. One reason for this shift is the new view of the endlessly receding ages in the endlessly extending galaxies. We know no specific beginning of time or of life, for our time and our life may be the most minute examples of the illimitable creations about which we know nothing. Our knowledge of the worlds in which we live has grown apace, but far more widely has flown our imagination. How can man any longer picture a God chiefly concerned with earth, who is definitely known by Incarnation in our kind of time, and who works salvation for man and all creation on some local Calvary? Our God is both too small and too great. Our view of Christ has grown, but not enough. The Church is about to lose the man who thinks, for he genuinely feels that the Christian faith is obsolete.

Yet am I convinced that when God revealed himself in Christ as faithful Love and as universal Righteousness he gave us a pattern through which to picture him, a model that can mould ever new knowledge; for such a view of Christ is indefinitely open-ended and inexhaustibly creative, even while providing a picture of God as near and as relevant as our smallest daily need. Such a view of God in Christ is not only as high as the heart of God, as wide as the world's need, as long as the endless Love of God and as deep as sin and all evil that resists his will, but it is also continually open to fit any circumstance of the new, however radically unknown to us at any time. But can we formulate from it any understanding of what traditionally is called the doctrine of the Atonement? Can we break clear of the Jewish sacrificial system and of all guilt-ridden formulations of satisfaction, and interpret for our own day the eternal truth of God's work in Christ?

Understanding the Cross as God's love suffering in history to win and to woo sinful man provides a starting point. The Cross as God's will to reconcile man to himself is as eternal as God himself. In this sense the Cross precedes creation. God created and creates the world because he loves and wants to share his overflowing joy. God creates to multiply his infinite well-being. God's creation is his sharing of himself. God creates in order to produce personal spirits within the Personal Spirit that intensify and bring to conscious distinction his own blessedness. Such moral and spiritual joy, however, never comes nor can come except through growth in understanding and through free acceptance.

Personal spirits of mature attainment in the depths of freedom and love cannot grow by fission nor be manufactured as products. Nor can they grow as vegetables or even as animals. Life on these levels may reach for, and find fulfilment in, the higher forms, but only the conscious life of moral choice and of creative community can foster developed moral and spiritual reality. Thus, as we saw in the first chapter, God set these finite representations of himself, made in his own image, within an environment where they could grow real and free by learning from the consequences of their choices, and where freedom could find satisfactory meaning and maturation only in the community which is always the contrapletal reality of the uniquely personal.

But God made man first to be set on self, individually and collectively, in order that he might become a real agent. The drives to self and to limited community are so strong in man that he cannot outgrow them simply by socialization. God put a cleft between his own kind of love and man in order that man might never find fulfilment until he would be quite broken of self-drives. Self-drives, moreover, simply do not disappear with increase in knowledge nor do they vanish at the command of will. In other words, man is in this respect naturally an unconquerable sinner. He cannot completely subdue himself, nor can drives to self or to ingroup loyalties which are fed by over-againstness ever be broken down by external force or manipulation. To become both genuine and free man must be willing to let himself be turned inside out by the wooings and winnings of love.

In order to become thus truly willing, he must come to understand himself, his drives and his situation. Then he must become frustrated in his seeking for self-sufficiency within limited drives and limited loves. He must learn to fear what he is and what he wants, as well as what will come to him as he either gets or fails to get that for which he strives. In order to want to be changed to something better man must have been both made for it and be restless for it. God so ordered man's nature in creating him. Oppositely, man must also experience the true satisfaction of living the life of love, first most partially and imaginatively, and then with increasing understanding and satisfaction.

This process of winning man over freely to his true self, which presupposes his being made for God and for all others in creative and concerned community, began with creation. Every bit and manifestation of love which man ever lived, he lived only because God made him for it and offered it to him. All human histories manifest some love of creation, some mothers' self-giving and some fathers' care. Even animals watch over their young and risk their lives for them. By creating, God implanted the beginnings of atonement. The process of atonement commenced with human history. Then as religions evolved, necessitating a sharing of the process of overcoming the mere will to self, the communities built on conflict were that far modified. No line of demarcation can in fact be drawn between religious and ordinary life because God was present in both to the same end, evolving selfhood and community, and softening both into creative openness as the leaven of love grew. Finally

God came to be understood as the living God of history as well as the Creator, and love took on broader and deeper dimensions with the widening of religious understanding.

In Christ the effective beginnings of grasping God as universal Concern entered the final stage of fulfilment. Jesus' going to the Cross was no external, mechanical or magical act. It was, rather, the Love of God persuading him, aided oppositely by his need for obedience and by his dread of yielding to what was contrary to Love. Love, duty and fear thus conspired to a climax in Jesus' going to his death. Thus in effect, since God was the moulding reality of Jesus' historic personality, it was predominantly God who went to the Cross. Love went all the way; Love could go no farther. Evil men's frustration, dreading the fulfilment of love, blindedly brought about the very fulfilment they meant to remove from human history. Meaning to kill love, hatred released it for its maximum. Since then it has been possible to understand that kind of love and, for those who know it, freely to choose it. Since then humanity has had an increasing way to know God, to know how to come to him, how to be forgiven and remade, and how to walk in a new kind of life by a new kind of power. God wants to cross over the gulf of sin in every man. This is his purpose in creating; this is therefore man's main need and the very goal of his life for which he restlessly seeks.

Some teach that God alone carries out the Atonement; this teaching misses the meaning of and need for creation. Some teach oppositely, that man—however God was then present and worked in him—placated God and made satisfaction of his holiness, making it possible for God to forgive him. Can we not say, rather, that God fulfilled man in Jesus as the Godman by crossing the gulf from man's self-drive to love's outgoing life and community? God and man belong together, the Creator and the created, the Father and his children, and the closer to each other they come, the more they work together for the fulfilment of his purpose.

In fulfilling man's nature and destiny, God never works merely externally. He comes to join us from within our lives and from within our communities. Love becomes involved with man and pays the cost of the new creation and the new community. The love that does not suffer as needed for the other is no love. Calvary as the climax of creation's redemptive suffering is thus the symbol and the summary of the total process of God's atoning. Can we not hold emphatically with Ernst Fuchs then that the crucified love in action became the true model of faith?

But this love could not be stopped by death. Once over the gulf from man's to God's side it stayed there in power to witness and to work from there. Sin cannot kill love, but love killed sin. Death cannot kill love, but love killed death. The reality of the Resurrection is the other side of Calvary. As Jonathan Edwards maintained, Easter is 'the first day of the Gospel'. Easter makes the day of crucifixion *Good* Friday. The Resurrection turns the memory of Good Friday into celebration, and celebration becomes thanksgiving, the holy eucharist of Love's continuing victory over sin, over death and over all of man's enemies.

This is the reason that the Cross of Christ requires our own cross. Unless we take up our cross we cannot be the disciples of Christ. To follow Christ is no external imitation. Following him is to become new creatures in and with him. 'Ye are all sons of God through Christ Jesus', claims the New Testament. Taking up our cross signifies that we have the spirit of Christ without which we are none of his. We share in his crucifixion and resurrection. His was the baptism with which we must all be baptized. Love must cross the gulf to us, enabling us to turn our lives inside out. We must be born from above, anew, by the presence and power of the new Spirit, by the power of the reality of the Resurrection. Thus we, too, have to face dreadful dying and joyous living. Thus we meet the Christ of Calvary and of the Resurrection, calling us to death of self for the new life in the Spirit. We have to be turned inside out for the world. In Christ's death and rising we have the high doctrine of sancti-fication, the New Testament's new life in the seed which must ever be our own goal. In such teaching we discover indeed the power of John Wesley and of his preaching the love of God in Christ for personal life and for society alike. In such lives God becomes the leaven 'until the whole loaf be leavened'.

I am convinced that when we recover the meaning for life and teaching of the full Gospel, and shed the externality of the mere myth that Jesus is God, we shall begin not only to reformu-late a more relevant Gospel for our day, with all the power of the glad news of yore, but we shall also begin to experience again the reality of God and the power of Christ. Once again, as in the New Testament, Christ and the Christian must come together. Then authentic worship will break forth into witness and work as we venture to break down the many roadblocks to faith that educated cleverness has put in our way. The weakness of God is stronger than the wisdom of man, for love's weakness is the truth the world can deny only at the cost of remaining in dark impotence.

The Christian faith, in this way, offers not a myth to worship but a life to live. The Christian life naturally centres in worship on its way to both work and witness, but that worship is of the eternal God, the Spirit who is Love, the personal Purpose who creates and fulfils. We know God himself through a human life that conclusively exhibited Spirit, Purpose, Love. Our faith is in God through one life for all lives. In Jesus God himself came to such fullness that love became real, life became free, the spirit became victorious. Through this life God became understood and available to man in the most universal way possible. Through this love God became disclosed as the final truth for man, the open-ended, adventurous creativity for an ever more zestful community. Through this spirit God entered man as the fulfilling power for true life. God has purposed in creation that man can reach mature and full life only when he comes into right relationship with God as the ground and goal of his life. Man is made for unconditional, universal love. This goal of all creation can be reached only through man's rightful being in God, only through his partaking of God's own Spirit at the centre of his life.

In the first chapter we discussed the living God of 'nowhere and nothing'. Such a transcendent Spirit, eternal and invisible, before, with and after all objectifications of a temporal nature; such a Love, the ultimate ground of all finite concern; such a personal Purpose, superdirecting all finite purposings by the way they are made and by the kind of pedagogical process in which they grow; such a God, the one, ultimate and only God, can reveal his own nature only in a life. He reveals a pattern, a model for understanding him and his way with all objectifications; but no finite existence under the circumstances of objective existence can possibly more than reliably suggest who he is. The categories of Purpose, Love and Spirit can help us organize, interpret and direct our own experiences in relation to the world we meet in those experiences. To be sure, we can have thoughts about God, but these never reveal more than ideas about God. We can also discern him in love's intelligent purposings. In this sense we can meet God in Jesus and in others. But the living God of nowhere and nothing can in the last analysis be known only in the Spirit. He must be known from within our lives.

Thus no teaching concerning Christ will be more than external ideas apart from his making Spirit available. Jesus himself spoke of this Spirit and promised his presence. Paul spoke of the Spirit of Christ. The more real God becomes, the more vital Christian worship and life become, the more stress is put on the Spirit. The Spirit is not apart from personal Purpose and Love, but he interpenetrates our lives, becomes co-subject with us to make us ever more integrated within the predestined fulfilment of our lives.

Albert Schweitzer ended *The Quest for the Historical Jesus* by pointing to a certain Spirit that can come to us. He was right. Until we become humbly willing to receive that Spirit into our lives in faith and to walk in the reality and power of that Spirit we shall remain guilty of absurd anthropomorphisms, of modern idolatries, of substance thinking, or of making cosmic process into a theological ultimate. We know God in Jesus as the Christ only when we are willing to receive, to understand and to walk according to that Spirit. He can never be reduced to cosmic or human existence. He takes on forms of being, but beyond them all is ever Spirit. The picture of God the eternal Spirit which we receive in Jesus as suggesting universal and unconditional Love, the personal Purpose of ultimate Concern, is finally only the colouring, so to speak, of the Spirit. Only when that Spirit reigns within as the life of our lives, the heart of our hearts, can there come to us that knowledge from within that affords us the conviction of being grasped, healed and fulfilled within the ultimate reality for which our lives yearn. In that Spirit alone can we both rest and work beyond anxiety and within full caring. When we thus know God in Christ we can say with Peter, 'Where else can we go?'

When we recall the living God of nowhere and nothing we

need not tie the eternal Spirit to Jesus alone while still recognizing that here he broke into the world as the fullness of time; the Spirit is the presence of God beyond all objectifications. All integrity comes from him; all truth comes from him; all love comes from him. When they become our own we are the more truly his.

All peoples in their religious realities are lighted and lifted by that Spirit. In Jesus the Spirit comes to clarity and explicit power, but before and after Jesus, in all lands and in all religious backgrounds, the same Spirit is at work. When the historic Jesus becomes an unnecessary hindrance to the multitudes who want to accept the God who fulfilled his life but who cannot honestly use him as entrance to God, for whatever reason, then Jesus is made use of in the wrong way. His own concern was for men to know God and to live in his love. Our concern must be the same. When his name can be used meaningfully, let it be so used to the maximum. When it gets in the way, let Jesus' own concern for men be fulfilled lest he become a hindrance. Then in all possible honesty as to history let all investigate the claim that God came in him as universal and unconditional Love.

Even though we can never fully settle that question, we ought to expect as much historical integrity as we do intellectual honesty generally. Essential to God, to Jesus and to the believers is that the latter find and accept the universal, unconditional Love that genuinely came in Jesus at a particular historic time. All other love, of course, is to be accepted with gratitude as coming from the same God who is the Source of Love. Even the historic love of Jesus must be tested and weighed in the light of this universal, unconditional Love. Ultimately our faith stands in God.

When we receive Jesus as the Christ in terms of the universal Spirit of God, and as the personal Purpose of his Love, our use of words in liturgy and in worship generally becomes less of a problem. No words can ever tell the full story of the Gospel. All words should aim at the universal Love of God the Spirit. We worship, then, not what is historically limited and humanly fallible but only the eternal God whose presence was the inmost, mature meaning and power of Jesus' life.

Merely to give up past poetry, however, in the interest of a literally minded, wooden honesty would surely be wrong. Not to examine, on the other hand, our use of terms and to strive for the creation of theologically correct usage is to deny honesty in worship its rightful place. Too much of past worship centres in the myth that Jesus was God. Too little material for worship celebrates Jesus as the Son of God. Far too little use in all forms of worship is made of the inalienable linkage of Christ and the Christian.

When we understand that in the life of Jesus we seek to see and to reach the reality of the living God of nowhere and nothing, of the God of eternity and of history, we shall be moved to create the kinds of worship that will celebrate this mystery in far deeper dimension and in far higher aspirations than ever before. We do not look for thin and anaemic forms of worship to cater to our sense of honesty; we need the overflowing sense of the unimaginable greatness and goodness of God whose glory we have nevertheless seen in the face of Jesus Christ. The Hebrew *shekinah*, as Roger Hazelton points out, was both a dwelling-place and a glory. God's glory cannot be settled in any place nor contained in any form of being, not even in a human person, and yet for us places of worship, forms of worship and human agents must all serve to point to God. The living God of nowhere and nothing can best be known in the kind of love that characterized the life of Jesus in a peculiar historic fullness, but only as the human concept of the Christ leads into the eternal faithfulness of God beyond our knowing and beyond our control.

Chapter III

The Bible and the Book of God

THE Bible is the Christian Scriptures; God's total speech to man is the Book of God. To find how the two are related and how we are to use that relation for our day is our double need: to be open to God's Word for the world and to be relevant to the world's questions. For contemporary Christianity and in today's world the Bible presents too many problems and offers too little healing power. Those of us who are vocationally responsible for the place and use of the Bible in the Church are deeply burdened by the plight of the Bible, and we are often at a loss as to how to remedy the situation.

I have no personal problem with the Bible. It has a cherished place in my life. I first learned from it in the devotional life of my parental home; then in a Swedish Sunday school where memorizing was obligatory; in the rigorous biblical and catechetical instruction of the Lutheran State schools; and, as I matured, in my own reading. As a boy of thirteen, when I left Sweden for America, my farewell gift was a Bible presented by the church Young People's Society. I still prize it. On Ellis Island, where I was imprisoned for eleven days because my immigration papers were not clear, I remember spending most of my time pondering this precious Bible, the one book I carried. Later, in high school, I punctuated my English themes by the style of the King James version, being ignorant of the Bible's history. In college I suffered untold agony in trying to hang on honestly to belief in its literal inspiration, its being a direct and final word from God. Through many years of family life we have kept reading through the Bible in family devotions and I have recently finished the entire Bible once again in my daily personal reading. As a matter of fact, I wear out one Bible after the other as I study it and write all over the pages. Each of my four children has a worn-out copy with margins full of my ponderings, and I have used many more. Every day I read the Bible, at least picking it up for brief meditation and

83

inspiration, in addition to my own daily morning study and our family use of it.

I want to impress this love of the Bible and my veneration of it on my readers before sharing my deep misgivings and problems concerning its actual and its proper use. If the Bible were only used by educated, mature saints there would be little problem! As it is, I believe that the Bible constitutes one of our major ambivalences, not only for the churches, but also for Western civilization. I am not revolting against the Bible nor struggling with it! What I am attempting to do, however, is to expose the problems of the Bible as fully as possible in order to suggest as competently as I can how rightly and effectively to make use of it both in the churches and for the world.

A poll on prejudice conducted under the auspices of Professor Gordon Allport, head of the Psychology Department of Harvard University, himself a responsible churchman, revealed that people inside the churches are considerably more prejudiced on the whole than people outside. If prejudice is defined as ill-will without sufficient reason for it, the poll disclosed that religion was correlated with much prejudice, especially the kind of religion that espoused such divisive teachings as revelation, election and theocracy. Anti-Semitism, for instance, has fed on the feelings that the Jews were responsible for killing Jesus. No one, I am sure, can have lived long in the American South-land (at least before the radical new beginnings in race relations) and have taken a progressive stand on the issue in word and deed without having received rebuke by word of mouth or in writing, perhaps in anonymous letters, defending segregation on biblical grounds. On the positive side, however, the Bible is used with unequalled power in Church circles to break down barriers and to establish understanding and co-operation. Those of us who have been heavily involved in situations of religious prejudice have found that no educational or social approaches can equal the biblical solvent in power if it is used with utter faith and integrity. Thus again we see the Bible both as a problem and a power.

In many and increasing circles, however, the Bible is neither a problem nor a power. It has become simply an irrelevant relic of the past. Most Western civilization is already secular-ized to such an extent that the Bible is virtually unknown. At least the Church people *used to be* familiar with the Bible. Now it has come to such a pass that even the students who enter our theological schools to study for the ministry are for the most part and for all practical purposes biblically illiterate. As a writer I have also discovered long ago that when I use biblical expressions or allusions I most often 'lose' my readers. Those who help in the preparation of my manuscripts occasionally call my attention to expressions which are clumsy, irrelevant or out of date. They gasp with embarrassment when I point out that these phrases are supposedly very well-known biblical expressions. Karl Barth has tried to revive the place of the Bible in Christian theology and Church life, but in spite of the popularity of his position among large sections of the clergy and among some thoughtful laymen the fact remains that, except for fundamentalist or evangelical perseverations, the Bible has become generally outmoded. Neither simply taken for granted nor at least acknowledged as the standard, it is no longer the authority for faith and life, for truth and conduct.

Can the Bible, then, be revived generally in the churches? Can it be revived in the world? If the Christian faith should resolutely find the reality of the living God, the God of nowhere and nothing, and if Christ the myth should be replaced by Christ the truth, could the Bible then become interpreted and used in a new light? Suppose we find, as I believe we can, that in order to go on to a creative and constructive civilization, we have to build new frameworks of interpretation that centre in the 'why' with full use of the 'how'; and suppose, further, that a deeper understanding of the purpose of creation as pedagogical process and of evil as necessary to that pedagogy, plus a far greater view of God and longer vista of his purposes, should let the New Testament categories of personal Purpose, Love and Spirit come fully into their own, might there not then also arise a far deeper and fuller appreciation of the Bible, not only in the history of ideas, and not only as a devotional book, but also as the bringer of the dependable truth upon which we must build both our knowledge and our lives? If this should happen I am sure that the Bible would no longer be hemmed in as some magically sacred book or some confessionally protected authority but would, rather, become the creative stimulus and standard for the ever-expanding, relevant knowledge of God for a maturing faith. In this way the Bible as the Christian Scriptures and the Book of God as God's total speech to man both for truth and for salvation would not only go together but work together. I shall undertake, therefore, to expose our real problems to radical scrutiny in order that we may understand the Bible as to both its inherent problems and its abuse, and in turn propose both the proper use of the Bible by itself and its central but seminal place in the ever-growing Book of God.

We shall devote two sections to the problems of the Bible, one pertaining to the problems resulting from its nature and one to those stemming from its abuse. I call this procedure to the reader's attention to ensure full awareness of the nature and relevance of the constructive suggestions which will make up the third section. The third section will serve a dual purpose by the discussion of both the proper use of the Bible by itself and its fuller use in relation to the Book of God.

I

The problems resulting from the nature of the Bible are chiefly three: the Bible is not a book of science, nor is it a textbook of doctrines, nor even yet is it a manual for morals. We are here, in other words, dealing with the mistaken views or uses; whereas in the next section we shall consider defensive or aggressive abuses.

For an educated, Christian readership it is a waste of time to dwell on mistaken uses which we have now generally outgrown. Nevertheless, for the full picture it is well to remind ourselves that God wants no absolute revelation of himself or of his will in human history. Revelation is for faith and not for knowledge. God respects our human minds and dedicated inquiry. God never teaches so as to undermine or destroy our need for responsible growth through the ever-incentive search for knowledge. Certainly there is no revealed science in the Bible. We have outgrown the Middle Ages and even the long, painful and losing struggle of the divines with the scientists. We no longer dispute the age of the earth with the geologists or the nature of the stars with the astronomers. In the actual space age of our times we consider the biblical picture of an angel shaking the heavens and the stars peppering the earth like fruit from a fig tree, as in the Book of Revelation, quite poetic and picturesque. When a mathematician tells us that π for the Hebrews was roughly 3 rather than 3·14159265358979 and that Solomon's porch could not possibly have been built by following the biblical specifications, we no longer blanch and feel that all of Christian authority is toppling. Obviously, we agree, the Bible must not be taken for a book of science!

Nor can the Bible give us a scientific account of human history, even of the people of Israel. We no longer worry about discovering the flood story in other literatures nor agonize if objective inscriptions from other civilizations fit imperfectly with Hebrew chronology. The Christian Church lost to Buddhism one of its strong potential thinkers when his Fundamentalist Church in Japan insisted on his believing certain historical events that as a university student he simply could not swallow. He is now one of Buddhism's ablest apologists, claiming that Buddhism as opposed to Christianity is scientific in nature and can unhesitatingly accept modern science. To be sure, on my doctoral examination I was scolded severely by Arthur Darby Nock, a Harvard professor of world-wide distinction, when in reply to his question as to who was the first great historian I ventured to suggest Thucydides. He pointed out that it was the authors of the Book of Kings who had the earliest sense of the meaning of history. The case for his contention is strengthened if with Leo Baeck in *This People Israel* we define history as human happenings with moral summons in them. The Bible contains great history, but such history must not be confused with science.

Obviously the Bible is not really a book at all. It is a collection of books from many sources and from many ages. It is a stately library of human experience under God. It is the story of a people called by God and the chequered response they made to that call. The same accounts are mentioned in different books with different colourings and in different dimensions of interpretation. The Books of Kings are far more modest even in the numbers they report than are the authors of the Chronicles. One creation story is far more primitive and less loftily and climactically conceived than the other. Nationalism, celebrated in the Book of Esther, is put under judgement in the Book of Ruth. The magnificent identity of goodness and reward which the deuteronomic author holds out is severely questioned by the Book of Job. Can one compare the spirit of Ezra with that of Second Isaiah? Enough! And amply enough for our purposes. There is no such unity in the Bible as could underlie and undergird an ever consistent reporting of scientific facts whether of nature, of history, or even of faith. The Bible is rightly and irrepressibly called the book of life. We should let it be just that!

Much confusion has been engendered by the idea that the Bible must be true in order to be dependable, in the sense that the Bible must be totally scientifically correct, both factually and propositionally beyond error, to the point that it is dependable not only as science but even as a textbook for doctrine. Many people have gone naïvely to the Bible to find out what to believe. They have thought that they can take whatever it says and thereby settle all their questions of faith. However well meaning, they have not understood that the Bible is not a textbook of doctrines but a sourcebook for faith. This faith must ever be worked out afresh in the light of certain guideposts which we shall examine in the final section of this chapter.

There is, for instance, no biblical theology in the Bible. In the beginning of the twelfth century there grew up what was called biblical theology and in the middle of the seventeenth century systematic theology as such came to birth. To be sure, biblical theology so-called and systematic theology so-called had been written, and in the grand style, long before those dates, but by then they had become self-conscious subjects. After all, the fight with scholasticism was intense and often discouraging! But to be honest, there is no one doctrine of God in the Bible, but many; and there is no one view of Christ, but many. There is no developed doctrine of such a central subject for Christian teaching as the Trinity. There are only formulas and suggestions. There are, so to speak, suggestive sources but no exact texts! Even so crucial a question as life after death or eschatology generally is both affirmed and denied with varying answers.

Nor can the Bible be used as a revealed record of historical theology. Some have excused the earlier portions as merely preparatory. To be sure, they have said, there are unworthy portions in this primitive part of the Bible, but such sections exist as the background of the later fuller revelation. After all, it has been claimed, God reveals himself progressively to faith and we must ever be mindful of that fact. For several generations there was much ado about such progressive revelation. Truth to tell, however, this kind of interpretation was mostly acculturation, largely an echo of the general theory of progress that dominated liberalism for a long time. To be sure, the New Testament is a new age, 'founded on better promises'; to be sure, Jesus towers over the personalities and teachings of those before him. But in all honesty and with requisite knowledge can we say that James improved on Jesus, that the Pastoral Epistles went beyond Paul, that Ezra went beyond Second Isaiah, that Esther went beyond Ruth, that Jude went beyond Jonah, that even Amos went beyond Abraham, or that Manasseh went beyond Moses? Christian revelation (or an approach to it) does not come by chronology, nor is it characteristically accumulative. New witnesses can use the old and God makes use of the past in the present, but the Bible is no example of continuous progress in revelation. We must not expect progressive revelation to be a hallmark of the biblical witness.

Nor can it ever be assumed that the Bible gives us systematic theology. God may use systems of thought in his larger pedagogy, but he never reveals his will directly through any such compilations. God speaks through life, and life uses words, but the words of biblical instruction are mostly the history of concrete experience, of human life, of rough or simple events, of parables and stories, of words of succinct wisdom, of psalms of praise. God's outlines seem very dim and confusing. He comes through acts, he comes to persons, he comes through words, but he comes for life, for faith, for inquiry, for concrete instances of need. The Bible is in no way a textbook but a sourcebook for theology.

Imagine what kind of book God could have written if he had wanted to give an authoritative, propositional revelation of himself and of his purpose! His outline and development would have been crystal clear and convincing. He would have revealed himself in a logical language beyond our imagination. A thousand lawyers trained a thousand years in unambiguous writing could never have rivalled his power of communication. There would surely have been innumerable footnotes warning,

'I do not mean this or that'. No denominational or personal disputes could possibly have resulted from the nature of such a Bible. In such a case Xenophon would have been correct in claiming that when God is our teacher we all come to think alike. But Xenophon was wrong in his view of God, while the Bible is right. God never intended us to know the truth in textbook fashion.

God never reveals himself perfectly for human life and human history. Even when he comes in his Son he comes in the weaknesses of the flesh and incognito. He is known for faith. He is known in the Spirit that gives life and not in the letter that kills. It is necessary always to keep in mind God's own intended method of revelation. They dishonour God who try to improve on his method. They want a perfect book; at least they want an objectively reliable record for life and truth, but God came humbly in his Son within the weaknesses of our common humanity, and he comes humbly within a book which is ever more a sourcebook than a textbook for faith.

There is a third problem that results from the nature of the Bible itself and which we must ever keep in mind. The Bible is no manual for morals and we sin against it when we try to make it so. When we do not understand the proper nature of the Bible we use it falsely and misleadingly. These, then are the three problems which result from the nature of the Bible itself and occasion its improper use: the Bible is not a book of science; the Bible is not a textbook of doctrine; and the Bible is no manual for morals. Abraham's living with his sister, for instance, provides no prescription for the limits of marriage in our day. Because Jesus came eating and drinking and was called a winebibber is no reason for us to justify the use of alcohol by his example. It is, of course, even more of a travesty on truth to use Jesus as an example for total abstinence! In a later chapter we shall consider such questions in greater depth, but even here it should be clear that we have no right to accept specific do's or don'ts from the Bible.

The Bible, indeed, does not even provide any cumulative rules of behaviour that may directly and invariantly be applied to conduct. The practice of fasting is both enjoined and made light of as a Christian duty. Even such a matter as divorce might seem beyond dispute—for Jesus explicitly forbade it—

but a deeper digging into the subject makes it quite obvious that the matter cannot be disposed of easily or finally. The Roman and the Anglican Churches have long histories of upholding what seems to be the plain teaching of Christian Scriptures, but when the fuller implications of the love of God for each and all are examined, the question springs back for both creative faith and reason. So it is with nigh every topic of human conduct. There is not only a new age of changed circumstances to which to apply the biblical standards of conduct; there is also a new appreciation of the complexity of the biblical witness both historically and existentially.

Further, the Bible supplies no invariant principles that can be applied directly, rationally and without the risk of adventurous faith. One semester I decided to teach Christian ethics directly from Paul's Letter to the Romans. I had become overwhelmed by the depths of its adequacy. Here I felt was a steady standard beyond relativities of human conduct. The more I studied Romans, however, in long and careful preparation for teaching, the more I found that its strong and straight principles were mostly contrapletal. Be concerned with your brother's conscience; but the more free you are of his judgement, yes, even of your own, the better. Such freedom with concern struck me as a happy solution until I came to apply it to concrete instances in 'case method' fashion. Don't hurt the conscience of the brother for whom Christ died; rather abstain—but blessed be he who has a strong conscience and does not judge himself in what he accepts as right.

If one is a public figure, one becomes aware of endless consciences not to hurt. One of the happiest experiences of our family life has been our Sunday afternoon drives together, the one time all of us could manage to be free and truly enjoy God's creation and the fellowship of the family. To my dismay I discovered that many people, and some in the community where we were living, consider pleasure driving on Sunday sin. Should one hurt the consciences of people observing us or should one go on innocently 'sinning' in the blessed freedom of the Gospel? Throughout the Letter to the Romans one can point out definite principles of conduct, but at the same time see concretely that taken together these principles enjoin real choices. There simply are no easy, invariant, directly applicable principles in the Bible in the sense of a manual for morals for external prescription. Yet how often, how many times, we come across people who in all earnestness quote the Bible as the final word of authority without in the least realizing what other principles are relevant or how many other passages of different import can be quoted as relevant to the same ethical situation. Before venturing, then, to suggest positive guide-lines first towards the proper use of the Bible and then towards its wider use within the Book of God, it is both well and necessary to keep in mind the nature of the Bible which, in itself, can occasion many uses of it that, even though not conscious abuses, nevertheless cause misunderstanding of it and impede its needful use.

II

In addition to the mistaken uses of the Bible, what of the definite abuses? An abuse may not be deliberate in the sense of a clearly self-conscious moral transgression; almost always, on the contrary, abuses of the Bible come from subtle rationalizations of which one is vaguely conscious during the period of conscious conflict or suppression, and which during the ensuing repression become only subconsciously present. The more such an abuse becomes a matter of repression the more deeply guilty the person will feel; not consciously and directly so, but only in such a way that he becomes zealous about the importance of the abuse and censoriously aggressive towards those who threaten its sanctuary. The Bible can thus be used either to excuse some narrow or hostile point of view or to justify its acceptance even by aggressively advocating it. How we read our Bible mirrors all too clearly our own depth dimensions. Let us examine three common abuses of the Bible in this defensive-aggressive complex of behaviour: The Bible can be used as a defence of (1) doctrines held for other reasons, (2) ingroup loyalties, and (3) moralism.

Many people defend as 'biblical' positions which no doubt are to be found in the Bible but which are far from representative of the Bible's main stance, let alone its highest. Thus for instance, the doctrine of eternal hell, or the eternal torture of the damned, is often justified on biblical grounds. Surely, too, it is in the Bible—unless one appeals to technical scholarship to point out that neither Hebrews nor Greeks had a concept of an eternally spatialized or hypostasized time. They thought of eternity, rather, as a very long time or in terms or cycles. Nevertheless the doctrine of eternal damnation, I believe, should be granted as one among several biblical positions, including no eternal life at all, life only in the Son, and God's eternal reconciliation of all things. But proponents of eternal hell do not for the most part hold the position reluctantly as a biblical doctrine but fervently and insistently, against all arguments and as the only possible biblical position. Pointing out the opposition to the doctrine voiced by the Fathers of the Greek Church is often not even noticed.

Unamuno in his insightful novel on envy, *Abel Sanchez*, very likely hit the nail on the head: 'Abel's successors, the Abelites, have invented Hell as a place for the Cainites, because, if there were no such place the Abelites would find all their glory insipid. Their pleasure is to see others suffer while they themselves stay free of suffering.' Advocates of the doctrine of eternal hell as Christians usually pick out some verse or verses from the Bible and hold on for dear life. Other verses, not only equally authentic but also more in line with the total logic of the Bible, such as 'God has shut up all men to disobedience that he might have mercy upon all' (Rom 11[32]) fall on deaf ears. Thus does defence of a doctrine abuse the Bible.

The same case holds for the biblical defence of war through the centuries, particularly in war-time. Although most of us are now beyond that unhappy practice, it is not yet entirely dead. Even those who manned the genocidal gas ovens could have experienced some satisfaction in citing from Psalm 137, 'Happy shall he be who takes your little ones and dashes them against the rock!' Ku Klux Klan preachers defended the bombing of Negro children in a church in Birmingham, Alabama, with similar defences! When one kills rattlesnakes in God's service, said one clergyman, it makes no difference what age they are. Blessed is he who dashed the *little* ones . . .!

Those who will countenance nothing but unconditional surrender and vengeance in war can pride themselves on emulating God's anger at King Saul for refusing total obedience to his express command to destroy all the Amalekites, 'to kill both man and woman, infant and suckling, ox and sheep, camel and ass'. Stealthy guerrilla killers can know the joy of Jael as she plunged the dagger into the unsuspecting Sisera as he slept. Those who long fan the flames of revenge can join the saints in the Book of Revelation who cry for vengeance day and night. These feelings and stands are in the Bible; there is no denying the fact; but it is an abuse of the Bible when they are resurrected in order to sanction similar evil feelings or positions in our day. The Bible, when sponsoring such evil attitudes and deeds, is for the most part dragged in rather than originally inspiring them. Worshippers who use the Bible in this unworthy fashion have never become open to its total and central message in Christ.

To take one more illustration of how the Bible can be used to defend doctrines, it is well known that the Inquisition fought heresies in unbelievably crude and cruel ways, by tortures and by sadistic killings. It is not so well known generally that the whole approach was considered biblical. Not only was Augustine's famous citation from the New Testament used, 'Compel them to come in', but especially important to the inquisitors in their nefarious business was the Pauline verse telling the Corinthians to deliver the body of the one who had misbehaved to Satan in order to save his soul! Yes, the Bible can suffer and has suffered frightful abuse when used to justify evils that have flourished on other grounds, or that are simply the expression of human sinfulness.

We need take little time to illustrate how the Bible can be used as a defence by denominational ingroups. All denominations subscribe to the Bible as authority and of late even the Roman Catholic Church is placing more and more authority, especially for the purposes of ecumenical discussion, in the written Word of God. Such use of the Bible can further the coming together increasingly of the separated brethren of every kind, but the practice of making the Bible the authority in Protestantism until very recently has resulted in the ever ongoing practice of sectarian splitting. Now sectarian backgrounds seem more and more transcended, to the point that at Montreal the Southern Baptists and the Eastern Orthodox were surprised to discover how much they had in common! Also the most unlikely discussions have been carried on across denominational lines, as for instance between the Episcopalians and the Pentecostals, even on the highest levels of confrontation.

Nevertheless, barriers are still justified behind biblical screens. Closed communion has been held biblical, as for the disciples only, and churches have even used the Bible to prove that they are in fact the only true disciples or the only true church. The same can be said for the Apostolic succession and for the practice of baptism. Both these ingroup defences have been justified by scriptural authority rather than acknowledged as prejudice historically and psychologically for whatever reasons. Certainly Jesus' almost offhand remarks about building the Church on Peter can in no way account for the practice of apostolic succession. Most of this practice comes directly out of historic precedent and intertwined ingroup feelings, or straight out of institutional behaviour and not out of directions from a book; nevertheless the Bible is dragged in to justify it.

Similarly there are many forms of baptism in the New Testament, in water for adult believers, baptism in the Holy Spirit, baptism of trial or even in blood, as in Jesus' exclamation, 'I have a baptism with which to be baptized and how I am anxious till it be accomplished', baptism of the conscience, not for the washing away of external impurities but for the cleansing of the conscience by faith in the Resurrection, as in the First Letter of Peter. But how many denominations will fully and unhesitatingly allow that all of these forms and meanings of baptism are biblical? How many will consider its own mode as only one of several possible kinds? The Baptists, the radical Pentecostals, the Society of Friends—all have their justifiable point of view as regards the Bible, but the history of Christianity is filled with invidious war over the subject, with all sides supplied by biblical ammunition.

I hope I have demonstrated the point that all such carryings on are abuses of the Bible and are usually not a matter of mostly obedience to a book but come out of a total set of ingroup loyalties and practices which sought support from the Bible sometimes with much and sometimes with less justification. The Bible is, then, used both to defend doctrines and to justify ingroup practices within a total context of defensiveness or justification of aggressive attitudes that are not entirely nor even mostly due to the Bible. At this point the Bible is not only used mistakenly but definitely abused. Nor is the line between mistaken use and rationalized abuse easy to draw. We human beings think and act as wholes, and at best we can grope but feebly towards the analysis of why we think and act as we do.

In addition to the abuse of the Bible by using it to defend doctrines and ingroup practices divisively as judged by the total spirit and meaning of the Bible as correctly understood and applied from the perspective of its highest pinnacle of revelation, is the abuse of calling it into the service of a defensive and haughty moralism. In the foregoing section we observed that the Bible cannot be used as a manual of rules for moral conduct. A still worse abuse of the Bible is to make it back up one's own self-righteousness, either as individuals or as churches. Self-righteous disdain of others is precisely what Jesus could not endure; yet how much of it is still with us. Some biblical Christians who were not like other people, certainly not like these 'modernists' who take no stock in the Bible, drove me through a city with which they did not know I was very familiar. How they berated the 'worldly' ministers and churches and how they praised the one who still 'stood by' the Bible.

'This minister,' they said, as we passed an imposing Baptist church, 'is very bad. He has no use for the Bible. He even lets his young people dance!'

I knew the man to be a near saint, humble, dedicated, searching constantly for God's will, but also one who cared to understand his people and to relate the Gospel concretely to their lives.

'But here we have a true, Bible-loving minister,' they said, driving by another church. 'He won't even let his people go to the movies.'

What a censorious, divisive, unloving rascal I knew him to be! How confused they were! In the Bible, dances connected with orgies and debaucheries and golden calves certainly are condemned, but surely not as dances, since the Bible also speaks approvingly of dancing unto the Lord. No, such use of the Bible is more than mistaken; it is dragged in to justify conduct which has been accepted on cultural bases and which has become a defensive symbol of correct Christianity. The divisive or abstaining practice has consequently become both a sign of separation from society in general and a means of self-approval that in effect condemns the rest of society.

Defence of moralism on biblical grounds need not be restricted to personal habits. It can refer to ways of worship. Some high church advocates of my acquaintance look down very long noses at the anaemic services of liberal churches that have become so acculturated as to no longer dare to revel in the rich symbolism of the biblical faith. At the same time members of the Society of Friends consider their biblical simplicity far superior, believing that their quiet voice within would be drowned out by the externals of routine symbolisms. I have heard the former characterize simple, direct worship as 'barn worship' and the latter call high church liturgy 'pagan practices'.

Somehow, in some settings and in some moods, Christians seem to have to justify whatever they believe or do by the Bible. Dragging in the Bible in a spirit of defensive-aggressive moralism to the point of feeling superior and self-righteous because one believes or does whatever one sets up as most biblical, is an abuse. The Bible with all its riches of thoughts and practices is exactly the easiest kind of book to be abused in this way. Just as most people and churches appeal to Christ without defining exactly what they mean by the term and therefore share a general point of common agreement without in reality having either to give up anything or to come any closer to one another, even so they appeal to the Bible. The Bible evades all strict standards for thought and conduct unless its proper use is rigorously established. But with such establishment, will it still serve as a point of common reference? Is the Bible our common compass because it can be used to point in almost any direction? Can it be a competent instrument to point clearly in the direction of man's true destiny? If so, will it be resisted and discarded or will it be accepted and used to bring in a new and better age for humanity?

We have now discussed sufficiently both the mistaken uses of the Bible as a book of science, as a textbook for doctrine, and as a manual for morals and also its culpable abuses, in the depth dimensions of man's decisional responsibility, as a divisive defence of doctrines, a rejecting defence of ingroup practices and a self-conscious defence of moralism. One set of problems arises from the nature of the Bible; the other, from the nature of man. The nature of the Bible and the nature of man cannot, of course, be held apart artificially but they can be taken up for inspection analytically. Holding all these problems in mind, and in particular remembering the far more serious threat of the Bible's becoming discarded as not only an evil to be resisted but also as no longer relevant, we turn to the basic reason for this chapter, our attempt to suggest the proper use of the Bible by honest and educated men and its fuller meaning within the ever emerging Book of God.

III

Considering these problems of both use and abuse, why is it not better to give up the Bible, write a new and better book, and face the future without the burdens and hindrances from the past? Two reasons appear: (1) The Bible is our heritage of Christian continuity objectified; (2) the Bible contains God's truth for the world.

Some seriously advocate that we stop using the word 'God' because it represents an outmoded way of looking at reality and at best is a confusing concept for modern man. This we may not, we must not do, because regardless of specific words and terms, God is, and only in his will is our peace. We could not be in the disastrous situation in which we now find ourselves except for our failure to believe and to heed the will of God. We found in discussing the living God of nowhere and nothing that the arguments used to prove his non-existence or non-reality are themselves spurious and have power only against false views of God which we must outlive and outgrow. In the same way we found that men rightly revolt against a Christianity which worships the myth that Jesus is God rather than accept the truth that in him, in his life and teachings, we meet the living God. But the knowledge of our meeting God in Jesus, in a kind of life, a kind of love, a kind of purpose, a kind of spirit, we find in the Bible.

There are those who speak eloquently to the effect that we may be right in our contention but wrong in the way we set about to implement it. Why make three letters, G-o-d, sacred, they ask. Why not rather let go of terms and ideas in order to be open to new and better ways of looking at ultimate reality and of becoming receptive to its power to help and to heal? Why put a needless obstacle in the way? Similarly, why not drop the name of Christ?

A deep-searching philosopher-theologian told us at a meeting of the American Theological Society that he had just returned from an interfaith conference of representatives of many religions, all of whom agreed throughout on such final matters as integrity, concern, cooperation, creative involvement and faith in general. At this theological society meeting, he complained, my address (the appendix of this book) had been advocating the same ultimates but had narrowed its appeal almost to impossibility by 'dragging Christ' into the discussion. Why not reach what Jesus sought for man, he asked, by letting him have his way of humility and self-effacement rather than making him into a false or needless roadblock to a common, desperately needed faith? And so also with the Bible. Why not accept its truth, its help, its meaning and message, without letting it get in the way of the faith and love which the world now must have in order to survive and indeed to enter into a creative new era?

My reply to the critic's request to leave out Christ was that far from wishing to flaunt him divisively in any way, I agreed, rather, that he himself would want to lose his name if that was necessary to communicate the reality which was his to show and to give. If we accept that reality, however, why should we not be honest about the way in which it first came with full impact into the world? Can creative integrity countenance historical dishonesty? Secondly, I returned, principles alone will not save us. The truths of love, of spirit, and of personal purpose are neither intellectual abstractions nor even general principles. They are merely descriptive of a kind of life, the life seen and self-revealed in the New Testament in teaching as well as practice. That life in turn is our best pointer in reality and truth to the living God.

Christ, then, is personal truth in history. In Kierkegaard's language he is a Christian moment, a truth so personal that to separate the message from the messenger is to lose and destroy the truth. For me, however, Christ is also a Socratic occasion or generalizable truth, for although he is life, that life is the light of men. He is not only Event but also Event-meaning: he is neither simply *theos* or *logos* but is rather the *logos theou*, the Word of God. According to Buddhist scriptures, of course, Gautama himself also claimed both to be and to speak the ultimate nature of truth. Such a claim is not unique, but there is a finality that came with the reality and meaning of the life of Christ, the life of love which at inmost characterized the personal purpose which is unique in both history and reality.

In the same way I believe that the Bible not only is our heritage which we need to appropriate in a fuller and better way, but also in some sense is the truth that is final for man. In suggesting this fact previously I used the word 'contains' rather than 'is' the truth. Which do I mean or do I mean both; and if both, in what relation does 'contain' stand to 'is'? I do mean both. Time and time again I encounter the contention that truth is a matter not of words but of personal relations. I hold this contention to be false. Reality is a matter of personal relations, while truth is our right understanding of those relations. A person can *be* the truth only if being is viewed on the context of communication. Truth can teach by example or exemplification as well as by words. Truth is correct understanding and communication of reality. Truth can be communicated through projects as well as through propositions. Spirit can reveal himself through being, acts or words. Thus God is. Or God is personal Purpose, Spirit and Love. Or God is *true*. But God is not *truth*. When we rightly understand God we know the truth that can make us free; we cannot know God until we are willing to know the truth that sets us free. Thus the Bible cannot be truth in the sense that it objectively contains or is God. That would mean conveying reality directly; whereas the Bible in itself is merely the objectified condition for communication. The Bible cannot be truth in the sense that it merely embodies or expresses true sayings. Truth is personal understanding. 'Tell me the truth', is a proper use of the word. Truth is reality conveyed and entertained.

How, then, could I say in the first place that the Bible not only *contains* truth but *is* truth? My contention is that the Bible is not merely an objective deposit of nature, i.e. print on paper. It is that, and conditions for truth would exist through it if it should be dug down into the bowels of the earth for a million years and never read. But the Bible is and conveys truth only as it is God's communication to man. The Bible is not merely God's past speech objectified, but more importantly becomes God's present living speech for faith and life. God speaks now, livingly, through lives and witnessings of the past, and peculiarly through the life and witness of Jesus as the Christ.

If God's speech has to be directly mediated, the Bible *contains* truth, for only certain strands witness to the fullness of the living God of the New Testament at its own highest. If God's speech comes mediated by faith and by faith's open world of obedience in interpretation, however, the Bible *is* the truth, for in this case the highest self-revelation of God through an objective container works with and on the rest of the material of the Bible (which is man's general experience) in such a way as to make God's speech livingly meaningful for the concrete decisions of actual experience. The Bible is then an objective deposit that mediates experience just as the rug on the floor can mediate the experience of colour. But even more than the colour varies with the light on it and the conditions of the experiencer, the Bible varies according to the light shed on it by the Holy Spirit and by the conditions of the responder.

Obviously I am using words in two different senses. Objectively, the Bible is the deposit of the conditions under which God's truth is properly mediated. In this sense we can say that the Bible 'contains' and at its highest 'is' truth. Strictly speaking, however, the Bible contains and is truth only for faith, for faith alone is personal response or appropriating understanding. Objectively in one sense, then, the Bible contains the truth of God and his purpose regardless of acceptance. The Bible, however, becomes the truth only for faith when man responds in utter openness to the will of God in terms of and by the power of the Holy Spirit. When this happens, if the central truth does not stand out strong and clear there is no authentic presence of the Holy Spirit and no full openness of response. Such a claim, to be sure, presupposes revelation as well as the work of the Holy Spirit and of faith. Knowledge is indispensable for revelation and for truth. Because of the human element involved in the response of both faith and obedience it is more correct to say that the Bible is truth rather than *the* truth; but

since truth can refer to the correct apprehension and comprehension of any reality, we had better also stress that the Bible
is the truth in so far as the correct response to it is to the truth.
Let us remember also that all human responses fall short of
understanding and accepting the truth which is experienced in
the biblical mediation of God's living speech.

The outline for the constructive third of this chapter will be
simple. Our first point will be a discussion of the Bible as the
Book of God (God's living speech to man) under three headings:
the pattern of truth, the process of interpretation, and the power
for application. Secondly, we shall deal with the Bible as
regulative of the Book of God. The third and final subsection
will consider the Bible as fulfilled by the Book of God. The
foregoing introductory statement is designed to prepare at least
suggestively the main issues for discussion.

The pattern of the Bible is, of course, Jesus as the Christ, the
kind of life he lived, the kind of death he died, the kind of
victory he won beyond and over death, the kind of purpose he
showed, the kind of love he made real, the kind of spirit he let
into the history of the world. The pattern is, then, more than
personality and more than principles. It is an open-ended
model of personal truth with inexhaustible implications for all
life and interpretation. The question will be asked of it: is it
literal or non-literal truth? Is this pattern statemental truth?
Is it propositional? Are the original propositions which the
Bible contains a matter of direct revelation? Or is the pattern
so much a matter of events, of personal spirit, that propositions
at best can only approximate or point towards the truth of the
life which affords us the pattern? Is the truth existential for
inquiry and decision? Or just how does this pattern relate to
both life and meaning; how does it relate to Jesus and to our
general understanding?

The pattern lies beyond both the literal and the non-literal
dilemma in its double relation to life and meaning. In the first
place, we have no infallible human language. All human
communication is touched with finitude and to this extent with
uncertainty and inexactness. Hans Küng, of ecumenical fame,
spoke at an Anniversary Meeting at Boston College on the
question of papal infallibility as regards possible reunion with
Protestants. He began by shocking us to the following effect:

Some Protestants believe that when the Pope speaks *ex cathedra* to the whole world on matters of faith and morals he is supposedly speaking infallibly; no thoughtful Catholic would make such a mistake. In the first place, Father Küng continued, there are no infallible human words. All human words are fallible. Therefore even if the Pope wanted to speak infallibly and had the authority to do so he could not because there is no language but human language. Secondly, said Father Küng, confessional statements may succeed in at least pointing towards the full truth, but all polemic statements in contramanding opposing statements (as for instance those of a heretic or a heretical teaching) deny the half truth which the heresy always contains. Papal decrees to safeguard faith and morals are polemic statements and therefore in the nature of the case cannot be expected to be infallible.

Listening to this, some of us were taken aback because we had thought that papal infallibility in the way mentioned was an explicit teaching of the Church, but we certainly could see and agree with Father Küng's point. There are no literal words of full and exact truth because language reflects the history of its thought, which is human through and through. Thus no language about anything can come literally, and thus infallibly, in this sense of exactness to the full expression of all truth in all its depth, in its every dimension of relation and in its inexhaustible implications. If 'literal' is to mean full, infallible communication of reality, literalism in any meaningful sense is indeed dead. Then the letter does kill!

The opposite, of course, is that all language is purely conventional, having no relation except historically and practically with the reality to which it allegedly refers. There is, then, no firm bond between what the Germans call *Sprache und Sache*, between speech and the content of speech. But if such were the case there would be no knowledge of any kind, and that is indeed a travesty on experience. In such a case a non-literal interpretation of the Bible would also be meaningless. Thus we are neither literalists nor non-literalists if the words have to be forced to their limits. But such forcing is indeed just that, *forced*. Such analysis is contrived and not real.

By 'literal', therefore, we mean generally reliable as to the representation of whatever reality is intended by speech. In such a case, for instance, I can ask my daughter to go into the garden house and bring me the red bag. In the garden house she will also find two white bags, a burlap bag and one blue paper sack. When she returns with the red bag I may conclude meaningfully that she understood me literally. To be sure, she did not experience that red bag quite in the way I had. We are not exactly the same persons experiencing the bag at the same time under the same circumstances and conditions. Literally we never saw the same bag if by literal is meant complete identity. But by literal we simply mean reliable communication for the purposes intended. She went and brought this bag and no other bag. Literal meaning should mean such reliability for speech. Then we can tackle honestly the question as to whether or not we accept the Bible literally.

A dog in Swedish is a *hund*. When my son was small he spoke Swedish as well as English. It would have been quite immaterial whether I called his attention to a dog or a *hund* in the next yard. The experience would have been the same regardless of the word I used. Thus if I call God 'Father' or 'Eternal Spirit', if they mean the same thing to me and to the one whom I am addressing, the words in themselves are not important but merely evocative of meaning. They direct attention.

Similarly, if I send a friend to buy a flounder at the supermarket and he comes home with a salmon, I can gather that the store was out of flounders but that he bought the nearest to it in the same general category, fish. But if he came back with a joint of beef and told me that that was the only kind of fish the market carried, I should take his use of the word 'fish' for beef as facetious. If I thought he was serious, my world would become confused. Either, I should conclude, he was suffering some mental malady or else I was losing my grip on reality. Words must reliably convey the reality intended. For the pattern of the Bible this fact of the reliability of words, call it literal or not, is of utmost importance. The pattern must indicate reliably what is intended. In this sense the pattern must go beyond merely suggested or symbolic truth to reliable meaning. At the same time the pattern does not deal with the concrete details of biblical meaning, whatever be the content of words.

In our next subsection we shall discuss this question under the heading of interpretation. The word 'literal' seems a rather

irrelevant word in dealing with pattern but a key term in dealing
with facts. The pattern must convey reliable meaning without
pointing to what is merely concrete or directly representable by
words. Can language perform such a service or must not
language be either directly reliable or else not truly statemental?
Can a pattern get us out of the dilemma between literal and
non-literal truth? Can we go beyond the problems of literalism
with regard to the pattern of the Bible and yet use the term
'pattern' effectively with reference to concrete facts, events or
beliefs?

My son, Frederick Ferré, wrote a book, *Exploring the Logic of
Faith*, jointly with another philosopher, Kent Bendall, in which
my son contended that a model does not convey statemental
truth, whereas Professor Bendall insisted that religion could
not have it both ways. Honest religion, Professor Bendell
contended, should claim statemental truth, however sophisticated in nature and in its defence of it, but should not hide
behind models or patterns that seemed designed to get religion
out of its problem of truth. My son's contention, however, was
to the effect that statemental truth in religion can never be
reduced to sentences with complete correspondence to reality.
Models are more reliably evocative of truth than are mere
propositions of correspondence.

In order to discuss this question of statemental truth with
regard to the pattern of biblical interpretation, let us look at the
problem of (1) propositional versus non-propositional truth, and
(2) propositional versus existential truth; thereafter we shall
seek as clear a verdict as the nature of the case permits.

Propositional truth means that words receive their meaning
from the total context of the sentence. Thus propositional truth
can be entirely analytical in the sense that it discloses only what
is logically implied in the sentence as such. 'Truth', however,
used in this way, is a misnomer. Truth is always understanding
of reality. Therefore there can be meaning but no truth in the
proposition as such. Immanuel Kant rightly called concepts
without percepts empty and percepts without concepts, blind.
Truth is always a matter of knowledge. Knowledge refers to
reality; propositions as such may not. One can speak of uni-
corns in propositions, but knowledge of demons would have to
be put seriously in question. One can refer to God in pro-

positions without the meaning's having necessary reference to reality.

Hume and Kant, therefore, both helped and harmed our understanding of truth, the correct apprehension and comprehension of reality, by their separation of meaning as such from meaning as basically referential to reality. Meaning should be applicable to both reality and falsehood, or to both reality and the works of the imagination whether as rationalization or as creative adventure, but the distinction between the central function of meaning as referential to reality and as referential to merely imaginary projections of the mind ought to be kept clear. Otherwise the 'feel' of reality is forfeited; and no more serious damage can come to man than for him to lose his sense for, and sensitivity to, reality. Perhaps the strongest and clearest safeguard against such loss is never to apply the word knowledge to either emptiness or blindness. Whenever meaning and reality are understood together, we should speak of knowledge of truth. There can be knowledge, of course, of imaginary works of the mind, but in such a case, that knowledge is recognized as imaginary in reference. Similarly there can be analytical knowledge, but such knowledge is understood to be empty and to have value only for purposes of the analysis of meaning. In other words, there can be knowledge *of* analytical truth but no knowledge *in* analytical truth.

We have seen, then, that confusion results when 'truth' or 'knowledge' is used in connection with either empty or blind references. Hume and Kant performed a service in distinguishing the merely analytical—logic and pure mathematics —from the knowledge of experience. They also aided the inquiry into human knowledge by showing that out of mere analytical knowledge can come no knowledge of reality. Qualifications like Hume's insistence that from the experience of certain colours of the spectrum intermediary colours can be conceived of without direct experience, thus granting some status to rational knowledge, or to the creative power of reason as such without direct experience, or Kant's deduction of *a priori* categories which are presumably presupposed by experience, are unimportant for our purposes, and I believe misconceived. Both instances presuppose experience. Kant himself had experience before he ever philosophized, and then he could go no further than to affirm that the categories were so universal and necessary that without them experience itself would be inconceivable.

For man there can be no getting before or behind experience as such; there can be only the proper use of it to find its true meaning and implications. There is obviously no truth apart from experience in the sense of human apprehension and comprehension of reality. So-called logical certainty in the sense of necessary analytical entailment is known only by human beings and therefore within and related to human nature and human knowledge as such. To call such entailment necessary *knowledge* is a travesty on human language. What is necessary is the finite knower, apart from whom there is no knowledge situation; and his knowledge of necessary, or merely analytical, knowledge is not analytical but experiential. Man knows as man and not as a proposition!

There can be knowledge *of* analytical knowledge, but not *in* analysis of propositions as such. Knowledge is always referential to reality. Therefore logical necessity has a certain analytical status of certainty for the finite knower, but no finite knower can know necessarily. Man may be mad. He assumes the validity of reason on faith. Man cannot prove reason by reason for it is man who reasons, and anything proved by man or reason is only as reliable as the tool and he who uses it.

The same is true of knowledge of the concrete world. The knowledge of my typewriter before me seems as certain as anything I can imagine. Still, the day before yesterday I received a letter, which for the most part seemed rational, from a man who (apparently in good faith) signed himself 'Jesus Christ', a man who sees before him with absolute certitude, he claims, realities that are foreign to my own experience. If suddenly I should see an angel before me bidding me to save the world by my writing, my trust in my senses would be in some ways shaken. I should want to inquire, yes, seek with utmost openness, what the truth and meaning of the direct experience was. If it was as certain for me as the experience of the typewriter under my fingers, I am afraid that nevertheless I should raise to myself, I hope not in unfaith but in faith's critical searching, the question of whether or not I was experiencing a moment of madness. I know people who have had such direct experiences and still I cannot trust them, and society has put some of them into mental institutions. All I am claiming is that direct experience needs the fuller meaning and testing of the wider experience. The reason I should be able to recognize the angel and understand his commission would itself involve a whole history of knowledge on the part of both the human race and of myself.

Propositional truth, then, is no light or easy matter to discuss, whether to elevate it into a privileged status of knowledge or to dismiss it as irrelevant for the revelation of religious reality or truth. Truth is the entertainment, experiencing or appropriation of reality through correct apprehension and comprehension of it. When Isaiah promised that God's people shall bless themselves in the name of God the truth or with God the truth, he declared that faithful followers of the truth shall know the reality of him who is himself faithful. When the writer of the Gospel of John cited Jesus as calling the Holy Spirit the Spirit of truth he consigned integrity to the Ultimate Concern, to the truth that can be known, and that, by being known, can set men free. Did not J. L. Austin define knowledge as a promise that can be trusted? To say 'I know', he claimed, involves a pledge ('I give my word') that accompanies the communication.

Although the advocates of revelation as event rather than as propositional truth claim that they have thereby safeguarded the personal or historical nature of revelation, they have only been talking in terms of superficial and false generalizations. No event can be known and no event can be communicated apart from propositional truth. To call such a position biblical is impossible because the Bible consists of the accumulation of propositions from Genesis to Revelation. Furthermore, God may reveal himself by act and by personal coming, by mighty deed and incarnation, but not only can God not be meaningfully known and communicated apart from propositional truth, the total context of human speech, but also the revelation that came in a life and in events is defined in the Bible both specifically, through propositions that refer to reality such as 'God is love' or 'God is spirit', and metaphorically, through terms like 'our Father'.

We shall soon come to a summary statement that will try to answer the entire spectrum of our first inquiry into the meaning of the use of the pattern of revelation, but at this point we had better simply affirm that just as the pattern of biblical revelation cuts through the dilemma of literal or non-literal knowledge in the Bible, so the same pattern refuses equally to succumb to any choice between revelation as propositional or non-propositional truth. We shall advance with confidence beyond the illegitimate and superficial distinction between revelation as event and revelation as propositional truth. The reason for the distinction is itself used for the wrong reason! In the next subsection, on the process of interpreting the Bible, we shall have to come to grips with the legitimate grounds of objection to the literal and propositional interpretation of the Bible. We have no right to broach this question, however, until we have discussed the pattern for understanding and using the Bible—the pattern for interpreting it correctly from its own highest meaning and power and in line with the truth of reality—which allows the Bible the kind of finality for faith which authentically belongs to it.

The third pair of relationships is that between propositional and existential truth. Here, too, we shall find that the pattern for interpreting the Bible makes these terms contrapletal rather than contradictory. The claim goes that liberalism fell prey to the interpretation of the Bible as ideas or truth about God. Even though the liberals avoided the evangelical drive to make the Bible a matter of infallibly revealed propositional truths about God and his will, they nevertheless still clung to truth as a matter of ideas. Along came Karl Barth, however, and trumpeting that what God reveals is not ideas as information about himself, but his own self. Then entered Rudolf Bultmann bassooning in a lower pitch that the Bible is a book for existential decision and not a textbook for supernatural revelation.

The truth is, of course, that if God is personal Spirit, if God is our Father, if God is love, no ideas about him can adequately reveal him. Revelation must then be personal supremely through a person and for persons. Buber would have us call it I-thou knowledge rather than impersonal, or objective knowledge. Kierkegaard would measure revelation almost directly in terms of the passion of faith rather than of the consistency of its information. Both have made needed points of protest. Obviously, biblical revelation centres in God's self-revelation and comes, therefore, basically through person and act. Faithful acts reveal the person more than mere words, and the highest revelation of a person is his own presence. Nevertheless much of personal self-revelation comes through speaking; words are important! I have no genuine objection to Bultmann's stress on biblical knowledge as decisional rather than informational. Ultimates are faith judgements that, in a world of unfinished process and in a world of freedom and sin, cannot be arrived at simply through information. Faith involves decision as well as knowledge through commitment and dedication to realities and ideals which cannot be fully proved by information.

It is not so much the affirmations, however, as the accompanying negations that we must watch. God is known personally, in spirit, experientially, decisionally, and in these senses existentially rather than merely rationally or factually in whatever combination. But such knowledge does not preclude propositional knowledge. Knowledge *of* is different from knowledge *that*, but the two are not contradictory. I may know a person directly but also know that he requires or desires certain things. I may know him experientially through confrontation but know also that he lives in such and such a place. Decision may be central to a relationship. Shall I or shall I not trust a man? But decision should not preclude information concerning him but, on the contrary, encourage all possible information that is relevant to the decision. This question we shall shortly elaborate. Here the point is that experiential knowledge is not contrary to propositional knowledge but, rather, presupposes it.

The objection, however, is to knowledge of ideas where the ideas receive their validity or their warrant as knowledge only through a total relationship or self-consistency of ideas. Knowledge then centres in the interpretation of the whole, in comprehensive coherence, in the fullest possible cross-correlation of ideas through self-consistency and constant empirical testing. Often Hegel's 'the whole is the true' haunts biblical interpreters to such a degree that they not only try to see the Bible as a coherent whole (whether of ideas or as a history of development), but even try to test the Bible itself by truth in general based on such whole-seeing, or synoptic vision. Hence springs the claim that we must interpret the Bible existentially, as directly applicable to experience and to choice, rather than through such a network of total ideas. What these interpreters reject is knowledge of the whole, of the totality of things. The Bible is existential for faith, worship and obedience and not a philosophical system of coherent ideas about either God or man's proper conduct. The Bible exists for concrete life and not as a world view.

Again, I believe the question is misconceived. Direct existential knowledge does not preclude a whole view on the nature of things. As a matter of fact, to be human is to make whole-responses. These whole-responses may not, indeed, be integrated and worked out to any extent, but living demands some kind of total configuration of what life means and what kind of world we meet in our experience. If we accept the biblical outlook (or one of its outlooks) as final we may find ourselves antiquated in world view as well as in philosophy of life. A modernistic view, on the other hand, may be shallow and ineffective for life. Better than either attitude is to have an open spirit and an open mind which is continually learning and revising while living in the meantime with commitment to the best we know. In grappling with linguistic questions in books of more technical nature (*Reason in Religion* and *Searchlights on Contemporary Theology*) I have concluded that, in any case, every view of the total that undermines the reality of riskful choice and of existential urgency is false and to be avoided. The Bible allows for no such complacency nor does man's best modern knowledge.

Bultmann's stress on existential knowledge as decisional is good in so far as it is positive. The trouble is that he reduces biblical knowledge to such limits. Decision, as we have said, is not opposed to information but requires it. The more and fuller the information the better, but in this kind of life and in this kind of world information cannot take the place of decision. This is all the more true in the case of ultimates. What really hurts Bultmann's position is his acceptance of a limiting and undermining existential philosophy that fights metaphysics as such and, in particular, any metaphysics of the kind implied by classical Christian transcendence. Metaphysics as rational knowledge, deductively or inductively, claiming to convey and to be directly related to the ultimate nature of things is impossible, but every faith judgement as to ultimates implies a metaphysical position. In other words, faith must choose concerning the ultimate nature of things. The more knowledge, both personal and cosmological information, correctly interpreted, goes into the preparation for such choice or into the making of it, the better.

Such knowledge, however, cannot take the place of nor hide the need for choice concerning ultimates. Bultmann simply sloughs off the issue by accepting a certain kind of existential philosophy and a certain view of science, bringing them both to the interpretation of the Bible. While I cannot here analyse either the false view of philosophy or the false view of science, as I have done at length elsewhere, the fact remains that there can be a genuine existential stress which neither does away with the proper use of consistent knowledge, even of one's world view, nor interferes with finding realms of reality that go beyond our realm of ordinary human experience in the world. Bultmann has given us a reductionistic approach which cannot be substantiated from knowledge in general or from biblical interpretation at its fullest and best.

Here all we can do is to hint at the nature of the pattern for biblical interpretation in its bearing on (1) literalism versus non-literalism, (2) propositional truth versus revelation through events, and (3) existential interpretation of the Bible versus either (a) comprehensive coherence (i.e. internal consistency) or (b) metaphysical thinking in the sense of some total world view, particularly as regards the Bible, in terms of some transcendent ultimate. How then can we best in the most succinct terms convey our understanding of the pattern for biblical interpretation with reference to these issues?

The pattern for biblical interpretation, the life, love and spirit of Jesus as the Christ, is neither literal nor non-literal in reference. It conveys reliably the truth of reality, the God 'of nowhere and nothing', the living God, the Love who is creative Spirit and personal Purpose. The pattern is not literal in the sense that no finite words, nor indeed finite imagining, can correspond directly to the nature and reality of the eternal God. Such a proposal is preposterous. Even so, it is reliably directive of thought. God is like this life, this love, this spirit of universal concern and unconditional faithfulness. He is the God of truth, of love, of life at their highest and best. These terms may only stammer the truth, but they do communicate that the truth is

THE BIBLE AND THE BOOK OF GOD

like what they represent, only more so and better. To walk in
the direction in which they point is not to be mistaken but to
find life increasingly fulfilled. The fulfilment is not only of
the same kind but also 'other', even as God is 'other'; but the
other only purifies, clarifies and transvaluates what is already
there. What little is first known of God's faithfulness becomes
understood as minimal and superficial in comparison to what
comes to be known, but the original knowledge and the following of it were necessary steps to the eventual fuller finding. Thus
we can both state as fact that God is unconditional, universal
Love and still recognize that no statement corresponds directly,
accurately or adequately to reality.

It might be said that now I am talking in symbols and myths
or possibly in terms of analogy. To be sure, these words can be
applied to my analysis but I prefer them not to be. The only
condition on which I can apply them is if they participate
literally in what they represent more than literally. Looking
back to our first chapter we recall that I can hold that since
God is directly present in Jesus (as Incarnation) we can use his
life, love and spirit as the sign within our symbol, the literal
presence of God which points to his unimaginable fullness.
With Paul Tillich I could hold that the symbol participates in
what is symbolized. Of such an analysis I approve part way.
This approach, then, would be like Karl Barth's *analogia
Christi*, and at its deepest utterance of love, *analogia crucis*.

With Tillich, however, the final category of reality is not the
personal Purpose, the Spirit of love of New Testament
Christianity; therefore his use of symbol does not carry through
for my purpose. Karl Barth's use of the analogy of Christ and of
the Cross would come closer, but Barth's Christology lacks the
full humanity of Jesus as a human being in the ordinary sense of
the term. With Barth there is a cleft between Jesus and us, even
in his humanity. Bultmann's myths never carry through to a
genuine transcendent reality; therefore his use of myth is
impossible for me. Besides, I believe that God is present in man
by the very potentiality of man as spirit, shared by God not
created, not a substantive spirit in some form of being, but an
innate capacity for irresistible grace that even in the form of
non-being and becoming is closer to God than is any realm of
pedagogical process.

Therefore none of the previous analyses will suffice. Nor will the Thomistic use of analogy, whether of proportion, proportionality, or of intrinsic attribution. All these approaches presuppose the category of being in some substantive sense. Closer to my understanding would be Barth's view of man's image of God as God's dynamic call on man, presupposing no substantive 'given' or matter in the content of the conscience. I should like, however, to dispense altogether with terms like symbol, myth and analogy, as far as the literal or non-literal dilemma is concerned, on the grounds that the pattern of the Bible is statementally reliable for its purposes of directing thought, affection, trust and obedience to God as he is found in the life, love and spirit of Jesus.

The fact that God is more and other than a human life or human history can convey is important in the forbidding of earthly idols. We cannot know any absolute absolutely in human life or history, but if the road sign is dependably true we have at least what symbol intends, the pointing ahead to the unknown fuller revelation of destination. If, then, on the other hand, the way of love, of life, of spirit is eternally ours for the walking in ever fresh adventure and fellowship, we have even now the presence of the truth directly and genuinely in a way that fulfils what the literalists are seeking. The pattern itself is made up not of the details of the historic Jesus but of the general directives of the life of the historic Christ. In this sense we are beyond literalism even in the sign. But the pattern is part and parcel of the right relationship to God into which we can enter even now, even while waiting for that fulfilment when what is known only in part shall be done away; for with the full disclosure of the life of God as Spirit and Love, there will no longer be need for such knowledge as is directive of destination.

True knowledge will no longer be needed when it has been used to direct man to its own fullness. Even the best map can be thrown away at journey's end. Thus, again, what goes beyond literalism also holds on to what is true in literalism: the dependability of the revelation not only as forecast but as directive, fulfillable presence. In this sense Christ as pattern is the way, the truth and the life, to the living God beyond the objectifications of pedagogical process, whose life affords the light which is man's dependable pattern for interpreting

the Bible, and, indeed, for approaching creatively all possible
realms of truth.

The question of reference to reality is complicated by the fact
that in Christ the joining of man's potential, pedagogical
nature and his eternal, fulfilling nature make a dual relationship to God. Therefore symbol, myth and analogy cannot be
used univocally or directly, and for our purposes in this book
we had better not launch into any technical or extensive analysis of the subject. The relation between revelation as propositional truth and revelation as event is no less difficult. I believe
that life, love and spirit are far deeper and truer terms than
event, or God's 'mighty deeds'. The deeds are secondary to the
life through whom the deeds came to their fullness. The lives
of the prophets reveal more of God than do their acts. The
analysis becomes exceptionally dangerous at this point, however, for it is not enough to say merely that no life can be known
without presupposing propositional knowledge and no knowledge of life can be communicated apart from the use of propositional language. Man lives in speech as communicator of
himself and of his ideas, and the contemporary German scholar,
Ernst Fuchs, is certainly right that the deepest movement of
man's speech is towards love, for man is made by God for such
love.

Life, however, although it may be the light of men, is not
merely light nor reducible to light. Life cannot be conveyed by
mere word. Words can help to communicate life, mostly in
general terms at that, only if life itself is presupposed as the
reservoir of experience that underlies and gives meaning to
the ideas. Ideas can help to introduce life but cannot take the
place of the confrontation of life. Therefore the life of Jesus
cannot be reduced to the biblical categories of Life, Love and
Spirit; nor can any biblical accounting equal the life itself. For
this reason we shall devote a later subsection to the work of the
Holy Spirit in communicating Christian reality and empowering its understanding and acceptance.

We are left, then, with the fact that while we cannot commit
the crime of separating event from proposition, or life from light,
neither can we equate them. The solution is neither choosing
one or the other nor taking both as equal and in the same sense.
The pattern is more life and event in its total impact than it is

mere propositions or ideas about God or reality. For this reason we have insisted that the pattern itself centre basically in the concrete life of the historic Christ (not in the details of the life of the historic Jesus) more than in the categories of life, love and spirit in general. The pattern should be as universal as possible but never at the expense of its personal and concretely historic nature. The historic nature of that life is a requirement of the Christian faith, as Paul Tillich insists in the second volume of his systematics, not as history but as theology. The ultimate is not a matter of ideas but of the One with whom we have to do, and the pattern of that revelation must therefore be *theos* before it is *logos*, or a matter of *logos theou*, of the Word of God. No mere Word will do. The pattern is the Word of God. Thus in this second instance (or propositional revelation of truth versus revelation through event) the pattern for interpreting the Bible again surpasses both while keeping the truth, intended or indicated, of both.

As to our third set of supposed opposites, coherent versus existential truth, we have already divided the question into two parts: (*a*) the internal total consistency of the Bible versus concrete existential truths and (*b*) existential reference to this present life concretely versus a supernatural metaphysics or transcendence. Regarding the former, in summary, there is no total unified truth covering the Bible as a whole, no whole pattern, and none can be had. No such comprehensive coherence can possibly be read out of the Bible or into it. To interpret Scripture by Scripture may be a helpful comparative method that leads to a widening of understanding but it must not presuppose any total unity of the Bible, for there is none. Such an approach may be devotional, mystical, even magical, but there is in fact no objective unity in the Bible. The Bible is made up of the whole gamut of human thoughts with all their internal inconsistencies and conflicts of ideas, facts, and points of view. Nor is there any total or whole pattern available that can be read into the Bible and make it a unified book by providing an overarching context for its understanding. Such an undertaking is illegitimate because, whether the approach be revelational or philosophical, it is untrue. The pattern for interpreting the Bible is highly selective, the reality and meaning, the Event-meaning of the life of Jesus as interpreted by the New Testament definitions of the God whom the Son revealed, but certainly not all of the Bible is consistent with the definitive pattern. The pattern comes, indeed, bringing judgement on much of the Bible as well as acceptance and approval.

The Bible, on the other hand, is not merely a collection of existential truths without recourse to a common standard or a supreme directive for thought and action. All existential truths, stories, myths, teachings, principles, words of wisdom, prophetic utterances, and historic events can be seen in relation to the pattern for interpreting the Bible and find their place within its context. The context does not make for any comprehensive coherence but it provides a supreme model for both understanding and action. This model unites in meaningful varieties, consistencies and contradictions, what cannot be unified into one consistent whole. The pattern gives directives for interpreting ultimate reality, for relating to God, for living together as men, for using nature, and for looking forward to the future —directives for life and conduct, for both meaning and choice. These directives are comprehensive without being consistent and they have a unified focus without being themselves unified. Thus experience is accepted in all its pedagogical wholeness and in all its eschatological unity without forcing either thought or decision into pre-made moulds. Within this pattern is freedom for creativity without a disintegrating and disabling final relativism. The existential is as stubbornly concrete and irreducible to mere or consistent meaning as before, while the pattern nevertheless gathers all existential truths into one focal perspective for truth and for life. In this way the pattern for biblical interpretation goes beyond the dilemma of coherent truth versus existential truths.

As to the coherent truth on the part of the Bible, which can form a supernatural metaphysics, versus existential clarifications of man's earthly experience, the pattern again refuses to be hemmed in by such choices. That the Bible centres in the living God and in the history of his people in the light of, and in relation to him, is simply fact. That Jesus and Paul, and, indeed, all the writers of the New Testament acknowledged, even took for granted the reality of God, prayed to him, and centred their lives in his will is another fact that cannot be denied. No pattern is biblical that rejects what is central to the meaning and the motivation of the Bible. Therefore to say that the Bible deals basically with anthropology or with the clarification of man's experience is to forfeit the claim to be biblical.

The story of the Bible is the story of God and of his people, of God and his Son, of the Son of God and his Church, not basically of man's experiences and history. Authentic experience in the Bible was a category in which God was central, not unaided man. But equally is it a mistake to charge that such an interpretation runs away from life into some magical otherworldly, escapist position either from ignorance or on purpose. The whole tenor of the Bible is God's concern for the world, all the way from his creating to his judging and redeeming it. Nor can man serve the biblical God by forsaking the world of creation and of history. Such false and unworthy charges are not facts but a sign of defensive belligerence. The Bible offers no such choice as between a sterile other-worldliness or a creative this-worldliness, between a supernatural irresponsibility and a worldly responsibility.

If transcendence is invalid on other than biblical grounds, so that we are compelled to forsake it for the sake of truth, the honest and open way to deal with the problem is, then, to say simply that the Bible's own pattern for interpreting its total truth is mistaken. Since there is no God, as is supposed, and no world other than this one, we shall take from the Bible whatever existential truths we can gather, recognizing that its main thrust is outdated and untrue. If, on the other hand, such transcendence alone can give us the fullest meaning of reality and the fullest directives for life, we need not shy away from the biblical pattern on non-biblical grounds. In our next main subsection, in which we are to consider the Bible as regulative of the Book of God, I shall at least suggest a way to handle this problem as a matter of truth in general; but at this point it suffices simply to affirm that the biblical pattern presents reality as more and other than this world and this life. But the biblical pattern is not arrived at speculatively. Rather, the Bible says most meaningfully that God (ultimate reality) is like the life, the love, the spirit of Jesus whom we meet as part of human experience and history and who relates relevantly to our own lives.

A biblical pattern bespeaking reality as more and other than man's ordinary world, in no way, however, precludes this pattern's offering man authentic existence in this life. On the very contrary, unless this pattern is rightly and adequately directive to the understanding of life itself, to what is wrong with it, and how it can be 'right-wised', to use Kendrick Grobel's good expression, this pattern cannot claim either to mediate reality or claim to be truth for man existentially. But in fact it does both. What is beyond man's control, indeed what ultimately controls him, offers to meet man's deepest needs as well as to answer most fully his most searching questions. The fact that some of these questions and answers are objective, such as the history of creation, does not mean that there are no existential questions demanding existential answers. The two categories are not contradictory but contrapletal. They do in fact involve each other and in the final analysis they even require each other. Therefore the choice between existential truths of the Bible versus the truth of its transcendent pattern is itself false.

Indeed, the pattern has the capacity to transcend and to fulfil the conflict between the literal and the non-literal approach to the Bible, between the propositional nature of revelation versus revelation through events, and between the existential versus the coherent understanding of the Bible. All these terms stand for needed truth. The truths, however, are not contradictory but contrapletal, opposing each other as they do only in some respects and in some senses, but not completely and finally, when lifted into a creative relationship to the pattern of God's love, life and spirit in Christ, which alone can do full justice to the interpretation of the meaning and the power of the Bible. Our next two subjects for consideration will be this meaning and this power, following which we shall turn to the two remaining major topics in our constructive section: the Bible as regulative of the Book of God and the Bible as fulfilled by the Book of God.

The first requirement for the process of interpretation is that the Bible be interpreted in full relation to the biblical pattern. There is no unity or pattern of the Bible as a whole, on the one hand; and, on the other hand, the Bible has more to offer and more need to give than mere existential, random insights and directives. The Bible offers a definitive pattern that gives full creative meaning and directive to life and thought as a whole. The pattern, to be sure, is Christ, and the whole history of Christian thought bears witness to his centrality for the Christian Scriptures. The Reformers, especially both Luther and Calvin, were emphatic and eloquent on this point. Just read Luther's preface to *Auslegung des alten Testaments*! Calvin may have stressed both the written word and internal revelation, but when the question was explicit the central meaning of the Bible was God's presence and work in Christ.

Christ has all too often been used as event without definitive meaning. From the event, however, there emerges the clear pattern of God's universal Love, eliciting the free, open, inclusive community of trust and concern. This God-centred, Christ-focused Spirit of Love who has shown his personal Purpose as our Father is unshakably the basic pattern for understanding and for using the Bible. Even though, then, we have already spent considerable space on the nature of the pattern in relation to literalism, event, and existential interpretation, I should be altogether remiss if I did not start this treatment of the process of interpretation by recalling that it is not the Bible as a whole, nor the Bible as existentially interpreted, but the whole Bible used in the light of its own highest and most inclusive pattern, Jesus as the Life, the Love and the Spirit of God within an authentic human life and human situation, that provides the definitive pattern for the fullest and truest use of the Bible.

This model, however, constitutes a reliable, yes, a revelational context for interpreting and for using the Bible. It can, of course, never impose any external truth on the biblical material nor change its original meaning. In its light the original facts and meanings can mean more than before but added meaning may not be permitted to deny, detract from, or distort the original meaning in its place and for its purpose. The correct and effective use of the Bible, therefore, requires careful study and understanding of what actually took place or what was meant by the original writers. There can be no glossing over their own intent, no smoothing out conflicting meaning in terms of other passages or writers. What happened, happened, and should be sought for on its own grounds. What was intended or understood by those who wrote the various books must remain forever what it meant when they wrote it, as far as what the Bible says exegetically. Fact is fact and meaning is meaning. Thus if Isaiah prophesied that a child should be born within six months as a sign to the people of Israel, even though the prophet would not himself tempt God by asking for a sign, that prophecy was meant for that day and may not now be considered a reference to Jesus on Isaiah's part. Such plain misinterpretation of the Scriptures must be avoided. How later biblical writers used such a passage, or what all the Fathers may have written concerning it, makes no difference. The passage has a definite historic context and must be seen in that light. If the Book of Ecclesiastes claims that dead men do not praise God, taking for granted that there is no vital life after death, no fuller context of later times or any wider pattern for biblical interpretation can change the fact itself. No allegorizing or symbolizing of passages by later writers or by modern interpreters can change one whit the original facts or the original intent of the writings.

Far more study of the Bible in historical terms would benefit clergy and laity alike. We need to know the history of the times during which the various parts of the Bible were written, to understand the changing thought-worlds of those times and to discern as far as possible what the original writings meant. There can be no new day for the Bible until it becomes a *well-known* book, not only by general reading but also by serious, detailed study of it. But, alas, this kind of study may lead us into another danger. We may feel obliged to interpret passages in terms of the exact meaning of the times when they were written!

All new thought uses old language. There is no other way for prophets and pioneers to communicate. Even seers of the highest order must use the common coin of current language. The only way they can go beyond the thought of the day is by the original way in which they use that language in terms of thought-forms, illustrations, parables or figures. People who accuse interpreters, therefore, of modernizing the Scriptures because they understand that new thoughts have come in, even though within old forms or terms, may have a rightful point, but they need even more to be warned themselves of the error of reducing the pioneers to the prevailing thought-forms simply because they cannot escape using the words and expressions of the day. The new must come with relevance to the old and in the discontinuity that relates to, and fulfils, the old approach to life and thought. Thus no amount of study of the thought-forms of Jesus' day can do away with the fact that his view of God and his understanding of life and love involve radical discontinuity as well as radical fulfilment, albeit often subversively of the *status quo* intentions of his times.

Whoever would know the original facts and meanings of Christian Scriptures, then, must understand the past more than woodenly, more than legalistically and literally. He must know it factually with all proper critical precautions, but he must also envision it creatively and even imaginatively. If scholars can spend a zestful lifetime without attaining such knowledge except in part, what hope is there for the layman, or even for the busy minister? He can study all he can, particularly at such points as he has concrete need. He can at least use the commentaries, disappointing at times though they may be, for both translations and commentaries themselves also reflect the dominant thought forms of fashion and prejudice. There are no helps directly from God to fortify the fully open seeker for biblical facts and original meanings! None the less we should seek whatever aid we can get, while reserving judgement at all points. The best way to conquer immediate conditionings of exegesis is to read diligently the entire history of interpretation. What did the Fathers think of these passages and what have different commentaries held during different ages? Such is the ideal of scholarship if one would free himself from the spirit of his own times. A thorough knowledge of languages can help, but words by themselves do not settle contexts of meaning. Each reader must bring to his Bible-reading, therefore, such understanding as diligent study can effect, first for the passage itself within its own context of specific writer and his times, and then in ever widening circles for comparison and enrichment.

Having studied as far as possible the original facts and meanings of the Bible passage, the reader is free to hold up his knowledge to the light of the pattern for biblical interpretation. The comparison of exegetical knowledge with biblical pattern does not destroy the original meaning but rather judges and re-evaluates it. The vengeful nationalist who gloried in the thought of dashing the children of the hateful foreigner against the rock stands stubbornly before the reader as a historical fact; in the light of the Christian pattern he also stands utterly condemned. His local loyalty may perhaps be condoned and even mildly applauded if viewed against its own limited background; but now it has become outmoded and judged reprehensible by him who told his disciples that whoever does the will of God is mother, brother or sister; who gave us the parable of the Good Samaritan; who lived and died for man as man under the one Father who was universal Love; who in effect died for the whole world. Thus the pattern changes no original facts or meanings but puts them into a different, higher context. It is this context which changes not the nature of the original meaning, but its evaluation. When Paul, for example, exhorts slaves to remain slaves in order to exhibit patience, his teaching of love may have been a leaven within the institution of slavery, but when his stand is put into the light of the Christian pattern he appears as an appeasing supporter of the *status quo* rather than as a prophet of God condemning evil unequivocally in the light of the Gospel of God's universal love for all men. Thus does the pattern add a new dimension of understanding and a new level for interpretation.

At this point we must exercise care, for the biblical pattern is a creative challenge to love, faith and obedience, not an illuminated arrow of instruction or of rules. Nor does it provide either the detailed map to get from one situation to another or the proper timetable for proceeding. There is room for patience, for understanding and for wisdom as well as for urgent concern for change. If the pattern provided a direct light there would be little opportunity for growth in grace, understanding and cooperation. The way of approaching our problems is almost as important as the result. The destination can be clear, if we will, and the road to follow can be charted in general. But the way of walking must still be in faith and love, not by the letter that kills but in a spirit that gives life.

Let us say, for instance, that integration of races is a Christian command, while segregation is explicitly sin. The open community for full, creative opportunity and for full acceptance is a Christian standard innate to its very faith. It is a direct disclosure from the Biblical pattern. But the way to bring it about may be a matter of most serious discussion and deliberation. When patience is enjoined as a substitute for ameliorative action, such advocacy no doubt comes from rationalization rather than on genuine love. If on the other hand, action is precipitate and ill-considered, or if faith is put in external conditions at the expense of human relations of free acceptance, action has become a substitute for the fuller works of love. Thus the biblical pattern, even when seen and accepted correctly, can yet give no merely external light. There is still call for creative human faith and cooperative participation.

The other danger is an idealism which in fact dismisses the need for creation. Thus the Bible can be used in such a way that the pattern itself takes the place of the Bible as a whole. The pattern should illuminate, explain and direct man's total experience. Often the evil in man's life, however, is left out in idealistic non-Christian interpretation. Thus we see the Bible sometimes used to justify war by piecemeal appeal to passages, with the Bible as a whole providing an indiscriminate standard for faith and conduct. We also see it used oppositely to identify God with peace only as though there had been no need, or were now no need for conflict. Where there are freedom, sin, and partial and opposing interests, conflict is bound to arise between persons, within families, and among nations. These conflicts have their place in man's growth as a self-being and in maturing groups. But they are not sanctioned as finally right and good by the highest use of the Bible. Some interpreters, however, rule out conflict as having neither meaning nor right within the biblical faith. In this way we can be left with either approval of war, on the one hand, and a sanctioning of creation as it is, or with a refusal of all meaning for conflict, on the other, and thus a denial of God's creation as pedagogical process.

For another example, let us consider the case of eternal hell. Some hold on to this belief as a Christian doctrine, hiding their position behind biblical passages, while others, condemning the wrath of God as inconsistent with his love, forfeit an effective doctrine of hell altogether. In God's full pedagogy, however, there is place for fear and for the frustration of fear in the making of self-being through genuinely free choices, even though neither fear nor frustration can be God's final word for and with man. The pattern should thus never be used with false over-simplification, for in this case its power to exhibit God's full truth for man in the widest and deepest possible relation to man's experience as a whole becomes forfeited. The proper use of the pattern for biblical interpretation, rather, affords the fullest light possible to release creatively the whole truth of the Bible, but it never can become external, or artificial; the Bible, properly used, must always be the living light of creative faith within God's concern for the world.

We need a pattern for organizing, for evaluating, for interpreting and for applying the Bible. The pattern of the life of Christ, as Love, illumines and puts into their proper pedagogical place all the varying, consistent and conflicting material of the Bible as a whole. What each part was originally intended to convey needs to be seen in the right context and used within the all-interpreting and all-directing pattern of the Christ. The God of nowhere and nothing, the living God beyond all created realms, has disclosed his Spirit and Purpose in the universal Love of Christ, 'the Son of his Love'. But the pattern and the process need the power; for the ever dependable truth of God's revelation in the pattern, and man's continuing need to interpret the whole of the Bible within its context, never come to their full fruition apart from the biblical power for life and light.

The power for biblical interpretation and use is the Holy Spirit. The Holy Spirit alone can make the living God real to us. No number of intellectual arguments can add up to the gripping conviction of reality. Calvin's internal testimony of the Holy Spirit is still needed. No human skill, however creative, in applying the pattern to the total process of biblical interpretation, can ever attain the motivating vision of the love of God which the Holy Spirit alone can create in our hearts. It is the Holy Spirit, who, to use biblical language, takes of the things of Christ and leads us into all truth. We must stop thinking of the Holy Spirit as a pious phrase and experience instead his meaningful and motivating reality.

Because the Holy Spirit can convict us of sin, he can lead us to forgiveness. Sin is the greatest obstacle to genuine understanding of the Bible. Sin leads us to rationalize. Sin lets us hide from the truth. Sin creates in us the tensions that make the truth difficult to distinguish and even more difficult to accept. From sin spring the doubts of needless conflict that lead not to growth but to distortion of the truth. Sin is therefore the greatest enemy of truth. Only the eyes of faith can rightly read the Bible; but faith cannot grow apart from forgiveness, apart from becoming right with God. The Holy Spirit can give us the freedom that follows forgiveness, which alone can lead to true faith.

Faith wrote the Bible; faith alone can read it; and faith alone can use the Bible. This claim is no promise of magical insight by some magical grace. It is, rather, the sober observation that just as there can be no forgiveness until the Holy Spirit convicts us of sin in the light of Christ, and just as there can be no freedom from the distorting tensions of sin apart from such forgiveness, even so there can be no faith empowering us to interpret and to use the Bible that is not the gift of the Holy Spirit. Man must seek faith and be willing to accept it, yes, to live by it, but finally the power of faith to understand the Word of God is the gift of the Holy Spirit. The Holy Spirit not only prepares for faith by the reality of forgiveness but also creates the enabling faith that receives, understands and lives the Word of God.

Forgiveness and enabling grace, however, are impossible apart from man's willingness to walk in the Spirit. The Spirit not only relieves the mind of obstructing tensions and opens faith's eyes, but he also strengthens the will to obey God's law. The law is a matter of right relations. The law of God is the total context of right relations to him, potential and actual. The law of Christ is the law of love. The law of love is the free acceptance and living of the right relations in God. Love thus fulfils the law, for implicit in love is always righteousness or holiness, the right relations to and in God apart from which love would be sentimental, distorted and unfulfilled. No one can rightly interpret the Bible apart from the faith that comes from the Holy Spirit as we walk with God. Where such faith is, righteousness is bound to dwell. Reading the Bible rightly involves living by it. To live obediently by the Bible involves trust in the universal Love of God, or the very nature of the pattern for biblical interpretation.

Forgiveness, faith and obedience are gifts of the Holy Spirit. They are his work, the fruits of his tree. But the Holy Spirit never violates our proper autonomy. He never comes to us except as we invite him. His presence awaits our free and full asking. The way we invite the Holy Spirit is through prayer. Prayer is the way of the Holy Spirit and the work of the Holy Spirit. Prayer is God's way to man from God's inmost nature to man's inmost citadel of reality. Prayer is whole-spiriting in God. Prayer is becoming authentic in life's central asking. Prayer is the self's reaching out in integrity for reality. Prayer is the self and the community finding freedom within the right relation to reality.

Prayer is no external exercise in words or attitudes, no internal seeking to control words and attitudes so as to be pleasing to God and to find an effective and satisfying life. Prayer is entering the life of God by the power and reality of the Holy Spirit. Prayer is becoming one with God and with his will for the world in the Spirit. Prayer is becoming genuinely oneself by accepting the purpose for which one was created, and the guidance of God within the process of growth. Prayer is openness to the Holy Spirit on his terms. Apart from prayer the Holy Spirit never gives power fully to convict, to cleanse, or to enable. Apart from prayer in the Spirit of Christ, or within God's universal love for the world, there can be no enabling faith. Apart from prayer as worship at the centre of life, in words and before and beyond words, there can be no full obedience that is beyond external conformity to duty. Prayer is willing in God through worshipping in God, generating faith in God and working for God. Prayer is the way to faith that dares to accept the pattern, that welcomes the work entailed in the process of interpretation, and that becomes open to the reality and power of the Holy Spirit. Through prayer the Holy Spirit leads us to the kind of integrity and concern where the study and the devotional use of the Bible turn into the practical living by the Bible within the concrete concern it generates.

The Bible must be studied. There is no avoiding the work involved in coming to know it, in the progressive understanding of it, and in the faithful use of it. The Bible must be used faithfully, then, in the service of the community and of the world as a whole. The Bible never comes alive from mere reading; it must be lived, and lived publicly, not privately. The Bible is the book of the community because it was written by the Holy

Spirit, God's unity in himself and among men. It cannot be used aright individualistically or in isolation from the world's needs. The Bible must be used within the community of faith and concern for the needs of the whole world as they impinge on the reader. The Bible, then, is pre-eminently a book for devotions, for worship, for finding God and reaching out to him. By that very fact it is also a book for understanding the world, caring for it, coming to know it, and entering into its concrete needs. But the need of the world above all else is to know God, to worship him, to come into right relations with him, to find his reality and the peace he gives, to find the final meaning of our fleeting lives within his eternity. Only the enlightening and enabling power of the Holy Spirit can help us use the Bible in all these respects.

In the first two major sections of this chapter we considered the complaints that modern man raises against the Bible. We observed that some of the problems resulted from mistaken uses of the Bible while others came from depth-conscious abuses of it. We are now in the situation where not only can questions no longer be settled in theory or practice by merely referring them to the Bible (for even theological schools no longer use the Bible in that way!), but also the world in general pays no attention whatsoever to the Bible as authority. Only among conservative Christians does the Bible occupy such a place or play such as a role, and even many of them are fanatically defensive or more persuaded themselves by the rational apologetic they bring to the biblical position than by the Bible itself.

Why, then, bother about the Bible? Are we so hopelessly tied down to it in liturgy that if we break its mythical or magical power over us the Church will seriously suffer? Should we be better off if we tried to revive the central place of the Bible in our thought and worship, or is such an attempt doomed to failure at the start? Why can we not or why should we not start afresh with clear Christian teachings and thus win the world, in so far as we can, for a new day? I, in particular, have to ask myself this question, since I believe that even while the heart of the Christian faith beats eternally true, traditionalistic theology is moribund. If the past has been a failure in its formulation of the faith, and if as churches we are steadily and perhaps increasingly failing, why should we not be willing to come out clearly and cleanly for the truth dressed in its most attractive form? Of what are we afraid?

The very fact that I have chosen to discuss the Bible in connection with the rebirth of our faith shows, of course, that I do not believe that we can simply discard it. We must go on and relate it constructively to all truth, otherwise we shall make no impact on our world or meet the challenge of a new day. We have two main choices as to truth outside the Bible: we can either deny and ignore it or we can relate it to our faith. To deny or ignore such truth is to deny that God is truth, the only ultimate truth from whom all truth finally comes. It is to deny the God of creation. It is to reject the God of all the earth and now of all the universes. It is no longer to bless ourselves 'with the God of truth', to think along with Isaiah 65[16]; it is no longer, I repeat, to accept Jesus' calling the Holy Spirit 'the spirit of truth' (at least as reported in the Johannine version), and it is to deny Calvin's affirmation, to which I return again and again, that to deny any truth is to insult the Holy Spirit, who is the Spirit of truth. But to reject truth in general is also to declare ourselves an esoteric group without relation to the world about us. It is to reject general education and our place among the inquirers for truth at all cost and in every way. Thus to be true to the Spirit in the Bible and to our Christian heritage at its highest and best and to remain relevant and real among our fellow men, we must cut loose from our ghetto psychology, which has been engendered largely by our biblicism.

Why is it that a preacher can take a text from Leviticus and people feel it to be holy, while if he spoke on a far higher truth from St Francis most worshippers would feel that the sermon was not really Christian? Is Christianity an ingroup magic, a narrow confessionalism, or is it God's truth for the world? How is it that we can read an imprecatory psalm for morning worship and feel its vengeful curses to be proper, whereas if we read from the highest insights of Radhakrishnan we should feel that we had been traitors to our faith? Is not hate, hate; and truth, truth, wherever it is found? The reason for our obtuseness is not hard to find. Revelation always outruns the human and makes what is different from it its strongest speciality. Thus many feel God closer in the reading of the King James version of the Bible than in the reading of the New English Bible. Somehow to many of the twentieth century the unfamiliar 'thou' makes God seem more real than the familiar and natural 'you'. Hallowed usage plays its large part, especially familiar usage of sacred language as opposed to varied usage of secular or ordinary language. The psychology of faith is deeply involved in this ingroup feeling about Christian Scriptures.

The worship of the canon is greatly to blame for this state of affairs. The selection of the books in the canon was determined rather by the contingencies of history than by a regulative doctrine of God's love. Thus books like Esther and Ecclesiastes were taken into the Old Testament and the Book of Revelation into the New. The inclusion of these should be justifiable only as representing what is contrary to the heart of biblical thinking, in much if not most of their import. If the pattern for biblical interpretation requires the whole of human experience for the full and proper exercise of its elucidating power and its guiding directives, the acceptance of such books can be justified. But as far as the Christian canon is concerned, the point was never made clear and explicit that the only standard for inclusion is the relation of the content of any book to the regulative Christian pattern of God's universal love in the life and spirit of Jesus Christ. In canon and creeds the Event was stressed at the expense of the meaning. The stress on *theos* revealed in history took the place of the *logos* revealed in love. Therefore the canon is void of final significance.

In so far as the canon helped to preserve and to focus historical heritage we have to be thankful for it; but it is likely that the books would have lived anyway because of the practical need for them, even without such falsely limiting fences as the canon provides. Indeed, they had lived centuries before the final fixing of the canon! To some extent, then, the standard and manner of the selection for the canon is to blame for the ingroup psychology of Christian thought and worship. We meet something of the same feeling in both Judaism and Islam where the situation and historic development have been similar.

If the stress in the selection of Christian books for the canon had been on meaning, it would have been far easier to avoid the confines of a closed canon. A closed canon or a limiting creed always makes for narrow confessionalism. I believe that one of the problems of the World Council of Churches in its otherwise highly significant and effective Christian work is its shutting itself off from the thought of the world behind a limiting confession which is not even defined in terms of *logos*. All one-sided, ingroup defensiveness suffocates growth and debars creative relations outside the group. All attempts to fence in the Holy Spirit are bound to erect the barriers that themselves limit outreach both in spirit and in fact. If the creeds and the canon had stressed the Gospel at its centre, the whole history of the Church could have been different and the main feel of Christian worship would have been more open to the God of truth. As it is, rather than being an open and opening book, the Bible became shut in and helps to shut in the Church. Some modern biblical scholars, like Albert Sundberg, are now creatively stressing the canon as standard rather than as content of Christian thought. If the standard is the Incarnate Word, the universal Love, there need be no problem at all in having a canon which is both definitive and open.

We have already given considerable attention to the question of the Bible as regulative of the Book of God. We have considered why the Bible has in effect been cut off from the Book of God, God's total living speech to men. We marvel that there has been so little relation between the Bible, which we have held to be God's revelation and truth in general. We have tried to understand why there has been such an esoteric attitude towards the Christian Scriptures, why there has been such a narrow confessionalism, why there has been a mood of ingroup defensiveness rather than an expanding witness in the welcoming of all truth from any quarter.

As we start the more constructive analysis of the Bible as regulative of the Book of God we shall not fall prey either to the idea that there is no final truth in the Bible, making all truth in effect relative and the Christian faith merely one religion among many, or to the opposite error that the Bible contains God's only revelation, thus denying God as the God of all truth and making the Christian faith in effect esoteric and relative, except for the blinded ingroup devotion of its unanalytical worshippers. Instead, I am going to affirm that the heart of the Bible—the Christian pattern, God's universal Love,

Life and Spirit, as reliably suggested by the total event of Jesus as the Christ, including the witness to it of the early followers—is indeed the kind of open-ended truth that no matter how much more is added to it remains in principle dependable. If God is faithful Love and competent Spirit, the eternal, personal Purpose, we can keep learning more from him in all eternity, but whatever we learn will be more of that faithfulness which we have trusted right along.

If such be the case, we must have a canon for biblical faith, the truth of this Event-meaning, the main meaning of this *logos* of the living Love, this universal, open Spirit of integrity and concern, that denies as untrue and unreal anything as ultimately less true than itself, and yet is continually open to what is more than itself, even to what is other than itself provided that the more and other be consistent with the inner core of its truth. Our canon, to be sure, would have to be equally open to all valid and adequate knowledge that denied its faith, for otherwise it would have to choose fancy and not truth. This means that in eternity there may be categories not even dreamed of from man's present narrow angle of vision. We do not under any circumstances deify earthly existence or earthly knowledge. We may some day meet inhabitants from other planets so far advanced beyond us that we can hardly glimpse their way of thinking. But we do have a full, reliable standard of truth for faith in terms of which we can discriminate among all new experiences and from which we can seek for righteous and creative relations among men. Therefore the Bible must 'come of age'. We must not be held back by a magical, primitive view of it. We must be open maturely and freely to all truth, even while knowing that as far as we can tell, both honestly and critically, we have the regulative standard for the evaluation and organization of such truth in the highest revelation of God in the Bible. The Bible taken at its highest and best is thus regulative of the Book of God.

It is true that if the canon had made *logos* standard as the criterion for Christian revelation an open faith engendering a creative theology, we should not now, at least in the same sense and intensity, be plagued with our present problem of ingroup psychology or of the magical authority of the Bible. But Christian theology cannot do without history, without the

Word made flesh. The *logos* in general, the Socratic occasion, needs the Word in particular, the Christian moment, God made personally present as Spirit and Love and to be made present as well, not merely in general or in principle, but in persons, in personal spirits indwelt by God as Love.

There are at least three criteria, therefore, which govern the relation between the Bible and its use as regulative for the Book of God. The first of these is the givenness for faith of God himself. The Christian faith (or any adequate faith) cannot do without the dimension of the transcendent, of ultimate reality, of eternity. Being-itself is a false abstraction; but God as the eternal Spirit who is seen in the Son of his Love is regulative both for the Christian faith and for all adequate rendering of truth as an ultimate category of explanation and as a final standard for conduct. In other words, the Spirit of Truth, the Ultimate Integrity, is also the Ultimate Concern. Not integrity alone nor concern alone in their human limitation, but integrity and concern as the final limits of human thought characterize the regulative relation between the Bible and the Book of God. Nothing less than such biblical truth will do for the Book of God.

The feel towards transcendence is found throughout most of the history of religions. Today we see it in Judaism and Islam, even in Hinduism, and not only in the 'theistic' Ramanuja. A wide and open approach to the question would analyse the inner drives of Buddhism, of Taoism, of Shinto and of the new religions of the world. The matter is exceedingly complex in thought and complicated in historic development, but both from wide reading and from personal discussion with non-Christians throughout the world I have observed a surprising openness for this foundational aspect of faith whenever we are willing to let go our own partial ways of looking at the problems. Historically we have lost the battle for truth at this point almost by default because of our insistence on false theisms. Referring again to the first chapter, the biblical view of transcendence can wing into a new and wider day when it sheds its confining cocoon of Western metaphysics.

As far as general truth is concerned, at least four main approaches indicate the truth of such transcendence. (1) The history of creation is the history of revelation. There can be no adequate accounting for novelty in the history of creation (in such a way that discontinuity is continually and fulfillingly related to continuity) apart from a prior ground of creative Spirit or Purpose. Although the incoming of the new is not easy on any hypothesis, no heuristic device can be more intellectually satisfying than the eternal Purpose, the creative Spirit, who is the source of significance as well as the ground and goal of cosmic process.

(2) No view of transcendence can more fully explain man's needs and offer to fill them than God as Ultimate Concern. In other books I have tried to demonstrate the nature of human needs and how the eternal Purpose when interpreted as Life, Love and Spirit meets them, not only as personal needs but also as the total meaning of history, the understanding of nature as pedagogical process, the grasping of the problem of evil in the light of suffering and healing Love, and the vision of the final destiny of man in and under God.

(3) Another indication of transcendence is vision. Those who have ever been grasped by the depth, comprehensiveness and intellectual persuasiveness of the synoptic vision of God's love in Christ as the ultimate for truth in general cannot but believe it and ache to share it with all others. The truth will stand up, however hard it may be to communicate it in its wholeness and in its seamless integrity.

(4) Finally, there is the power of participation in the Spirit of truth. All ultimate truth is spiritually discerned. Those who have been convicted and convinced by the Spirit of the truth they cannot deny, or who have ever been 'beyond' this life in terms of authentic ecstasy, cannot but affirm and confirm their experiences. The two objective categories above, then ((1) and (2)), although they have a real independence for examination and communication cannot find their full meaning and power apart from the two subjective, contrapletal approaches, and similarly the two subjective approaches ((3) and (4)), cannot convince those interested in general truth apart from their being persuaded also through objective corroborations that are intellectually sturdy.

Having spent much of my life on this question of faith and reason, I can in this connection hardly do more than point towards the fuller truth and ask you, the reader, to pursue it along your own lines. I am convinced that the biblical faith in

God, its view of transcendence as the living God of creation, history and providence is an indispensable aspect of truth. I have never found any candidate for ultimate truth to equal it in intellectual robustness. The biblical criterion of such transcendence is regulative for the Book of God as God's total, living speech to the world.

This personal Purpose which is the first criterion from the Bible as regulative of the Book of God, this steady nature of transcendence, this acceptance of the living God of creation and history, who has been understood the most clearly and steadily (although not exclusively) in the tradition of the Western religions, needs to be supplemented firmly by the reality of Spirit. As we shall see, the three categories of the biblical pattern are the very categories of the first chapter that most adequately express the living God, the God of nowhere and nothing, and the same categories that most effectively spell out the meaning of the life of Jesus in Chapter Two. With the incoming of thoughts insistently and with intensive propinquity to the East we shall increasingly need fuller understanding of the non-personal, the non-manipulative, the true suchness that characterizes all reality. Thus the intellectual and moral transcendence of the *personal* Purpose of the God of Love needs the total meaning of his *impersonal* presence, his non-self activity, even his constant capacity for non-being. The category of Spirit alone can perform this function authentically. The biblical category is no substitute for being as substance; it is no subtle way of using spirit as a word to perform the uses of substance. Substance is defined, definite, formed self-being, static or dynamic, that is itself in such a way that where it is nothing else can be. It can, of course, be amorphous or porous (as all matter is in some sense of actuality or potentiality) and thus capable of being penetrated in the sense of being interlaced or interwoven, but any overlapping of substance, however refined, is still a matter of external relations.

Spirit, however, is reality of identity beyond external relations, in itself incapable of objectification, where true overlapping or interpenetration is identity beyond discrimination, a root-unity anterior to being. Paul Tillich would call this the 'ground of being' or the power for harmony of being. If he took his own thinking seriously enough he would arrive at a supernatural reality (or call it a transcendent reality, which is no transcendent realm). He has a right to reject the term 'supernatural' if by that is meant a false objectification of the non-objectifiable. His ultimate, as he has told me personally, is no mere sum and substance of all finite objects and persons and no mere dimension of depth potential for such a world of experience. It is, rather, the reality, creatively and redemptively, which that world presupposes.

If Tillich abandoned, then, the category of being and being itself, which is a contradiction in terms of his own analysis and which he has to change in nearly every new volume, and accepted instead the category of Spirit, as he does terminologically in the third volume of his *Systematic Theology*, he would come up with an understanding of reality where one may call God neither 'a' nor 'the' God as an entirely separate category, nor especially the supreme Being (as we saw in chapter one), but where also the Spirit can both have a total focused consciousness in himself and a supreme personal Purpose and yet also be the Self of selves and the Nature of nature. In other words, Self or Personality would be no ultimate category as would Love, Spirit and Personal Purpose; but such an ultimate, directing consciousness would neither be merely the creation of other consciousnesses as their sum total nor merely a distinct consciousness as categorically apart from them, but would, rather, be Spirit as the ultimate unity and identity of all Reality while yet open both to the reality of their being in the Spirit and to their being genuinely distinct, finite spirits with an authentic measure of self-reality.

As we enter into the new world of fuller thinking on a worldwide and planetary scale we must keep the biblical criterion of the kind of transcendence that can be reliably known as more-and-other, and as totally directive Concern, the personal Purpose which is expressed metaphorically by the term 'our Father' which gives unity to this and to all creations, but does so not at the expense of a true category for immanence in nature and incarnation in human life. Thus the personal, or non-overlapping category of external relations, the category of genuine transcendence, needs the spirit, the co-inherent reality of unity and identity which allows at the same time sameness of reality, in truth and fact, and distinctions within that reality.

The biblical category of transcendence is astonishingly rich for creative developments in many directions which have as yet scarcely been surmised. It burgeons and boils with the intellectual suggestiveness which we have seen only from a distance. It would indeed be folly to listen to the voices that now advocate 'the wholly other', the Hebrew God of majesty and mystery beyond all creation, as representing the total posture of biblical transcendence. This transcendence is there and must not be neglected or obscured even though today there are drives in this direction, too. But along with biblical transcendence must be maintained its contrapletal category of Spirit as immanence in creation and incarnation in life.

If we neglect this second category, of immanence and incarnation, as regulative of the Book of God we shall not only push away from us the creative needs of the Eastern thought-world, but we shall also cut off and cut out the truth that alone can make us whole; for personal Purpose and Spirit in their dual relationship to reality are not only *intellectually* a matter of external and internal relations but personal Purpose and Spirit are also, and even more importantly, the categories of *personal* relation to God in terms of encounter and inner experience, of Christ for us and in us; in fact they are therefore of equal importance to the meaning and power for ethical living and for social relations, the two topics which remain to be treated in following chapters.

The third criterion from the Bible as regulative of the Book of God (God's total speech to man, God's constant living communication of himself and of his will) is love. In most theological quarters today the category of love is a popular one. Love is extolled both by the advocates of transcendence and by the devotees of a new, radical approach to doctrines and morals which is in revolt against this transcendence. Support from all sides is all to the good if love is honestly accepted and competently applied to both faith and life. There can be no serious question that love is the central category of the highest meaning and power of the New Testament. Unfortunately, however, 'love' is a term that lends itself to abuse in both thought and life as easily as, and possibly more easily than, any other.

The love learned from the Bible is the God-centred, Christ-focused, person-oriented, universal concern for the creative fulfilment in God and with all men of each and every creature.

It is this love which must be regulative for the Book of God. This love is an unlimited and unlimitable as well as an unconditional love. It is not a general good will through some general will for all. It is, rather, a concrete, particular care from God for all, under particular circumstances, under all conditions through each and all in every concrete situation of need and fulfilment. It is a love for people in the ultimacy of personal relationships where the reality of what is personal precedes in primacy all study, all action and all growth, while fully encouraging all of these in their proper places and perspectives.

Thus love is a matter of neither quietism nor of activism. It is no mere question of being or of doing. In reality we can be with God today in paradise. The 'now' is primary as the locus of relationship and acceptance outweighs in the scales of reality all preparatory work for it and all subsequent growth in it. But acceptance is never a matter of isolable self-satisfaction or escape from constant concern, either in terms of the continuing responsibilities for self-fulfilment in all needful ways or in terms of the duties for others in our common situation of communal need and communal attainment.

Love, then, is a full, open trust in God, engendering creative zest and satisfaction in the now, a resting in God, a living reality in the present. Love is at the same time an inclusive but particular concern for all, especially as they are relevantly related, that all may find reality in God. Love allows us to become willing to let others alone as they need, or to carry out such study, work or giving with them and for them as will most effectively secure for them their highest fulfilment as fellow creatures of God. Love like this will, indeed, mirror all the problems and failures of our finitude and sinfulness, but, if genuine, it will the more importantly participate in the immeasurable reality, help and healing of the personal Purpose and the power of the Spirit.

I believe that these biblical categories, final for faith, must therefore be authoritative for the Book of God. They form a dependable biblical base for creative, adventuresome truth, both effectively motivating all attitudes of relationships and also reliably directing immediate action and further search. Indeed, these categories provide us with an open Bible. While keeping the Bible creatively central to the Book of God, we also enjoy the flexibility to consider and to accept all truth from the total Source of Significance. We need not be defensive or aggressive in relation either to the secular world or to other religions. The biblical truth must be ever more rigorously tested in the arena of creative thought and power for life.

The world is moving towards a new day. We err when we tie ourselves down to a falsely authoritative Bible as a whole instead of accepting the full freedom of the heart of the biblical message which will regulate all other truth, not by external authority or by magical claims, but by its very power to order our total world of knowledge and to foster the universal human community in creative, co-operative adventure. Thus we free the Bible to be itself at its own best even while we set ourselves free within the truth that releases ever more creative life.

The Bible at the heart of its message is regulative of the Book of God. It points to a finality of faith that is an open directive to reliable destiny. It offers truth for the seeking and the finding which grows in depth, in height, in breadth and in length even though the direction of growth has already been indicated. But in another sense the Bible must be fulfilled by the Book of God. Our final, brief subsection must end on this topic. It must conclude on the note of openness towards vistas not yet spied. How can one describe in advance the country one has not yet reached? And yet we know that human beings must discover not only truth anew but also new truth, no matter how much reliable truth has been granted us on which to build. We have had a taste of travelling and we have maps to point us towards the land to be explored, but that country beckons us for pioneering more than present knowledge suggests.

The Bible, after all, is only the history of a small rural people and of its prophets and seers. Even he who most fully envisioned and experienced the universal God and the unconditional Love, did so against a limited background of experience and had himself a primitive apperceptive mass for interpreting what he experienced. For this reason, recognizing the shallowness of any period of time by itself and the inborn finitude which will always beset the best of human knowledge, we must never rest content with deifying what is inside the covers of any book. The wedge between the sacred and the secular as exhibited by our inadequate use of the Bible must be done away as we mature into the freedom of the truth which centres in life, love and spirit, however much these then must be exemplified and exhibited in concrete life.

Three areas particularly serve for fulfilling the Bible by the Book of God. The first is our view of God. The Bible's view of God as Shepherd is idyllic, but more picturesque than real for modern man. Its view of God as King is too authoritarian. Lord and Ruler are concepts that go ill with love. 'Father' is by far the best term, but even the family becomes a tiny concept in the light of the billions and billions of galaxies. We live in a space age so startling that even the word Creator needs radical refining, and Fatherhood of the illimitable universes stretches the family concept to the breaking point. There is no denying the truth in any of the traditional terms but neither is there any getting away from the fact that our deepest and widest concepts of today hardly fit into the smaller and milder connotations of traditional worship. Perhaps all we can do is to be faithful to the open yet reliable biblical categories and wait for the new ages to coin the proper terms for God and to fill these terms with the appropriate affective content.

Head and heart must go together. Meaning and motivation must reinforce each other. We must not be disturbed, therefore, when new thinkers challenge the old patterns. What we need to watch is the spirit of that challenge. Is it personal, invidious, irresponsible? Or is it weighed down with concern for man and truth in all their depths of interrelationship of need? Are the harbingers of the new aware of and appreciative of the meaning and power of our human heritage and of our Christian past or are they merely revolting out of restlessness and confusion? Surely new and better thoughts must come, and the Book of God will need to be written ever afresh and in terms of the new scenery, but if the God of the Bible is the God of truth such new ways of truth will only engender sturdier thinking and more awesome worship.

The larger view of God will surely have to keep growing and developing new language to fit the new facts. We shall also have to become more keenly aware of our technological revolution. How can biblical language be fulfilled by technological terms? How can automation be used to illustrate the works of God in creation and providence? Already creative thoughts are swirling in my head on the subject, but no one of us can provide more than the first suggestions towards the continued writing of the Book of God. To be open to God's voice for today and to appreciate the living Word of God's present speaking is our task. Much atheism simply leaves God in the dead, irrelevant past and never sees his work in the present acts of his love. What, for instance, of the revolution that will come through leisure? The Bible has no genuine God for the world of sports. What a need! Nor has the Bible developed a view of God as Educator of children and adults in an age when education will have to occupy increasingly main stretches of life. A world of forced leisure, moreover, will find us with no genuine view of God in terms of the arts. Most aesthetic views of God fit ill with what we know of him totally. Art will be made part of general life as more and more time will be devoted to it. How can our understanding of God relate the arts intrinsically to all of life? Will worship occupy the centre of the future? Man must live by both meaning and motivation in ultimate dimensions of depth and not merely by what is material and human.

Most important to the Book of God, however, are the blank pages of today. We can suggest areas of need, but only our total history under God can provide the answers. We have regulative relations for destiny. We are not left in confusion to drift. We must use the Bible in line with the best authority for interpretation we have, we must leave room for the mystery of the living God of nowhere and nothing beyond all dependable knowledge for faith in our world of creation, and we must have a view of Christ that lifts our vision into the ever growing future of life, love and spirit; but we can never stop writing the Book of God except with the directive, 'to be concluded'. Even our interpretation of eschatology will have to grow. At present we cannot see how. As the eternal why of God's love is brought more and more to bear on the how of our knowledge there will surely be more light.

Perhaps the fundamental creativity of our age will have to be devoted to working out the relation between the why and the how. We have seen in previous chapters how our age is turning significantly from the questions of how, from which we have learned accumulatively with untold profit, to the questions of why, the challenge of the future for the fuller living meaning-fulness of all knowledge. We may soon face a strong temptation to turn from the dull and laborious how's of the past to some more exciting explanation of over-arching purpose in terms of why. But no why can ever take the place of the how. The Middle Ages made this mistake. Since then the opposite mistake has been made, namely to substitute the how's for the why's. The more laborious task which now confronts us is to see all history biblically in terms of the ultimate why of personal Purpose without forfeiting God's grace in the great measure of independence in creation which can be answered only in terms of patient how's.

Even the nature of fulfilment itself will need radical rethink-ing. The Jewish notion of life after death in late Judaism and the further embroidering of it by the Christian doctrine of resurrection are realities for faith that are death to lose. But they are no final formulations. We must look at the teachings of all religions and come up with some answers that will more fully satisfy our best knowledge and our deepest possessions of spiritual vision. Paul Tillich has led the way by affirming that death is neither the continuation nor the cessation of the individual. He has also wanted to synthesize the Christian view of resurrection with the Buddhist teaching of nirvana. Both these confessions contain deeper implications than most people surmise. The Christian view of destiny is neither of place nor of condition in any external sense but of the fulfilment of the finite spirit within the infinite Spirit in constructive meaningfulness. God himself is heaven, but what can it mean to have eternal life 'in God' without mere meaningless merger in him and without the continued separateness that spells restlessness and unfulfilment?

Other religions offer numerous suggestions as to destiny. Consider, for instance, *The Wisdom of Lao-tse* on this subject: 'To have been cast in this human form is to us already a source of joy. How much greater joy beyond our conception to know that that which is now in human form may undergo countless transitions, with only the infinite to look forward to?' or we can find creative newness in terms of the development of our own faith, but I can assay neither of these approaches in this volume. The Buddhist doctrine of nirvana, for another instance, may not mean being 'blown out' in the way of extinction but rather being blown out of the kind of existence which now denies 'true suchness'. What is the true suchness of nirvana when we are beyond the limitations of this life? The subject calls for complete openness to possible new developments. If these developments come, we must still know that from this side of eternity we need mostly to be open for what God will show us concretely in his way and time as to what he holds in store for us. We might even think of God's having a Sabbath rest for our age to be followed by a quite new era of unimaginable creativity!

Thus our view of God, our view of the kind of world in which we live, and the view of the end, the final destiny, indicate three areas in which the Bible will increasingly have to be fulfilled by the Book of God. My deepest conviction is that such fulfilment is even now beginning. God will raise up prophets and sons to perform such a task. When the Book of God is written for its own new day, however, we shall surely find that the central message of the Bible remains ever creatively true and constructively regulative of the Book of God. In one sense God has spoken once for all his saving truth in the Word of the Bible. He will never deny his own faithfulness. God will just as surely speak whatever further saving truth man needs for every age in the ever open and ever dependable Book of God.

In chapter one we saw how the living God of nowhere and nothing can be known trustworthily only by the double relation of encounter and indwelling; in chapter two we found that Jesus was the Son of God because he lived this double relationship to God and into human history; in this chapter we have observed that the Bible can be understood adequately and dependably only when it is interpreted within this double relationship of its own dimension of depth, the Incarnate Word, confronting the eternal Word who transcends all telling. The Bible is the concrete, historic heritage of the Word made flesh with relation to and for all flesh in a creative, regulative confrontation with the Book of God which is ever being written afresh in terms of the 'more' of the heart of the Bible and of the 'other' than the Bible which contrapletes such moreness. This view of the Bible combines naturally the fully open mind with the ever worshipping heart.

Chapter IV

Moralism or Morality

THE living God of nowhere and nothing, the personal Purpose beyond all objectified existence, who is the Spirit of Love, who has shown his very nature and will in the life, teachings, death and resurrection of Jesus, 'the Son of his Love', has given us a Gospel not only for faith but also for conduct. Our day needs a Gospel for conduct. We are desperate for an interpretation, rooted in reality, which can be authoritative without being authoritarian, and which can give meaningful motivation without being either externally imposed or internally undependable. Our approach to ethics must avoid alike an arid objectivism and an irresponsible subjectivism.

For the purposes of this chapter, I shall define moralism as any and all unauthentic morality. According to dictionary usage in both English and American (if we may employ the *Oxford Universal Dictionary* for the former and the Webster *New World Dictionary of the American Language* for the latter) the word 'moralism' means ethics without religion, or conduct not 'spiritualized'. To my surprise, I could not find the theological usage, meaning a false trust in conduct as a way of salvation or a self-righteous self-satisfaction on account of one's fulfilment of a prescribed code of approved conduct, in any of the three dictionaries I consulted. Nevertheless this connotation is currently so general that I shall make free and frequent use of it. In any case, the standard definition for our purposes will be false morality whether or not it is explicitly connected with religion.

Moralism, then, is the abuse of morality whatever the conscious or subconscious relation be between the intention of the act and its grounding in reality, whereas morality is life in the truth, that is right understanding and free acceptance of reality. Moralism fails of such life in the truth either because it lacks true understanding or full acceptance of reality (the moralism of externality) or because it lacks a free, spontaneous motivation elicited by a releasing relation to reality (the moralism of internality). We can look at moralism as conduct only externally rooted in religion or as conduct lacking adequate rootage in reality. The right moral relation to reality, on the other hand, would involve a releasing openness to reality, combining an authoritative directive with an understanding, willing response.

The first main section of this chapter will deal with the moralism of externality; the second, with the moralism of internality. It is interesting to observe that according to my definition of moralism as any and all unauthentic morality there can be no true morality without right religion. Right religion is right relation to reality. Right conduct is life in the truth as the right understanding and free acceptance of reality. Religion in itself, of course, solves no ethical problems. Religious practices exhibit an immense amount of moralism. But conduct outside religion, although it can be good, cannot be fully good. It lacks rootage in reality both for meaning and for motivation. It lacks total context.

Kant, for example, taught moralism rather than morality. He sought a false freedom of man apart from man's reality as spirit beyond all objectification. Kant's concept of autonomy fails to be grounded in reality; his ethics does not derive from the nature and will of God. He even tried to found his religion on morality. That is sheer moralism. Kant even went so far as to ground morality in the practical reason, a procedure which amounts to moralism intensified; indeed, it involves the substitution not only of man for man-in-his-universe or man under God, but of reason as a practical function of life (with whatever categorical imperative) for the whole man reasoning in his ethical response to reality.

Here is no place, of course, for technical discussion either philosophically or ethically, although there is great need for it elsewhere. I merely hint at Jaspers' committing the first of Kant's mistakes, dismissing religion as the ground of ethics; but Jaspers at least accepts the whole man as reasoning ethically. If only he could think of religion not merely as historically particular and therefore as limiting necessarily the complete openness of philosophy, but consummately as the universal 'Encompassing', requiring the full integrity of openness by its very nature, for which he ardently keeps seeking! In any case, the theologians keep giving him mountains of ammunition.

By the end of this chapter, however, I hope to demonstrate that there can be not only a view of reality that releases full freedom for integrity of conduct, for a community of co-operative maturation and increasing maturity, but also a historic ground for conduct which ethically in particular demands the most universal standard possible. We shall indeed see that the *external* relations of our three previous chapters, demanding creative encounter with an acceptance of reality, will have to be intrinsically contrapleted by the *internal* relations of identity and co-inherence in the Spirit which make for an ever widening, inner reality of freedom both for self-fulfilment and for community. In between lies the whole process of divine pedagogy and human growth which accumulates the product of love's freedom.

Kant's three universal laws for morality (that each one act so that his own act could become universal law; that all be treated as ends and not means; and that all be both fully free and slave in the kingdom of ends) are, of course, only an analytical transcription of the Christian requirements of the ethics of love: universality, the full centring of concern on the other, and perfect freedom in full service. Kant's laws lack, however, the total context of 'the encompassing' Reality as the primary data for ethics. After a few remarks about the concrete problems of morality we shall turn to our two sections analysing moralism. The word 'mores' will be used simply as the amoral acceptance of what is generally considered proper. Mores may be the most frequent occasion for moralism, but mores by themselves are not moralism.

Mere generalities will not do, for morality is a concrete as well as a critical issue. Can anyone nowadays know concretely what is right and do it? According to surveys, not only do large numbers of Methodists in the United States take a drink but even the Methodist Church, at least in its responsible commit-tees, has begun to look at the problem of drinking less externally. Can the Methodist Church come up with an answer that is morality rather than moralism? British Friends look with less horror than they used to at homosexuality and other so-called unnatural practices, and even suggest that pre- and extramarital relations might be less evil than a husband's rape of his wife when unwilling. Does all this mean that society is breaking down and going to ruin, or as some stoutly aver, that it is throwing off its shackles of moralism to create true morality?

I wondered about this when I was invited to address a large university student group on the question 'Sex Before and After the Pill', referring, of course, to the widely used oral contraceptive. The leaders of the group told me they wanted 'a creative view of sex', none of the old Ten Commandments moralism, none of the old do's and don't's of traditional Christianity. This group was too mature, they wrote me, for reverting to the customary inhibitions of sex morality, centring in marriage as the end-all. Somehow they wanted a creative, Christian view that would be morality and not mores.

What is the present situation? Surely the old inhibitionist moralism that curbed little and mostly produced guilt feelings will not do. Traditional Christianity has been poverty-stricken in the field of morality. It has forgotten and generally forfeited the freedom and vitality of the original Gospel. All too often people have rejected the prohibitions of traditionalism and have lived as though faith did not matter, while others have shrivelled into slaves of duty without either the fun of 'freedom' or the joy of spiritual release. Even many church folk have made their choice either going to church and doing what they pleased or going to church and please don't! Is there any solution? Must man be either uninhibited or frustrated? The choice lies between moralism and morality. But does either choice escape the dilemma?

I

In our discussion of the false morality of externality, we must dismiss as either moralism or mores all conduct based on external authority. Mostly to obey orders is not moral action. Children, of course, have to learn by doing as they are told. When such learning is necessary it naturally is both right and good. Obedience, to be sure, is living by law and not by the Gospel. While not mature morality, obedience has its place in God's pedagogy as well as in the pedagogy of parents. The law and obedience to it have their proper functions. Mental and moral defectives, for instance, are also 'minors' in that they are

incapable of adult morality. For them, mores must be prescribed; they must be told what to do.

Conduct dependent upon explicit tutelage, however, lacks
true morality. When children have grown they should no
longer have to be told. Many churches, however, treat people
like children. The Roman Catholic Church in the past has
trained its priests in innumerable moral rules or prescriptions
for concrete situations. Parishioners marvel at the consistency
of the counselling they receive in confession from Roanoke to
Rome. But telling people what to do helps to undermine
morality in so far as it fails to encourage a creative, vigorous
morality. Morality consists in learning to discern and to make
moral choices. When choices are ready-made for them people
are in effect treated like children who never are allowed to grow
up. They are back under the rules and regulations of the
Pharisees and not within the freedom of the Gospel which is the
essence of mature morality. To be sure, the best in Pharisaism
and in Catholicism goes beyond such tutelage; and today, as
in its great moral theologian, Bernhard Häring, there is a clear
clarion call to the ethics of love.

The Roman Catholic Church further dampens morality,
however, when it claims to be able to assess, punish and forgive
sins according to some definite scale of guilt. Such appraisal
magnifies externality if it permits people, however subtly, to
feel that now, their sins forgiven, they are free to sin some more.
Unamuno, in his novel, *Abel Sanchez*, declares that people under
such a system can sin more gracefully and tranquilly. The
seriousness of sin, as a personal act in freedom under God which
only he can forgive, and of inner as well as outer consequences
which only he can assess is, if not entirely removed, at least
dangerously reduced. The externalizing of morality tends to
paralyse it. Confession is often an aid to mental health but it
may also unwittingly help to increase immorality. True morality cannot be externalized without turning into either
accustomed mores or a self-satisfiable moralism. The Catholic
Church is now facing this problem in depth and, one may
hope, will become increasingly free from the externality of
conduct.

Many Protestant churches are no better off, but their failing
is of a different nature. Conservative sects make even personal

dress a matter of morality. Some churches forbid their youth any worldly pleasure or conformity with custom. When bobbed hair first came into fashion, a church of my acquaintance expelled all the girls from the choir for having their hair cut, even though in order to forestall just such dismissal they had banded together in committing the 'crime'. I remember that on the day I was baptized as a boy in Sweden a visiting minister preached on the text: 'If it were not so I would have told you', explaining to us that Jesus 'would have told' us if he had wanted us to dance, smoke or play cards, or particularly attend the movies. The taboos were simple and straight: Do these things and go to hell. Otherwise 'touch not the unclean thing'. Churches like these, few though they be today, preach moralism but know next to nothing about morality.

A soprano soloist, herself a Methodist in a Southern city, told me of her experience in being invited to sing at a special celebration in the church of a 'holiness' sect. The choir director met her with a prompt warning, 'We know you are a Christian, Mrs. T., but to keep the choir from thinking that you have lipstick on, would you please go and wash?' She washed off her lipstick in chagrin.

Upon her return he said, 'There is something else unbiblical about you,' and indicated her ear-rings. Off they came.

'Something else I fear the Bible does not allow.'

'Whatever can it be?'

'Rings on your fingers.'

'But they have never been off since my engagement and wedding day!'

They pulled hard for the sake of Christ and high morality, but the sinful finger was shamefully grown or swollen and the rings did not come off.

'Then turn the diamond around so it will be inside the hand while you sing.' (Hidden sin is more moral?)

The sermon that day, continued Mrs. T., consisted of the minister's ranting against poison that killed a specified number of people each year. The congregation was bid to view a small, casket-like box but warned not to get too near. Poison is dangerous. What was in it? A package of cigarettes! To be sure, modern medicine will back up the preacher. All together now for high and holy morality.

Then what? More poison. This time the poison that is a stench in the Lord's nostrils. This time a tin of coffee. Then the climax. The devils trembled. Immorality was routed. Out came the bottle from behind the pulpit. What degrades more than the bottle? Especially that bottle that had its birth in the American Southland. What bottle? Coca-Cola! Lift high the banner of Christ. Blow, clarions of morality.

That congregation, being told what not to do, remained little children morally. Morally immature, they relished the safety of knowing how to walk to heaven without having to learn morality.

Catholic and Protestant churches alike thus in bits or overdoses often unwittingly conspire to keep their people from learning morality. Being told what to do, the faithful are kept moral children all their lives. The extreme illustrations I have used are true incidents personally known to me. Even though they may seem to caricature moralism, they serve to bring into focus a general tendency to substitute telling people what is right and wrong for letting them learn morality.

Another way of keeping people from becoming moral is establishing principles for them to follow. The Church may not say outright, 'Don't do so and so, because we have decided that it is wrong, or because the Bible tells us that it must not be done.' It may, rather, simply say, 'We stand for principles.' These principles then become equated with mores or become used moralistically.

The clergyman father of a graduate student at my own seminary, a young man who had already received his B.D. at an outstanding university divinity school, breathed hellfire and purpled nearly to apoplexy as he expounded to me the 'principles' that he felt any Baptist minister must have. I could hardly believe my ears as he choked out, 'I would rather strangle my son with my own hands than have him smoke'.

Likewise, when the question came up as to how to advise students about to leave for study abroad, where theological discussion often centres around a glass of wine or a mug of beer, some Canadian churchmen immediately settled the issue, 'You must not even discuss the matter. We expect theological students to have principles.'

Sex, also, is a simple matter with such an approach. When it was discovered in a church college that an engaged couple had been carrying on intimate relations, the solution presented no problem. Students who are not Christians, who have no Christian principles, it was generally agreed, have simply to be thrown out. Sin is utterly simple for such people, who reduce morality to a matter of church mores, or who substitute Christian 'principles' for morality.

'I always lie,' cheerfully proclaimed the brilliant, affable principal of a British theological college. 'In my opinion telling the truth is not only boorish but often harmful. Sometimes a doctor must soften the truth in order not to kill the patient almost at once. I always try to encourage a student beyond the actual situation, and sometimes I pull him through.'

A breach of honour? But listen.

'I lie,' went on the principal, 'because I believe in concern more than in the truth. When I have to act on one principle rather than on the other, I choose to act in love.'

Can we act thus simply on principles and be moral? The principal obviously had a point, and a Christian point; but have we the right to select thus arbitrarily among principles? Concern, affirms Emil Brunner, is more important than character. Is love, then, perhaps above all principles? If we grant this contention, do we not land in the morass of subjectivism? Cannot love when treated as a principle become an excuse for not living up to the right? Do we not rationalize when we choose love instead of principles? Our third section will wrestle with this knotty problem.

Principles as absolute rules put a damper on morality. They solve moral problems prematurely. A principle seldom fits any situation concretely. Principles make people self-righteous in their claim to know and to do the truth. Certainly rules and regulations called principles are externally imposed and thereby make conduct a matter of mores or moralism rather than of morality. Principles can be based on the summations of past conduct and thus focus present choices or they can be based on creative presuppositions generating pioneering attempts at action. Can principles, however, relate man dynamically either to releasing reality or to free motivation in response to such reality? In any case, principles govern conduct externally without recourse to full reality, and elicit an internal response of obedience which never rises to the free creative motivation which reality releases when it is rightly apprehended.

To live by custom, in the third place, is quite as external an act as to live by tutelage or by principles. What is conformity to custom but the abdication of genuine morality? It is a matter of mores, if unthinking; of moralism, if deliberate. There is no authentic freedom in doing what 'everyone' is doing for the sake of not being 'different', or for the sake of being 'accepted', and surely there is no releasing rootage in, or creative response to, reality. Currently strong stress is put on peer prestige. One must do what is accepted as right by one's peers. I heard it seriously suggested in a graduate school that senior students ought to be made 'teaching fellows', on the grounds that these students considered even their young instructors too old for their proper peer group. Students would not take seriously, it was suggested, the teaching of anyone outside their own peer group.

Similarly custom dictates in the matter of sex. The question of premarital sex relations to the group of college students I mentioned earlier was not one of right or wrong; it was not even a matter mostly of possible consequences, either externally or within the students themselves. The only question that seemed to matter (and it mattered tremendously) was whether it was 'done' or not. If promiscuity, or at least sex relations among those 'going steady' was the approved course, how could either parents or teachers expect girls in particular to risk their 'belonging' by being prudish? The discussion was thus not about morality but about mores. As a matter of fact, the question of right and wrong apart from the judgement of the peer group seemed a matter of theory or 'abstraction'. After all, they shrugged, who is to say what is right and what is wrong? Mores thus define morality.

Mores may, of course, amount to practices which affect the very livelihood of people. I know of a baker who, upon his conversion, decided to follow scrupulously all laws pertaining to his business. By taking no shortcuts and by observing all sanitary regulations and rules as to ingredients, he found to his dismay that his cost of production exceeded the usual way of doing things accepted by his competitors in the business. On the edge of bankruptcy, the baker decided to abandon his new-found Christian faith and once again was able to make a living. Morality may be not only costly but a most complicated affair. External customs and considerations modify the circumstances of morality. The conditions of the situation under which choices are made become different. What then? To have accepted the illegal practices customary to the profession would have been moralism, acting apart from and contrary to the demands of reality. But when those demands seem excessively costly, how can reality be called motivationally releasing? Such concrete problems will call us to account in our third section.

A young idealist upon receiving his degree from a leading graduate school of business administration determined to keep personal integrity in business no matter what the cost. After a few years he confessed to me that he had found personal scruples to have little or no place in the world of 'big business'. Policies with which one does not agree are determined at the top, and one either conforms or is out. While working for a large corporation, after much humble struggling to be both practical and creative, he tried quietly to call the attention of his superiors to certain practices that he felt were morally wrong and could be corrected. All the thanks he received for his moral observations was to be called an obstructionist. Soon afterward he resigned his position to open his own small-scale private business. When mores are binding to the point that participation in practices we believe to be wrong are necessary to our livelihood, how can we possibly be moral?

Thus on the level of social custom some mores are taken with punitive seriousness. Join us or leave us, seems to be the prevailing attitude. On the level of business or professional practices the morally sensitive are hard pressed to know how both to keep their job and yet to avoid doing what is personally offensive but generally done. The tyranny of custom brings on a morally paralysing conformity. Moralism, as conduct not rightly related to reality, takes a stranglehold on life. If all conduct based on external authority without deep inner understanding and approval is a matter of moralism or mores and not of morality, what chance does the ordinary person have to be moral? Has the Christian faith a way out? Must life be either a matter of obstructionist defiance or of pliant conformity? If moralism and mores have such strong hold over people socially and practically, how can we go beyond both to morality?

This first section has pointed suggestively to the problem of the moralism of externality. Shall we call it a pressure towards the abuse of morality? Obviously such externality is only a partial truth since all conduct involves people whose inner selves cannot be left out of any intention or action. There is no such thing as *mere* mores. All accustomed actions have some constant relation to both the meaning and the motivation of every agent of action. We are aiming not at an all-or-none analysis of ethical behaviour but rather at a suggestive understanding of the over-emphases or under-emphases of certain phases of the total ethical relation. To this end we have considered, in this section, the dangers of tutelage, of principles and of custom, the major temptations to short-cut and short-circuit the full inner response of understanding and riskful decision.

Tutelage is for children and as such needful; but often institutions offer or even demand courses of action in such a way as to obstruct maturation. Principles, furthermore, can become not only isolated from their source in reality that releases steadiness of authority and power for motivation, but also divorced from their creative call on the moral agent for fruitful scrutiny of moral problems and for the inner appropriation of the ethical meaning of moral relationships and actions. Principles, then, can occasion either mostly mores or mostly moralism in conduct. Moralism in this case may be a matter either of conduct without religion (with no recourse to reality) or of self-righteousness in terms of accepting the principles themselves as satisfying the demands of both truth and action. Custom, moreover, seems to contribute mostly to habits that hardly touch the moral consciousness. Out of custom men act simply for the reason that this is the 'proper' thing to do. But whenever such customs are threatened, the degree of defensiveness or even protective aggressiveness that results reveals the depth of moralism that lies behind mores.

Naturally I have only suggested the issues of false morality, not in order to describe them in either depth or detail, but rather to bring out the problems, I hope honestly and not in caricature, in order later to demonstrate the power of the Christian Gospel for human conduct. To highlight the issues somewhat I have in this instance used several concrete illustrations. In the next section we shall follow the same procedure with the moralism of internality.

II

If all conduct based on *external* authority is thus a matter of moralism or mores and not of morality, conversely, however, there is nothing *within* man that can attain full morality. There is also a moralism of internality that cuts off relations to reality. Often we hear it said that conscience is a safe, even a true, moral guide. Some people have gone so far as to equate conscience with the voice of God. But conscience in itself is far from being the voice of God. By itself conscience is not even the will to right conduct. Surely it is not a spokesman for creative morality. Conscience by itself is mostly the reflection of one's concrete moral situation and one's accustomed response to it. Conscience is man's side of the image of God as God's concrete call on man. To rely on conscience as it is, is to rely on mostly the accumulated standards of human customs rather than on the ever creative, convicting image of God which although generally hidden from consciousness reflects reality directly. Reliance on conscience as such is a prime example of the moralism of internality. If any slogan deserves our suspicion, it is 'Let your conscience be your guide'.

In a pastors' school where I was teaching, for example, a hot discussion arose about the need to take progressive measures with regard to a specific situation. One reactionary, recalcitrant minister after another, a small group of minority diehards, stood up to protest by saying, 'I think ideally this ought to be done, but I am going to vote against the action, because my conscience just won't let me.' After considerable discussion back and forth I was asked point blank for my opinion about conscience in a matter like this. My answer was immediate: 'To hell with conscience!' This reply shocked some of the men, accustomed as they were to hide as a final refuge behind the authority of conscience. There is no warrant, not even biblical, for so doing. At least the New Testament states that 'if our hearts condemn us Christ is greater than our hearts'. Doubtless I should have couched my answer positively, 'To Christ with conscience', but the negative was startlingly effective!

Conscience can be the refuge of moral laggards and of reactionary do-nothings. Conscience generally reflects the prevailing *status quo*. It helps to keep from acting below its own level; at least it twinges if we do. But nothing encourages moralism more than this very dependence on conscience. Jesus hated sham; he could not bear Pharisaism. The good, respectable, yes, the 'best' people kept society in the state it was in because they had adjusted to the *status quo* and approved it. Not only that, but they preened themselves on doing so. They felt not only satisfied but superior. They were the good people, even the people of God. Painfully true to conscience, they thereby killed true morality. Robespierre, according to Stanley Loomis in *Paris During the Terror*, was the most dangerous and destructive leader of the French Revolution because he gave himself and all others a false sense of religious idealism based on his continual reliance on and reference to his conscience. Open sinners have no such refuge as have moral Pharisees; Jesus saw them as less morally reprehensible than those who hid behind conscience to escape God and authentic morality. The Pharisees made morality 'of no effect because of their traditions' and customs, the mores that made up the content of their consciences.

Let me cite a deplorable yet wryly amusing example as told me by the Bishop of Oxford about his predecessor. At the occasion of the Oxford Ecumenical Conference the good bishop had to fight long with his conscience before he could feel right about admitting to Holy Communion those who did not belong to his own ingroup. One of those who had received the invitation after the bishop had searched and conquered his conscience, was the president of the Southern Baptist Theological Seminary in Louisville, Kentucky. He in turn paced his room for hours fighting *his* conscience, in the end being conquered by it. Thereupon he wrote to the bishop to this effect, 'Having searched my conscience after receiving your kind invitation to participate at the service of Holy Communion I have come to the decision that I must reluctantly decline, since my conscience will not let me take the Lord's Supper in the company of some who have not been validly baptized.'

It is necessary to live beyond conscience if we are to live morally. Unless Christ, as universal concern, is the criterion of

conscience and the Holy Spirit its driving motivation, conscience is not trustworthy. A Free Church minister of my
acquaintance suffered qualms of conscience even when he was
to kneel at the side of Archbishop Berggrav at the Oslo Conference to receive Holy Communion. But this minister spoke
roughly to the prejudices working through his conscience. He
conquered his conscience by the reality and power of Christ.

Many people suffer needlessly from the tyranny of conscience.
Driven by guilt, they experience constant conflict without the
healing rest of the freedom of the Gospel. People have 'conscience' about everything. Sabbatarians can make Sunday the
worst day of the week for countless young people. Some people
feel guilty about sleeping eight hours a night instead of praying
more or reading more. Some feel guilty about having too much
sex and some about having too little. Life is full of guilt.
People seem always unhappy, suffering over what they do or
don't. People are kept apart and progress is held back because
of conscience over the wrong things. Only God, so to speak,
could go perfectly by his conscience. We human beings are too
steeped in our own juice of moralism. Over and over again
when I hear trivial matters discussed as major divisive issues I
feel tempted to shout once more, 'To hell with conscience.'
Get rid of its prejudices and move up into the world of morality.
The guilt feelings of an oppressive conscience, causing unrest
and division, must be burned out if not by the fires of hell, then
by the hot love of Christ for persons that they may find moral
freedom.

If, then, individual consciences are as varied as the wind and
far from faultless moral guides, can there be an inner way of
being moral without any such dependence upon conscience?
After all, conscience is, for the most part of the time, merely the
internalizing of what we have learned objectively from parents
or from the peer group. Some people who discount the reliability of conscience believe in inner-directedness. They claim
that there can be an inner quality of life, a progressive maturity,
which can be moral and go beyond the relativism of conscience
as the inner representative of the mores. Usually they provide
almost perfect illustrations of the moralism of internality,
conduct without religion or conduct without conscience. What
of such inner-directedness?

Most of these inner-directed people think of themselves as morally mature, even morally creative. Unfortunately they are all too often little more than moral odd sticks. When the group goes one way they turn their face in the other direction, feeling proud simply not to be part of the herd. All they are doing, however, is to revolt against the general conscience as the content of community mores. They are sometimes morally radical, showing their independence in the disdain of traditional morality. They are moral sophisticates. On the other hand, if most people take a progressive moral stance, they are just as likely to stand pat on the traditional, for they are determined not to be morally dictated to by anyone or by any society. Inner-directedness is usually individualism rather than mature morality. Inner-directedness apart from religion, apart from receptive relation to reality, amounts to sheer subjectivism. People so directed have no moral compass. Neither are they weather vanes; they simply never want to accept the weather.

A large city church working for church union, a high moral aim that seemed beyond dispute, took a final vote on constructive action. One of the church officers, a man of high repute, stood up to say, 'I believe that everybody will now probably vote for this measure. I have to admit that I myself have long been convinced that we ought to unite. But I am not going to vote for union. It would trouble me greatly if everyone had to act with the herd. Just to prove that there are independent thinkers and not merely puppets in this church I am going to vote against the measure.' His negative vote spoiled that feeling of final triumph when after years of study and discussion a divided group, having at last come to see the issue straight, was eager to take a progressive step, even to the point of unanimity. The vote would have been unanimous but for such an odd, inner-directed personality. For him, morality was to act contrary to the group, to be in the minority, even if in the wrong! His act was symbolic; or, shall we say, it represented the inner-directedness that pays attention to neither conscience nor reality. Such is the nature of the moralism of internality.

Some people who cannot go with external standards for morality, or with externally induced conduct, who do not fall prey to tutelage, principles, customs, conscience or inner-directedness, believe that true morality depends upon following a *reasonable* way of living. What of reason as a moral guide? Can genuine morality be built on man's reason? Is not reason a way of going beyond both merely external standards and internal feelings?

The simplest answer is this: there is no such thing as 'reason'. We may neither reify nor deify reason. Reason as such never tells us what is right or wrong. Reason is only man thinking. Reason is a person reasoning. How a man reasons depends centrally upon the person he is. Reason is man's reaching out to know the world around him or to obtain what he needs. Man reasons in order to understand and to satisfy all other needs. As life grows more and more complex, he uses reason in accordance with his evaluations in previous experience. The way a man evaluates the world and informs present experience in terms of his evaluation depends mostly upon the kind of person he decides to become. Reason in itself never comes equipped with some moral compass or Geiger counter. Reason is not a moral gyroscope for steering life's ship. Reason is the servant of self. Man can be helped by accepting evidence from experience and by directing his future value judgements in line with his interpreted experience, thus using reason, but the weighting of the evidence still depends on what the self seeks.

Using reason, man decides from past experience and in the light of the present situation what he wants and how to obtain it. If he seeks to promote or merely to protect the self he uses reason accordingly. In such a case the moral judgement becomes one of prudence, or, if beyond prudence, a shrewd weighing of issues with the maximum gratification of self in mind, however subtle may be the rationalization. The self may focus reason on how to obtain the maximum power, recognition, or gain. The goal of reason itself is not morality as such.

Some may strive honestly and patiently for the common good. They may call concerned living beyond self 'reasonable'. In such a case reason is used to serve not the self but the common good. The morality, nevertheless, comes not from reason, but from the person. Reason is only an instrument in the use of self. When the self is stressed, rationalization ensures; when the self gives way to Spirit, reason secures increasing moral light on man's problems. If the self has inner resources for seeking the common good, he can indeed make use of reason in the interest of true morality, but true morality does not spring from the brow of reason. Thus genuine morality cannot be built on reason alone. We can never stress enough the distortion of ethics that issued from Kant's false isolation of the use of reason for morality from both the whole self and from God. Reason is never dependably directive apart from right religion.

Those who use reason for the purpose of enlightened self-seeking, whether defensively or aggressively, arrive more at prudential moral maxims than at true morality. Their moral evaluations become mostly moral rationalizations. Those who genuinely strive for the common good, however, can use reason in the interest of morality, but they have the morality before they have the reason. They use reason to ensure wise action for the common good because they already are moral at heart. Those who appeal to reason, therefore, either use prudential maxims (whether as external grounds or as internal justifications) or, genuinely seeking the common good, merely use reason in the service of morality. Kant, as I have shown already, attributed to reason universal moral maxims that he derived straight out of his Christian, and in particular his Lutheran, heritage.

It is fine talk indeed, then, to say that morality comes from reason! Morality is a way of living, and reason is simply in the service of life. Morality, to be sure, needs the full use of reason, both critically and creatively. Reason is God's gift to man, to be accepted and used with all critical and creative care and thankfulness. But those who try to reduce the self to life by reason apart from the productive power of will and the nourishing flow of satisfying emotions, are for the most part starved selves who need to understand and to attain the full life of morality. For them, too, morality tends to be counterfeited into dry rules of conduct and wizened directives for living. Whoever turns mostly in on himself in moral conduct commits the grievous sin of moralism as internality and suffers the restrictive consequences of such false inwardness.

In this second section I have tried mostly to suggest the moralism of internality. I want the analysis to be more than a foil. We in the West often do not learn sufficiently from the negative, even though we are greatly guilty of it. Many people, often ignorantly, accept the dictates of conscience as what is finally sacred. The Catholic Church with great liberality has been stressing conscience as inviolable. Conscience can be man's last defence against institutionalism. Ebeling, a contemporary Protestant theologian, even makes conscience the main hermeneutical principal in a day when hermeneutics has been nearly central for theology. But we must be extremely careful on this point. Conscience must ever be in the context of the Christ as unconditional, universal love, engendering a creative, co-operative, open community. By itself trust in conscience is either the fruit of individualism and commits the moralism of internality, or it is more subtly the crime of deifying the context of an earthly community as the source of conscience rather than man's rightful use of conscience with the worship and service of the true God. Thus conscience can cut conduct off from the community, and even from reality.

Inner-directedness, on the other hand, is usually the sin of secularism, as conduct without religion, which is the very nature of moralism as it is centrally defined. Inner-directedness is even more obviously a cutting off from community as well as from reality. As a process of maturation in creatively freeing the self from the moralism or mores of the herd, such inner-directedness has its place, even as does man's freeing himself from God as an external authority. God is never releasingly real until man knows that his deepest self is of the nature of the eternal Spirit in such a way that to find reality is implicitly also to find freedom in and for the self. But most inner-directedness falls far short of the full, free response of self as spirit, to God as Spirit, within the freedom of love and the common, creative, personal Purpose which is the ground and goal of reality.

Finally, reason apart from right religion is patently moralism at its sophisticated, most immature stage. Not only is such use of reason the objective cutting off from the nourishing meaning and motivation of reality, but it is often the occasion for the kind of theological moralism which lets man feel superior about his moral autonomy and his honest reliance on reason. Many cannot genuinely grasp how by such thin reliance on reason they have truncated ethics and sinned in their sophisticated pride. Such reliance on reason is engendered by a combination of intellectual earnestness and moral ignorance and immaturity. We turn, then, from the moralism of internality to our third section, a constructive look at the Gospel for human conduct.

III

What, then, is morality if it is not a living by objective authority, not a matter of living under tutelage, principles or customs, and if it is not a question of being guided by some inner monitor, some inward power or ability like conscience, inner-directedness or reason? True morality may have need of any or all of these and does use them in the proper place and way, but is finally not to be equated with any of them.

Morality is based on man's releasing relation to reality. The Christian faith offers reality, releasing both freedom and fulfilment. Christian morality interprets reality as God whose purpose for man is that he might find fulfilment in freedom. God is the kind of love that bestows responsible freedom on man. Man is made to be free as God is free. God is free in love. Because God loves the world he has made it for freedom. Love, being a relation which requires freedom, sets the other free to be himself. Love cannot be forced; it must be won, it must be elicited, it must grow from within. Love grows only in the soil of freedom. God's Love is the sun; freedom the soil. But between the sun and the soil must be a real person with genuine responsibility. Both by nature and by choice, man must be free to be unfree, he must be free to refuse his freedom. In his freedom of choice man is, of course, free to deny his nature and thus to be unfree. He must be free to run from love, to flee from love, to fight love, to refuse love. Man must be free to be unfree and thus to be loveless. But finally man is made for fulfilment in love, and he can therefore be fully free only within the finding of love.

Morality is living according to one's deepest nature. Morality is to be free at the depths of one's spirit. Morality is to be rightly related to reality and to act accordingly within the freedom of reality. Christian morality is to be free 'unto God'. God has made us for himself, which means simply that he has made us for love. God is love and to be wholly for him is to find freedom in love. Man cannot manufacture, force or earn such freedom, for freedom is the gift of love. Only the lover is free by nature. Only the lover is free to be himself. Only the lover finds genuine self-being. Only the lover finds authentic existence, for only the lover is truly 'unto God' who is Love.

To be 'unto God' (*coram deo*) is to be unconditionally. It is to love without limit. Freedom is boundless love. To limit love is to limit freedom. To hem in love is to deny one's true existence; to hedge out love is to deny God. People become addled about freedom. Somehow they fail to understand that man is basically spirit. Man comes from God the Spirit, should live unto God the Spirit, and will return to God the Spirit. The Spirit is free because the Spirit is love. To deny freedom is to deny man's spiritual nature; to deny freedom is to refuse love. To reject love's freedom is to reject God. To reject God is to forfeit the Spirit.

Most men live in what they consider freedom. They want to do what they please, with no responsibility and no limitation on their actions. They want to share no burdens. Therefore they want no love, for love is responsible, pleases to do what is needed, limits and focuses its actions by its objects of concern for maximum being with, and, if need be, helping the loved ones, and willingly carries the burdens of others. Wanting to be free by rejecting love is seeking basically to be unfree by nature. It is to become slave to self. It is to serve desire. It is to be anxious in the face of others. It is to fear being 'put upon'. To seek irresponsible freedom is to find unfreedom. It is to be dissatisfied with one's deepest life, to court meaninglessness, to take flight from authentic existence.

The self, then, seeks an external master. Man clamours for the freedom of belonging. He wants to prove to himself that life is not meaningless and that he is doing right. Thus he chooses the unfreedom of service. He seeks to do right, he begs for tutelage, he hands over his freedom of desire for the sake of dependable duty. He hungers for law. He craves righteousness. He tries to do what is right for others by conforming; he escapes morality in the service of mores. But all his efforts leave him lonely, unsatisfied, anxious, for man cannot succeed in that way. He can never be totally right by either external or internal standards. In that way lies the thraldom of moralism. First of all, man finds he cannot keep the whole law of righteousness, whether monitored by people or by principles. He fails, feels guilty, spoils his own image of himself. Man craves to be free and cannot find freedom in terms of mores. He cannot find freedom within the moralisms of either externality or internality. Man is made not for mores or moralisms but for morality.

Nor is there escape for man within himself. His conscience keeps accusing or excusing him. He can never be sure that he has done right. Licking his moral wounds, he wonders and worries. He cannot correctly read his internal gyroscope; it shows a confused and frustrated mechanism. Reason refuses to be a final arbiter, and after conduct has been acted on according to reason, conscience still keeps burning and hurting. Man is restless still. He cannot find freedom either by doing as he pleases or by pleasing to do what is directed either externally or from within. Poor man, guilty man, sick man, lost man!

Morality is being free for God; it is being free for love. A distinguished psychiatrist, Clemens E. Benda, in *The Image of Love*, reveals that man in himself cannot love. He tries to love but finds himself at the centre. He forces himself to love and does only his dry duty. He presses after love and finds that he is mostly a hypocrite, making himself believe that he loves when all he is seeking is himself, his way, his success, his security, his satisfaction.

Man *can* love, however, because he is made for love. He cannot love in full genuineness except in God, for God is love and all love is of God. We love only because God first loves us. Trying to make God in our own image, we find him neither real nor helpful. When we magnify our sense of right and call God Lord, we encounter nothing but a taskmaster. We now fear our fear and dread God's wrath. Unless we are convinced that wrath is an eternal aspect of God we cannot believe in him because what we believe in is not so much God as our sense of duty made into God. We have created a god out of our own guilt, and God is not really there, only a sense of dread of him and a longing to placate him. We make up myths and doctrines to make him seem more real and to satisfy our need for him; but God never comes alive, for we do not worship the true God, the God of freedom, who is Love, who is Spirit.

When we open to love we open to God. God is neither a philosophy nor a system. God is the personal Spirit who is Love. He is the living God of nowhere and nothing, the God of the

Incarnate Love, the God of Spirit beyond objectification, the God of the living Word of the Book of God. God is the source of freedom. God is also the source of significance; hence for life to be meaningful it must be free in love. When we rightly relate ourselves to reality, the love of God is poured into our lives by the Holy Spirit. We become free unto God. We become able to love. We find that we are spirit and live in the Spirit. We are new creatures, new beings, new!

Freedom does not come without forgiveness. Forgiveness, to be sure, is not a final relation to God. Man is made not for right but for love, not for law but for good news. For this reason forgiveness is not at the centre of man's relation to God. The forgiveness of our sins is a prerequisite for right relation to God because we must repent and renounce our self-centredness, our trying to live by self-sufficiency and self-satisfaction. Our self-security must prove false. We must own up to the alienation in which we find ourselves, our estrangement from God. Because we have sinned by putting ourselves in the centre of life, we cannot become free without forgiveness.

Man cannot find love, consequently, without reconciliation. Man cannot know his spirit restored to the integrity that God gave him in creation apart from forgiveness. Only God can forgive at the depth of our being. Only God is ultimate and eternal. Of course, we must be willing to forgive without limit even as God forgives; otherwise we cannot be forgiven. Of course, we must be willing to live out our forgiveness in restoring and repairing where we have done wrong. Of course, being forgiven means joining all others in the common responsibility of putting things right before God and with one another.

Being forgiven results not in the freedom of servants, however, but in the freedom of sons. It is the forgiveness not for service, but for love. It is the restoration beyond obedience to friendship. We can have responsible freedom to go our own way; we can abuse our freedom. We can have responsible freedom to learn to obey. But no such responsible freedom in itself can attain true freedom. Authentic freedom is fully responsible but responsibility cannot achieve freedom. We become free indeed only within the reality of the Gospel. Then our very maturity becomes a matter of love's freedom. We are free no longer to serve God but to become co-workers with him as sons.

We need to be free from external moralism in order to learn mature morality. We need to be free to try living from within until we find out that such living is not authentic existence but false isolation from existence. To be free is to be freed by love from all external and internal moralisms in order that with perfect willingness and with understanding openness we may give our lives as free sons to God, who lets us keep them precisely in the new freedom of mature sonship. There is no full morality apart from such living in God, when we are right with reality, being the more ourselves the more we are in line with the very ground of our being and the very goal of our lives. Morality comes only with the free, understanding acceptance of the releasing reality of God's love for all men. Morality is the freedom of the spirit which is the willing, understanding living in love. It is finding our deepest nature precisely in the companionship of our Father God and the limitless community of our fellow men.

Morality is the free and full expression of one's nature in terms of love. It is being free spirits, free 'souls'. Genuine conduct is the spontaneous expression of maturity. It is living the life of love which works no ill to its neighbour and therefore fulfils the law. It is living the 'royal law' of love. Such morality does not bind the self; it releases the self. It frees the person. It lives the law not as law but as love. Love creates right relations whether of being, of doing, of helping, of freeing. Love never bypasses but fulfils the law by overflowing it. Love creates the right relations which are the nature of law. Morality has all the ease of doing what one pleases when one pleases to do the right. Love creates the motivation of spontaneous, even joyful concern. When morality rises to its full height of love, it enjoys the liberty of duty done without the task's being felt as duty. Morality is fullness of life through rightness of life. It is living the truth which is right relation to reality.

Morality dares, furthermore, freely to accept suffering. Suffering comes and is hard to take. The ordinary self suffers and rebels against suffering. To be moral is to dare to face suffering not only as part of life but as the pedagogical fire that cleanses, as the harsh pruning that results in growth. Suffering is still hard. It never becomes easy no matter how many years we live with it. But suffering is met by a different spirit when we

166

understand how God is using it for our good. We can accept our suffering, not gladly or easily, but with a free spirit and with gratitude for God's love. We can also face and help others to face the world's suffering. We can become free to care. We can learn how to be ready for other people's trouble. We can truly feel with them, understand them and often help with some aspect of their total situation. How welcome to a sufferer is a visit from a former sufferer who has been helped to love's freedom through his suffering.

Genuine morality is daring to love and to be loved. It is openness to others. To be free for love is to be free for entering into companionship with other lives, and above all with the Father of lives. It is to find meaning precisely in being of help. Christian morality means freedom to give out of love and to receive in love. The lesson is almost impossible to learn, for subtly we see our motives as better than they are. We are more driven than drawn, we more long to be recognized than to recognize the worth in others, we more want to be known than to know. Above all, when we are continually frustrated by suffering, spiritual realities tend not to be real to us. Our convictions fail to free us and to lift us beyond ourselves. We live dull, drab lives of doing the ordinary, and wistfully keep looking for some relief to come into our lives. We do not yet know that selves *as beings* have to endure the frustrations of falsity of relations, while only selves *as spirits* can be free.

We need the exhilaration of morality. This often comes through suffering. In one sense the worth of a man is known in his inhibitions. He must learn from them. Morality becomes known in struggle. It comes in the bearing of burdens. It comes in disappointment and defeat. But Christian morality lives beyond all these, finding partial fulfilment in the present and even more in hope. It comes as the fruit of the Spirit. What are better than love, joy, peace, patience and self-control? The Spirit is Love, and he who is in the Spirit bears the fruit of love. The joy of the Spirit is joy's freedom to live for others and to expect in hope. It is to know the reality of present being in the Spirit and therefore of at least beginning to walk in the Spirit. Such peace is not the absence of trouble nor the dearth of problems. It is knowing the right relation to reality whence come the perspective and power for the eventual facing and overcoming of troubles and problems. Patience, gentleness, self-control—*humanly* these fruits cannot be richly borne. They come from the source of significance in the Spirit.

The secret to morality is thus the Holy Spirit. The Holy Spirit is no pious phrase, no agent under the control of narrow Christian doctrine. The Holy Spirit is God's love for us, for all of us, reaching out to mature us in community. God sets us free from himself in order that in finding ourselves we may find the freedom that can be real and responsible only as it is in line with reality, with him who is Love and whose purpose for us all is to live and to be fulfilled in that Love.

The test of morality is the fruit of the Spirit. To be moral is to be free in love. It is to become mature in spirit. It is to trust God for himself and his purpose without ulterior motive. It is to love him for himself because he is Love and alone fully worthy of love. It is to enter freely into life and the lives of others. It is to will to do the right, not as duty or principle, nor as conscience or reason, but as a fellow-privilege within the great family of God.

For some, this celebration of Christian morality will remain mostly words unless it is buttressed with a more careful analysis of how it can be achieved. Let me offer some concrete illustrations to suggest the living meaningfulness of Christian morality. How can morality, Christian conduct, be appropriated? Let us approach this topic under three headings: the objective aspects of morality, their counterparts in man, and, finally, man's own part in Christian conduct. My assumption is that the Christian faith reveals, releases and relates reality. I beg no pardon at all for my faith; I offer no apologies, for I have honestly tried to find all the faults I can with it. The main fault I find is that it is too good to be true; but I have to live by faith and I have found no other that can equal Christian faith as truth. Therefore I accept it and rest in it. Declaring it comes from having seen and lived by it and having, indeed, found the greatest obstacle to it to be my own failure to live and trust it enough.

The first topic, the objective elements, we may consider under three subheads: (*a*) Christ, (*b*) the image of God, (*c*) the Christian community. Christ is God as we know him in human history, in a human being, particularly in Jesus as the Christ.

The final, objective authority and standard for Christian conduct is God; but God is not known generally in nature, history or experience so much or so definitively as he is known in the life which first revealed his universal Love and released its reality for human history. We need not repeat here that we are concerned not with the historic *Jesus* in the particular details of his life but with the historic *Christ* as a kind of life, a kind of love, a kind of spirit.

The God of nowhere and nothing, the living God beyond all objectification, finally beyond all human limits of thought and experience, can be known only directively in the model or pattern which reliably indicates the directions of universal love with no claim to finality in itself. Jesus lived such a life and pointed beyond himself to the perfection of the Father. For him no one was good, finally, except God, but he knew God to be Love, to be Father, to be Spirit, the inner reality and power of his own life. We have, therefore, in the life of Jesus and in the pattern of his teachings a seminal model which elicits universal, unconditional and eternal love. Such a pattern can judge us and direct us continually without ever becoming exhausted. It is unfulfillable even as it fulfils. It is final in its creative incompleteness. It is definite and definitive in its constant call for ever widening, ever deepening, ever heightening concern. Christ as model calls to action and indicates the nature of the action without ever spelling out the details or the means of action, in such a way as to leave the moral agent definitely directed yet also creatively free. Jesus lived ultimate concern concretely. To follow Jesus is to live ultimate concern under concrete circumstances. There can be no rational or historic, direct carry-over; yet what refusal to follow or flouting the moral demand means is clear to the willing moral agent.

The pattern calls for unconditional trust in God who is *for all* to help all to be their best; thus faithlessness as lack of trust is ruled out. The pattern calls, further, for love; therefore lovelessness is contrary to the pattern. The model of Christ calls for living this concern into creative, right relations among men. Therefore not only lack of trust and lack of love, but also lack of loyalty cut athwart the pattern for Christian conduct. The pattern calls, furthermore, for integrity since the Spirit is the Spirit of truth. The pattern calls for openness to all others;

therefore whatever creates barriers among men is avoidance or defiance of the pattern.

Concern calls for concrete giving, helping or leaving alone as the need may be, and therefore indifference and individualism are ruled out by the pattern. The pattern calls for the love of all which includes self-acceptance in creative concern and freedom within a community of creative responsibility and loyalty. The pattern is thus generally directive and yet existentially empty in calling for creative choice. It cannot become external tutelage, a matter of principles in terms of rules and regulations, or a sum of customs, and yet it can use all of these creatively when the person must face for himself or the group the concrete choices which the pattern only generally suggests.

The pattern, furthermore, has an objective impact on man in terms of the image of God. The image of God is no structure of the self, no substantive form within man. The image is the dynamic call of God on each man according to the pattern of Christ. The pattern has a flexible form, like a dressmaker's pattern, for each person. The image is no general reflection of God as universal love; it is Christ for and in each man. Jesus as the Christ is the image of the invisible God in particular because he lived concretely the Love of God. Jesus made the image of God real in history. God's universal love became particular in his life. But Jesus Christ is only one consummate, pioneering realization of reality in the reflection of the image. The general call of God received a particular form in a concrete life. But Christ as Incarnate Love is the universal Word for all men. All are made in the same image. For this reason the New Testament speaks of Christ being not only our 'clothing' but 'formed' in each man. It speaks of perfecting Christ in each man. Such use of the Bible is in line with its central nature and purpose. Here God and Christ, the Bible and Christian conduct come together.

The image, then, is not subjective but objective. It is God's presence for and in each man, first as his call; then, as accepted as his presence through that image. Morality, therefore, is not without both its historic and its personal standard, both of which are objective to man, even though in and for him. Only life lived in love according to the pattern of Christ is right relation to reality. Only such life finds that reality fully releases freedom for fulfilment. The image of God, to use more technical language, is God's presence in creation, calling each man and all men to himself in accordance with his own nature and his own purpose for man, and also God's presence in redemption, by both encounter and indwelling, that increasingly fulfils the reflection with reality. The image is love called for; the reality is love lived. God is love and has made us for himself; no man can escape that fact. God comes to each man with a pattern for him, his own image, that can be realized only through a process of understanding, acceptance and growth, in both encounter and indwelling. The pattern is the image of God, seen concretely in Jesus as the Christ as a kind of love, a kind of life, a kind of spirit, offered to each man through God's love, for God's love, to be realized finally only by the presence of that love.

The historic pattern and the personal pattern, the historic image and the personal image, can be creatively regulative and releasing only in relation to the Christian community. The pattern is always one of love, and love is ever a matter of communion. I say 'communion', for 'community' is a collective word while 'unity' is singular; but communion combines union with community, or the one and the many. Love is never mere unity nor mere community. Love is the reality of communion, the kind of community where creative cooperation in both sameness and diversity is released through the kind of unity which underlies it. The image of God has to be worked both into and out of man within Christian community. It has to be worked into man because the pattern is God's call in creation from beyond man for man. It is thus objective. But it also has to be worked out of man since man is so intrinsically made for it that his inner nature can be released and fulfilled only when its potentiality is actualized or realized concretely in human history. Such creative accepting and releasing of the image of God comes only contextually.

Contextuality is neither merely finding the revelational context in Christ and growing towards it as a community, as though the image were merely objective in historic terms, nor merely discovering an inner call for persons or community by means of some group dynamic for concrete growth in community. Rather, contextualism in Christian terms is the constant dialogue of encounter and interpenetration, of externality and internality, wherein the colour of the Christian conduct, so to speak, is taken into the resulting community both by its steady regard for Christ as the historic standard of creative cooperation within the trusting of God and the trusting of truth, and also by its insistent concern for the freedom of man's community in creation which God as love has faithfully bestowed upon man as man. As I shall point out later, there is no substitute for man's part in Christian conduct. Choice must be both genuine and creative. But no contextualism is Christian that reduces ethics to a standard of *koinonia* in terms of human good will, however good its kind of community and customs may be. The Christian community is basically a matter of acceptance of reality; secondarily it is living that reality in its own style. Christian community is primarily release in reality, the gift of God's presence, the creation of the Spirit; for this reason I have made it co-ordinate with the historic pattern of Christ and the objective personal call of God, the concrete image of God for and in each man, as the third objective precondition for understanding and living Christian conduct.

Before going on to discuss the objective counterpart in man of these preconditions, not now in terms of the objective realities man encounters, but as the indwelling or interpenetrating realities that are presupposed by man's own response, namely the work of the Holy Spirit, the personal agent, the prompter and the enabler of Christian conduct, I want to provide concrete illustrations to show the freedom of the Gospel for human conduct.

At a Senior Common Room at Oxford everyone except me smoked. I decided, however, to remain a non-smoker not only to please myself but to express the freedom Christian conduct provides beyond mores or moralism. I could see no reason why I should not be free to live my life without either judging others or without 'belonging' in that sense. Mores can separate in both ways. We should be beyond mores, if we know the reality, the power and the freedom of morality. Has not Christ set us free, and free in all these realms of mores as well as in the power of responsible, concerned morality?

As a non-smoker, however, I have smoked deliberately and for a purpose. In former days smokers on the seminary staff where I taught were the exception. One spring many years ago during a faculty retreat at Professor Philip Guiles' summer home, the question of smoking came up for more than joking; it was becoming almost an issue dividing us. At the height of the tension Dr Guiles took out a cigar and in effect almost pleaded, 'Nels, you don't smoke, but do show your Christian charity by joining me in a cigar.' I enjoyed that cigar. The divisiveness among us went up in smoke. That night Dr Guiles asked me to drive him home to his physician. We had had no idea that he had been in pain. In a matter of hours he learned at the hospital that he was suffering from cancer. How thankful I was that I had not stiffly spurned his friendly offer of a cigar, that my acceptance had paved the way for intimate conversation on the long drive home.

I have said little directly on matters of personal habits and nothing at all in my writing because, much as I loathe the power of evil habits over people, even more I hate the moralism that keeps them from accepting life in freedom and makes them frustrated judges of others. I have marvelled over the New Testament ethics which is not a puritanism of principles prescribing concrete prohibitions, but an inner freedom and an outgoing concern that put all matters of habit or custom in their place. The Apostle Paul averred that we must do everything unto the Lord and therefore whether we eat meat offered to idols or drink wine or not, we must eat and drink unto the Lord, remaining sensitive to our brother's conscience but not judging either him or ourselves. Paul believed in the freedom in which all things were pure in themselves and relative to the place, circumstance and spirit of their use.

Love is neither freedom from nor freedom for the law. The law is a matter of right relations, often creatively chosen, and therefore must be a matter of directives. Love, too, needs directives. But the directives are neither external duties nor internal burdens. Love seeks directives in order to grow as the plant seeks light. Love is not hemmed in by boundaries, but its boundless overflowing is ever controlled by directives. Love loses fear in finding concern, finding joy, finding fulfilment. Love knows law not as an enemy but as a guide. Love knows disciplines, neither as external nor as internal imposition on conduct, but as the concerned control and direction of motivation. Love finds; that is its very end. He who is still seeking and never finding is like the hovering hummingbird outside the flower. Love finds and enjoys life's nectar. Therefore love is the faithfulness of morality beyond moralism and mores.

We have examined the pattern for Christian conduct in Christ, the image which comes objectively from God's reality as a structural reflection, calling for life in the spirit and in love and the Christian community which comes to the moral agent as a creative, objective challenge to make love real under concrete circumstances. That love should make for freedom, for flexibility, and for responsible fellowship under God for the world. Let us now proceed to discuss the objective counterparts to man's encounter with God in Christ, in the image and in the Christian community under the general heading of the Holy Spirit, and under the three specific subtopics of the Holy Spirit as (a) active agent, (b) moral prompter, and (c) motivator or enabler of Christian conduct. The most important matter to keep in mind is that the Christian faith is a Gospel for conduct.

The Holy Spirit is probably the most neglected and misunderstood reality in the Christian Church today. He has dwindled to a pious term or even to a sign of spiritual oddity. What robust, active, normal person nowadays indulges in pietistic shibboleths like the 'Holy Spirit'? But, on the other hand, who can possibly understand the faith and not know the centrality of the Holy Spirit for Christian belief and life? Can one know the lives and thoughts of the Wesleys without recognizing the place of primacy of the Holy Spirit in their message? The love of God was for them, as with St Paul in the Letter to the Romans, 'poured into our hearts through the Holy Spirit which he gave us'. Christian life for them was, according to the model of Christ under God, a matter of walking in the Spirit, a matter of being perfected in the Spirit, a matter of assurance in the Spirit. Today we shall get nowhere (and certainly not to the living God who can be bound by no place or space) unless we recognize that Christian morality is attainable only on the conditions of the Holy Spirit.

The Holy Spirit, for our present purposes, we define as the personal agent who acts in human lives and history. There has been a period in theology when a false fear of not being scientific has silenced us. We have been guilty of scientism. We have in effect surrendered to a world view of closed, causal continuity according to which if God acted in life or history (and particularly in nature) he would be 'interfering'. But there is no such world as a total network of closed causes except as methodological presuppositions of a limited and limiting scientific method. There is, naturally, such a realm in general. If there were not, there could be no dependable prediction in science. But this realm of causal continuity, at most, is equal to the description of the physical world; and even here mechanical models have no longer the acceptance or degree of power for explanation that they used to hold. To charge that God interferes in his universe when he acts in it is like protesting that we interfere in the universe when our purposes and thoughts through our bodies redirect chains of causation, cause reversal or change in the flow of energy, and, indeed, initiate new chains of causation. God, however, is far more intimately and intensely related to his universe than we are to our bodies. Therefore to bow God out of his universe on the ground of the laws he has made is a quite inadmissible argument. To lose the faith that God works in his world and can work wonders there is to suffocate the Christian faith at its effective fullness.

Thus the Holy Spirit, knowing lives and history incomparably better than we do, works with all creation in line with his total purpose towards his final goal. All of nature and history are pedagogical. The Holy Spirit as such works only wherever he is understood and accepted as universal concern. The Spirit has also other functions in nature and history in general. In *The Christian Understanding of God* I have called these functions 'Spirit in general' and the 'Spirit of God'; but at inmost there is only one Spirit although he functions differently according to the needs for 'condescension', or for relating himself to the medium in which he is to work. Thus when anyone understands, accepts and lives the Holy Spirit so as to be effective for God in human history, the Holy Spirit works through his other functions in nature and history to prepare the best possible situation for the moral agent who is a new creature in Christ.

Nature and history are both open to God and on these preparatory levels he does 'manipulate'. He never manipulates the free spirit, of course, but nature and the unfree spirit are both subject to his working. The Holy Spirit thus opens doors for those who are ready to walk through them. Nations, peoples, and nature are far more subject to the work of the Spirit than we can imagine. Jesus did heal where there was faith. The more the moral agent is interpenetrated by the Holy Spirit the more power there is to change nature and history as these are relevant to the agent of faith. Wherever faith is a factor it is always a prerequisite for Christian conduct. Where more than one person is involved there is more than one faith to consider. God alone knows the complexities of nature and history, but I am convinced that our faith is the most relevant key to their possible change. Our faith, however, is not the active agent. The active agent is the Holy Spirit, who works in prevenient grace operatively before he works cooperatively. John Wesley, as few others, depended upon and invoked the prevenient grace of God. He knew that the Holy Spirit is the active agent in his world beyond our ever knowing.

The Holy Spirit is not only the active agent; he is also the prompter to Christian conduct. Alfred North Whitehead worked out an entire system of special providence through the primordial nature of God, wherein God alone sees the total pattern and therefore works in and with all moral agents for the greatest possible creativity and harmony. In Christian thought, too, the Holy Spirit is not only the convictor of sin; he is also the lure to good conduct and the provider of the best choices possible. The Holy Spirit has no prefabricated morality to offer. He respects the inviolability of those who seek to live genuinely for the common good. He respects all moral agents, of course, but until this point is reached the Spirit must deal with people pedagogically according to the needs dictated by their stage of development. Where there is understanding, acceptance and willing seeking of God's will for the total good, however, he creates continually situations for life that can be chosen by those open to him. Thus there is a dynamic plan of life for each agent, not prefabricated, but as a cybernetic series of creative moral choices.

The moral agent cannot know as the Holy Spirit knows and therefore he is free partly through ignorance. But the more he enters into and understands the way in which the Holy Spirit would have him walk, the more his freedom of choice begins to coincide with his freedom of life as he finds fulfilment by walking in the best way for the common good. Nor is that way merely an external road upon which he enters. It is, rather, partly a way that he himself helps create by his openness to the Spirit and by his concern for the world. The moral agent is thus not only prompted by the Spirit towards moral choices which the Holy Spirit as active agent has worked to prepare, but he is also guided into a genuine personal and creative choosing which changes the very nature of the world itself.

That the Holy Spirit does not work externally, we know. He works, rather, through co-inherence. The pattern for acceptance that he creates is worked from within the dimensions of depth. The objective opportunity ensues. The door opens; no one knows how. Some people call it coincidence, chance, circumstance. Those who live and walk in the Spirit, however, perceive a pattern. They are not surprised when the door begins to open. They walk in constant expectation and acceptance, and their way of appraising is not at all the way others see the same situation. The Spirit also prompts from within. It is as though we heard ourselves utter unknown or surprising realities. But besides producing patterns for situational acceptance and besides prompting to creative responses, the Holy Spirit enables us to carry through our Christian conduct. God speaks and we act. We do what seems humanly hard or impossible with an ease that astonishes others.

Most conduct is motivated by fear, by self-protective or self-promotive desire. Christian conduct means God's acting in love in the particular locus of our lives. We also have to respond as we shall find, but God makes our seeing possible through the forgiveness of our sins and the removal of the tensions which block our understanding. Our eyes cleansed, we behold new things.

The Spirit not only cleanses our eyes, however; he gives us eyes of faith. He provides new eyes for seeing. We perceive new choices and behold new creative paths before us. More than that, the Holy Spirit also provides enabling grace, co-operative grace. Some find certain moral battles impossible to win. They find their imagination stronger than their will. They discover that the harder they try the more dismally they fail. But if they throw their lives in faith on the Holy Spirit, *mirabile dictu*, they find their lives lifted to new possibilities.

Their seeing, their desiring, their cravings, their satisfactions have been radically altered.

Who of us has not really let go his striving, contemplating that God wants our best far more than we do, without finding not only a new power in his life to encounter God but a new power to lift, to strengthen, to inspire the total self? Christian conduct will amount to no more than fine words until we are lifted and let beyond the struggles of self up to the new plateau of the Holy Spirit's presence and power. The encounter without, then, becomes ever more demanding, but instead of being overcome by it we are released and encouraged as we find that the Spirit never makes demands that cannot be met in the Spirit. The Christ for us, the image of God for us, the community of Christian people with and for us become for us creative encounters when the Holy Spirit becomes the active agent, who, having opened doors outside us by his work in the objective situation, then enters within our finite selves, guiding and enabling, prompting and motivating our spirits.

The human response, moreover, must never be lacking. No Christian conduct is real without a free moral agent who decides responsibly for himself. God never substitutes himself for us. God never does for us what we can do and should do for ourselves. Instead he provides the opportunities that make for fuller freedom even on our part. If I should do my daughter's mathematics assignments (even if I could!) I should cramp her educational opportunities. I should be hampering her. But when I make it possible for her to attend college in order to learn I increase her range of freedom and responsibility. Similarly, God never does our homework but he does make it possible increasingly, if we let him, to go to school and to ever better schools. For our purposes I am going to suggest three of the many kinds of responses for which Christian conduct calls. The first is prayer; the second is study; the third is creative choice of action.

Since I have spent a good part of my life writing on prayer and the devotional life in the belief that they are crucial both to understanding the Christian faith and living the Christian life, I shall not here pursue the subject at any length. (My most careful statement of the topic may be found in *A Theology for Christian Prayer* published by the Methodist Board of Evangelism in the United States.) I have come to believe that prayer, too, like the other subjects we have considered, can be understood only in terms of the dual, dialectical relationship to God in terms of external and internal relations (or in terms of the encounter of God the Father in prayer and the indwelling of the Holy Spirit in our lives) and according to the pattern of the historic Christ, the Universal Word of Ultimate Concern, the Incarnate Love of human history. Prayer is the living with God that makes him become real to us in understanding and in acceptance. Prayer makes words become Word. Prayer can turn historic statements into present, personal realities. Prayer is the opening of one's life to the Spirit who can convict, convince, and even convert the self, who can make him into a new creature. Prayer is the life with God that makes human freedom real.

God comes neither as external nor as internal, but as the personal Purpose that he is and has as Love and Spirit, in such a way that identity of reality and will is achieved along with freedom of personal will and distinction of personal consciousness. We are both ourselves and more than ourselves. In becoming more than ourselves we also become more ourselves. Peter Taylor Forsyth was right in holding that the coincidence of the divine and the human in Jesus was a matter of being held together not as metaphysical substances but as the dynamic relations within the life of prayer. He who does not know prayer, he who does not understand prayer, he who does not use prayer in the spirit of Christ, in trust of God and concern for man, is neither modern nor wise. He has not yet caught up with the Gospel of God for human conduct, and still lives in the foolishness of self-striving which always in the end remains self-defeating.

Just as neither the objective Christ nor the indwelling Holy Spirit can ever take the place of man's moral response, even so prayer can never take the place of study. Study is not merely or mostly a formal, bookish pursuit of knowledge. It is, rather, taking thought to discover all the necessary facts which have bearing on moral decision. Some of this knowledge can be found in books. There is a deep, permanent need for more thoughtful and diligent study of moral issues in general. But most of the facts impinge on moral action too immediately and existentially for general analysis to be precisely helpful. Principles will often be highly relevant, but they usually conflict, and can practically never be applied directly. Life is too concrete and too complicated for that! Both general knowledge and the grasp of the specific aspects of a moral situation are necessary conditions for mature and effective moral choice. Some moral choices even evaporate upon fuller knowledge. Let me illustrate.

For some time I was a thorn in the flesh of the president of an institution where I taught. I was young and idealistic, with ears open to the longings and complaints around me. In this attitude of concern I learned that our theological seminary was paying substandard wages to the charwomen and to those who worked on the grounds. With vigour and virtue I protested and complained to the president. Finally in disgust or desperation he appointed me a temporary member of the small finance committee that decided the distribution of funds. I rejoiced over this victory and the opportunity ahead of me; but when confronted with all the facts I found that the seminary, during these days of the Depression, was financially desperate. We were paying our teaching staff far less than comparable graduate institutions. We were putting out only a few hundred dollars a year for new books. Buildings would crumble without repairs. Gladly would the committee increase the wages of the workers if I would take full responsibility for whatever else in the budget had to be cut out or pared down. Crushed and crestfallen, I beat a hasty retreat from committee membership. Never again did I criticize from such a lofty place of moral eminence. Facts at least taught me humility and respect for the integrity of others.

I should already have known better, for in my first parish after being graduated from seminary, I had in a sermon denounced 'capitalists' in scathing terms. One of my loyal deacons, a manufacturer of neckties, came to me after the service, profoundly disturbed. He was a deeply committed Christian. He took me to his home and opened his business account books. He explained that because he could not bear to compete with some hard-hearted companies that had lowered the wages of their employees even below subsistence level, he had been losing business steadily and had, in fact, just lost contracts to two of the leading national chain stores. He was paying something like eight dollars a week to his workers, most of them women, many of them widows with families to support. He offered to let me make the choice for him, of either lowering the wages or going bankrupt and out of business in a short time, leaving these women with no employment. Again in bewilderment I begged to be excused. Happily, Franklin Delano Roosevelt's minimum wage law came in time to save the business. I learned through this experience that to understand moral choice one must know both the concrete facts and the total context. Thereafter preaching became harder and scolding from the pulpit less triumphant. I began to read economics with ardour; I even contemplated taking a doctorate in the field. The more I read, the more clearly I saw that human nature, history and economics are intermingled, precluding any easy answer.

In the next chapter I shall confess some of the convictions that gripped me as I studied and learned the concrete, relevant facts in economics. Christian conduct is not mostly a matter of personal habits, although they are seriously a part of life, but neither is it right to centre Christian conduct in the objective conditions of public life alone. The two spheres, elusive and complicated as they are, with subjective attitudes playing a highly important role, belong together as expressions of a common life.

The Christian good, however—the love of God and man—involves discovering what is true and right in any situation. The pattern will not tell us this in some merely objective manner, nor will the Holy Spirit take away our privilege and responsibility of intelligent search for proper answers. Often it is necessary to curb our feelings in many matters, both personal and public, until we have availed ourselves of the God-given chance to find the truth in its fullest and most particular context. It may appear that the Fathers were mistaken in including Wisdom Literature in the Bible. It seems off-hand and prudential, but it is not! Fanaticism and sentimentalism feed on the half-truths that an inadequate viewing of the total picture suggests. Hate and intolerance spring not a little out of sheer ignorance. We tend to see nearly everything in stereotypes. In prayer we become willing and in study we become wise to break the stereotypes, to come closer to understanding the deeper and more complex problems, and to grow more sympathetic with those who labour under difficult moral decisions.

Prayer and study enable us to face the need for creative decision. No creative decision is merely human in nature nor do such decisions issue from moral negligence or sloppiness. The Holy Spirit will help us only when we are doing our responsible part in preparing for and making the decision. The old saying has it that creativity has more perspiration than inspiration. I doubt that; but without moral effort we have no right to depend on the Holy Spirit for help. The motivation of inspiration is a mostly unknown subject. There is creativity in all fields of human endeavour. The secular and the sacred come together in what is uniquely creative. Usually creativity comes to those who have cared much and worked hard, but no amount of care or hard work by themselves can achieve creativity.

My own experience shows a mixture of results. The parable of *The Sun and the Umbrella*, for instance, a small piece of writing that has received considerable attention, came to me after prayer early one morning in Oxford as an address for the Old Boys at Mansfield College without any specific preparation whatever or even the slightest inkling of what was going to come. Some of my most acceptable writing has come almost in a flood of inspiration. Then again, at other times when I have dedicated myself the most in utter abandonment of prayer and spiritual preparation, working at my typewriter almost with my face turned continually up to heaven, the results have been rightly depressing to objective critics. I have found that preparation in reading, long pondering of a subject, caring for the people for whom it is meant, and freely letting go while actually writing has produced the best results. But writing is only one kind of moral decision, a determining before God what one is to bring as truth to men. All creative work demands decision and even ordinary life has its moments for creative decision. Then a person must commit himself and take the consequences in faith.

May I be permitted one more personal illustration? When we moved to Tennessee, my wife and I, as Northerners, were ignorant of the racial situation from the inside and wondered just how we were to respond. I had visited in the South long enough to have come to love it and too long to think in terms of mere brittle principles, of mere do's and don't's. We decided that we would live in full, forthright witness for the transcendence of racial lines, but that we would try to act only according to the pace, the proportion and the power of the Holy Spirit. Friends advised us that it would be impossible to have our home open to Negro visitors, as we had been accustomed in New England, to speak frankly, to maintain full acceptance by both Negro and white communities and still keep living in the South. At least, they said, we would become nervous wrecks in trying to overcome such an ingrained and deeply-felt situation. But time proved that creative Christian decisions are possible. We never made a 'cause' of anything. We never told our neighbours what to do. When we first invited Negro friends to meals or entertained them overnight, both the Chancellor of the University and my colleagues warned me. I never felt defensive or over against, and with my wife and children kept praying and rejoicing. We met each situation as it came up, never pressing any issue, always willing to wait if waiting furthered good will, constantly trying to witness in word or deed when the time seemed right. To our joy we saw barriers go down. During my first lectureship Negroes attended public meetings for the first time in the history of Vanderbilt University. Soon other faculty members and church folk were opening their homes to Negro guests. A neighbouring Methodist college and the university Divinity School became integrated. Large churches and even one of the hotels served dinners to newly integrated groups such as the local United Nations Association and the American Association of University Women. All this was only a part of a great movement under the Holy Spirit. He was in charge to do or not to do. Where causism would have created wounds hard to heal, Love's concrete concern became constructively creative. Love's action both witnessed and healed.

I am personally convinced that in the final analysis there is no better approach to the race problem or to any other problem than the creative work of the Holy Spirit. Our wounded world needs it in all relationships of life. External and internal conditions, external opportunities and attitudinal acceptance, need to go together. Law and sanctions have their place, and perhaps even revolutionary force, but none of these can create full moral choices or mature social conditions. We can have a new age, however, if we dare to accept the full Christian Gospel for conduct. If we trust God enough, we can take up the world's heaviest burdens and tackle its thorniest problems with healing help and with inward joy. It is high time that the Gospel be applied precisely to conduct.

The objective Christ—God's universal Love Incarnate, working through our encounter of his image in us as God's objective purpose for us, and in confrontation with the Christian community for the world—needs the understanding and acceptance of the subjective Spirit (both objective to our spirits and yet co-inhering within them), the active agent who prompts to moral decision and provides the power for it. Both the objective Christ and the subjective Spirit call for our response through prayer, study and creative decision.

From a lifetime of trying I know, as far as I can know anything significant, that the Gospel for human conduct is true. It comes with reality, power and joy. I often feel with Nietzsche that God is less concerned with our sins than with the niggardly way we treat our hopes for the future. Ours is a heritage that calls for an effective history now for faith's future. That history cannot come until we dare to face the communal task of the Church and world history. Therefore it is to this critical topic that we turn for our concluding chapter. The illimitable, living God of nowhere and nothing, the ever dependable Love, whose Son came for all the world and for all conditions of men, is beginning even now to write a new chapter in his Book, not alone in ink and paper but in human conduct, both personal and communal. In such an understanding and with such expectation we turn to a consideration of the Church, communism or Christ-community.

Chapter V

The Church, Communism and Christ-community

THE living God of nowhere and nothing, we found, is beyond all objectification. He can be contained by no space and by no thing. In Jesus, the Son of God, however, we found a reliable indication, a true road sign, to God's nature and purpose. In a human life we have met a kind of love, a kind of spirit, whose Source and Significance must forever be beyond human imagining, but whose purpose gives us a dependable suggestion of who he is. Although no book, moreover, can ever describe the Life that God is, God keeps speaking on our level of understanding through his ever freshly written Book that must be creatively regulated and finally interpreted through the biblical pattern of God's unconditional, universal Love. Christian morality, too, centres in God's love, the free, creative responsible concern for each and all.

Personal goodness, we saw, is not enough. Our day in a new measure calls for public morality. Our age of crisscrossing institutions, public and private, with its technological sweep and its scientific-secular spirit, demands some understanding and control of the super-involved way in which modern society operates. God loves not only persons but peoples. God loves the world in all its complexity. He loves men as individuals and as groups, but he loves all unconditionally and forever. He loves them under all circumstances, simple or superlatively complicated, fragmented or too thickly interrelated. Confusing complexity tempts us to reduce reality to function or to substitute relevance for truth. But it is reality that functions; and for health and healing nothing is more relevant in the surviving last than truth itself. We turn our analysis for our last chapter to the meaning of the Christian faith for our collective life.

God has kindled a hot fire for freedom in our era. Suppressed people all over the world are rising, demanding a new age. The Christian Church, by the most basic definition of its own nature a free, open, inclusive community of creative concern, should meet this demand. Instead, the Church all too often and far too much has become acculturated and has aligned itself with the *status quo*, whereas in the meantime communism has been identifying itself the world over with the welfare of the struggling masses. Democracy, too, in spite of its very nature as the government of the people, by the people, for the people, has fallen captive to the capitalist system. What, then, can be done? How can intelligent, concerned people best work for a new day in the contemporary scene? Three institutions clamour for allegiance: the Church, capitalism and Marxist communism. How shall we relate ourselves to them?

I suggest that we cannot bypass the Church, as many seem inclined to do, because its ground and goal is the reality of the love of God for all. To bypass reality costs too much. But the Church must be shaken loose from its bondage to capitalist ideology in order to align itself with the aspirations of the people for a new day of freedom and fulfilment for all. Its fear of communism must not hinder its general identification with the people for their day of freedom. In particular, the Church must espouse the goal of economic democracy, be it called 'democratic socialism', 'social democracy', or by whatever name.

At the same time, by its very nature the Church must likewise refuse Marxist ideology, especially its intermediary means of class conflict and totalitarianism or dictatorship. It must, indeed, preserve from the capitalist era of world history whatever workable truth there is in political democracy. Above all, it must give the world the meaning and motivation that come from a faith that is rooted and grounded in God. The Church must, in other words, root its community in reality and truth, in God's complete, all-embracing concern for humanity in each and all of its members. Thus the Church, rather than having to choose between capitalism and communism must seek a kind of democracy—political, social and economic—that corrects and completes them both.

This critical, central issue for community in our day will form the focus of this chapter. We shall discuss the question of Christian community itself, both as demanded by its inherent nature and as it has become abused by acculturation; we shall consider the relation of the Christian faith and community to the other faiths and communities of the world; but the main issue will be the confrontation of Christianity and communism.

Marxists insist that no change can come about until the power structures are altered. For this reason, they hold, revolution in general, or at least conflict of power, political or economic, is almost always the only way to a new day. Since I believe in God, however, not only as Ultimate Concern but also as Ultimate Power, I believe also in spiritual reality as itself the final and most effective force. Only Jesus, perhaps Gandhi and a few rare spirits, have ever dared to trust spiritual power. But I am convinced that when the Church dares to accept its own nature as the inclusive community of concern and when an increasing number of believers work in education and in political life towards the goal of a total democracy, God will give us a new day where peace and plenty can bless and not threaten the world.

Many keen critics, however, believe that teaching trust in God is only another form of sanctioning the *status quo* and of holding back the day of the people. I am writing, however, on the premise that God's will is not only ultimate but can be immediately effective in human affairs, if we let God use our dedicated faith and freedom and allow the future to judge the result. I believe that we face a new era and that in order to usher it in, Christians should align themselves throughout with democracy as the day of the people: with political democracy as it has arisen during the age of capitalism and with economic democracy as it is arising during the age of communism; but that we must go beyond both in the quality of faith that directs and sustains them. The true Church should fully identify itself with genuine democracy, with freedom and faithfulness in fellowship based on the universal love of God for all.

God himself, I repeat, has kindled a fire of freedom for a new day. Neither political nor economic democracy can reach its own fruition or effectiveness apart from an authentic faith. Democracy must be born of, directed by, and sustained within a genuine and robust faith in the living God of nowhere and nothing, the universal Love that is both the word of Creation and the Word of Reconciliation. If the Church under God dares to live out its own faith independently and vigorously into social and political action, miraculously that faith will itself flourish anew. It is not first of all intellectual problems or doubts, however real and strong these be, that are killing faith today; the blame falls ever increasingly on the guilt of complicity in an evil social and political order.

There is no easy solution to the coming of a new day, but I hope that this chapter will provide at least general directives that can be effective: faith in God as Ultimate Concern; the Church as the free, open, inclusive community of that Concern; democracy as an implied form of communal life, generated and made viable by that Concern; the all-embracive nature of democracy, spiritually, politically, socially, educationally, economically and racially; religion for 'one world' in effective unity with no sacrifice of enriching variety; one world under law with creative opportunity for all, in whatever groups and regions might minister most fully to human need. Of the three primary contenders in our day: capitalism, Marxism and Christianity (including in its widest sense whatever is true, or truth yet to be discovered in other religions). Marxism and the Christian faith are both eschatological; they point primarily to the future for a verdict as to their reality. I am not undertaking an abstract discussion of these topics, but I am trying, rather, to face the future from within our concrete situation, with faith under God, and to recommend such measures for Church and society as seem not only desirable but also genuine options for political action.

We live in perilous times. The knowledge that our age is unique in that we can end our own existence not only as individuals but as a total civilization has driven our society into a nearly pathological state. Small wonder that many go in for unbridled pleasure 'while they can'. Others turn to crime. Still others fill our mental institutions in numbers as never before; and who knows how many more are living on the edge of their mental resources in our age of tension, where violence and world conflict characterize even what we call peace? Whatever easing of international tension and efforts to cope with the total destruction that threatens all we may encounter from time to time, such truces can come to a sudden end in a world so full of basic conflicts and so characterized by corruption that civilization itself is touched by death. Destruction can come suddenly and unexpectedly, or if not destruction, at least a flare-up of cold war tensions sufficient to pressure us close to insanity.

Meanwhile communism has been spreading throughout the world like a prairie fire. We may hold it back by American arms and economic enticements or threats, but the hidden veering towards communism in the minds and hearts of the people of Asia, Africa and South America appears to be moving fast towards a consummation. External conflicts or 'coups' are only breakouts of the steady inner growth. The rest of the world is trying to hold off the old corruption of the West. It observes that the West is sick unto death without apparent strength to recover. 'The American way of life', to us a slogan of pride, is for much of the world a contagion to be avoided. The free enterprise system of which we boast represents to them the reactionary tyranny of the have's over the have-not's—a tyranny which can be maintained away from home only behind military dictatorships or economic oligarchies propped up by American financing. Such a situation is at best insecure. We of the West may be destined increasingly to lose both influence and friends. Unless something happens!

The West is losing out also as far as religion is concerned. Christianity is rapidly being discredited as the religion of the West. Even in Europe it has been largely repudiated; in Sweden and to a great extent both in Britain and on the Continent. Such discrediting is also growing in America, especially among the young.

Some blame science for the death of Christian ideology. They claim that we can no longer believe the biblical myths and must face the truth of day. But such claims, as we have seen, are only partially true. Most people now understand that the Christian faith is not tied down to biblical mythology. If it were, human intelligence would have thrown out the Christian faith long ago. The Christian faith stands or falls, rather, not with its myths but with its view of God as Ultimate Concern and as Creative Spirit. Even these ultimates have deeper truths behind them. There are no real secular rivals to such faith. The Christian faith is being discredited, rather, as a practical way of life, whether personal or public. The Christian faith, in so far as it is dying, is doing so mostly by default. We are too ill to believe. We are too sick to have faith. We have no energy for great believing. We are too corrupt to dare to affirm the Christian view of God.

The Church is being discredited because after two thousand years of talking about power for peace, or the universal community of God's love, we are still threatened by war, even the war of annihilation. In addition, we are experiencing unheard-of race violence throughout the world. Even religious wars are not out of the question under some unexpected nightmare of human tension, beyond man's ordinary endurance. Whatever threat the future holds, we can be quite sure that the institutional Church has greatly failed mankind. Some may say, of course, that it is we who have failed the Church. We have failed Christianity. There is some truth to such a claim. The true Church cannot fail or fail the world, but we have made Christianity what it is, and our man-made Church has failed man disastrously. The Church as it is for the most part is not God's creation but man's. This acculturated Christianity, this depleted Church must die; and die it will if our true Christian faith, by whatever name, becomes genuinely operative in the world.

How can we choose a name that will communicate the meaning of the true Church of the Living God, especially in its task for public life, as distinct from the weak, warped and culture-bound Christian Church as it is today? The God who loves all made us all for himself in order that we might live in creative community. But for the fact that Marxism (which owes its power not a little to the part of the Jewish-Christian faith which it borrowed, truncated and distorted) has unrightfully been permitted the exclusive use of the term communism, we might meaningfully employ such a term as Christo-communism, restoring to it the dignity of those early believers who in their simplicity thought the Sermon on the Mount could be lived. Water will eventually remove labels from a pickle jar; perhaps time and holy water might succeed in clearing communism of its Marxist connotation. We cannot afford to wait that long.

Not the Church as a defunct institution, representing a dying, thoroughly corrupt *status quo*, but Christian community, Christ-community, based on God's full care for all is our hope. I assume that I may at least use 'Christ' and 'the Church' as realistic rather than as merely pious terms. My aim is to rehabilitate for proper usage such terms as Christ, communism and church. First, then, we turn to some elements of failure on the part of the institutional Church; then in the second main section to the way communism (as a general word beyond Marxism) represents the drive of the people for freedom and for a new day. The third section will deal with the nature of the true Christian community, the genuine Church itself, in relation to the concrete problems of the world which now confront us.

<h1 style="text-align:center">I</h1>

The Church that we have made is divided and divisive. Having split into Orthodox and Catholic churches, it proliferated Protestant denominations. Lately it has spawned innumerable sects. The Church as an institution has thus modelled for the world its own inherent fragmentization. We complain of our culture's splitting to pieces in education and in social life; the primary split is in our religion. We have been crumbling gradually and steadily at the very foundations of our civilization. The Church is to blame for much, if not most, of the West's divisiveness which we are exporting all over the world. The Church has not provided the West with a viable faith, whether on the intellectual or on the practical level of life.

It is tragic, for instance, to see Christian missionaries tearing continents to shreds by their sectarian mania. In the Philippines, I have been told, some sixty new sects have been introduced since the Second World War, each one denouncing the others almost as antichrist. What vicious pamphleteering! Some who are familiar with the South American scene say that the sects are quite as harmful there. This kind of 'Christianity', this kind of church, is a curse to the world, a shameful betrayal of peace for individuals and for the nations.

The currently much discussed ecumenical movement is a source of both encouragement and hope. Almost impossible progress seems at times nearly within reach. I have not only been privileged personally to participate in some of its vital phases but have had some of the happiest family celebrations in connection with ecumenical victories. Every day the cause of ecumenism is in my prayers. There have been significant unions taking place all over the world. None the less the going will be at best slow and frustrating. Ecumenism will not move far as long as some denominations are sectarian enough to insist on bishops (or no bishops) and others on infant (or adult) baptism as the normative mode. How preposterous in an important ecumenical negotiation for one large denomination to hold up discussion on the use of wine versus grape juice in the communion service! Some of the major American denominations cannot take even the first really positive steps towards union.

Seeing the world going to pieces, how can intelligent people put any hope in such small minded sectarian institutions as the Christian churches, which only help further to mangle the world by their divisiveness, and move together mostly only under dire threats from without? Without denying or belittling the good influence of the Church and the strong, positive part it plays in many respects, it is safe to say nevertheless that in the perspective of our total problem of today's worldwide revolution, the Church has proved to be utterly backward, a basic, almost irremediable social lag. If the Church cannot even reform itself in line with the will of God, how can it possibly help the world to become one constructive, cooperative, trusting whole?

Furthermore, the ecumenical movement in the World Council of Churches has slowed its progress by adopting for its central path a mythological formula that, as the world becomes increasingly educated, will become increasingly unacceptable. To expect the world, let alone Christians, to worship Jesus as God will prove hopeless for the long future. Once the ideological blindfold is removed and Christians see clearly how superstitious and mythologically paralysed they have been, they will come alive to seek a faith that is real and that can be believed intelligently and honestly. In the meantime millions repeat a creed they either do not believe or do not understand. By leaving out Jesus' humanity, the World Council has cut down its rightful claim to relevance and reality. The World Council, however, is a changing movement of history and is free to move from myth to Gospel. We dare not count any movement out until history itself proves its own point.

It may also be that no institution on earth has done more to damage man's moral sense than has the Christian Church. Its theologians have double-talked the Christian faith, often blaming their deviousness on the need for symbols and myths, until the believers are confused and upset. To be sure, most church folk and, for that matter, most ministers neither read nor think. But the few who do are the ones who count. No wonder some of them are recommending suicide for the Church. The current cry, 'Smash the Church!' is more than a slogan. It bespeaks a guilty state of mind. It is the sign of inner emptiness and weariness.

Words in the Church are often loosely used and slippery. Few expect even a theologian to say what he means. For example, in reviewing my book, *The Christian Faith,* Charles Clayton Morrison, then the editor of *The Christian Century,* wrote in obvious astonishment, 'here is a theologian who believes the Christian faith is *true*' (italics his). I know no ultimate more true than that of the Christian faith (not to be confused with traditionalistic Christianity); but I recognize also that such faith occupies a lonely theological position. A divided and divisive Church has split the world, undermined its unity at the very foundations, and introduced not a little the lying and dissembling spirit. Is the world helped or hurt by keeping such a Church alive?

The institutional Church, unfortunately, is far less Christian than it is the product of culture. In America, as a matter of fact, the Church makes no bones about this. The use of the national flag is one test. According to official usage, when the United States flag is placed on the right of the speaker and on his level, or on the right of the congregation if on their level, it occupies the place of honour; it stands for supreme loyalty to country. The Christian flag similarly stands for Christ and his rule over men. When this flag is placed on the left of the speaker on his level or on the left on the level of the congregation the meaning is unmistakable. There are notable exceptions where God is put in first place, but by actual symbolism we are generally Americans first and Christians only in the second place. Most American churches, judging from their flag usage, believe not in God and country but in Country and god.

The implication is God is all right if he is on our side. In any case, let us make sure of it by subordinating him beyond all doubt. God had better stay a means to our ends, for we will not change our ways to accord with his. We demonstrate this concrete and complete decision on the most effective level of human communication, in the very symbols that express our depth conscious. While the institutional Church calls itself Christian it is far more the expression of culture. The sanctification of the *status quo* is a leading function of the Church. We do not like to think so, but so it is.

We scarcely need mention how the Church has supported segregation where the problem has been most relevant. Not even a bishop could be admitted to a certain church when accompanied by his fellow bishop, a Negro. And unsegregated bishops' wives have landed in jail for trying to enter a restaurant together where segregation is the way of life. The Christian conscience has been at work, of course, and we are thankful for persons like Martin Luther King and places like Selma, Alabama, as symbols of a new Christian concern and concrete action. Even so, the Church has been stimulated also by non-Christian examples like Gandhi, or pushed by the fearsome pressure of communism in the background of the entire modern world. Government and business as well as the Church are now listening to justice, however reluctantly and grudgingly. If the Church had been Christian even at its stronger edges the race situation could not have developed in the very regions where people flock to church in the greatest numbers. What if, instead of following culture patterns the Church had listened to the voice of God's universal love in Christ?

Much the same can be said of property. The Church blesses 'free enterprise', which for the large part means the protection of the profits and privileges of the few. Under the shelter of such a system the strong use the law to oppress the weak. A poor man can get years of imprisonment for stealing a few cents; a rich man can literally get away with murder, especially if he holds organized political power or perhaps happens to be a prominent gangster. The Church mostly slumbers on, uncaring. I have written to a bishop inquiring about a concrete case of injustice and received a reply with rationalizations aplenty. A letter to a state governor brought forth more and other rationalizations.

The Christian faith holds that we belong to God and to one another, that all we are and have is for the common good. Each person is precious not only for himself but also as a member of the community for which he was created. Thus from the Christian viewpoint all motivations ought to be for the common good. Man ought to be indoctrinated, by the very way he lives and makes his living, to be concerned for others. What do we generally find, however, in the capitalist way of looking at life? A cynical disregard for others, where to beat them out is to be smart. Business is largely cut-throat unless it be the conspiracy of a few to hold up the rest by raising prices together.

Many business people I know are frank to admit that one cannot be a Christian in business. Others have had their moral sensitivity so dulled that they can coolly talk about unemployment as the 'labour pool' that is 'good for business', with no conscience about caring for these unemployed. For to care is 'socialism', the terrible Welfare State. (Socialism has indeed become a dirty word.) Only selfishness works. Take away private gain as the main motive and people will be lazy, lose initiative, and degenerate. I have heard such talk over and over again from the lips of prominent Christian laymen, and I know some clergymen who unfortunately subscribe to the same beliefs.

Democratic socialism is no cure-all, but it aims at least at an economic system controlled by the people for the common good under democratic processes. Capitalism, on the other hand, in practice puts stress on the clever head and the hard heart. One would think that the Church would say: So, we were mistaken about concern. It is not really practical. The cynical people are right and we should shut up shop. Let us nail up our doors; we are done. Far from it; Sunday after Sunday the voice from the pulpit abjures us to act out of love, out of concern for the common good, while blessing unashamedly a system of private property that makes mincemeat out of its Gospel. If it is true that one cannot be a Christian in this 'free' economic system, as God is real, why not change the system to accord with his will? The Church, with its privileged status, profiting often as a bystander is perhaps more sinful than those who are defending the system from within. These latter may be blind, but the Church cannot help seeing; therefore its sin remains.

It is no news that the Western world is disintegrating from corruption, rotten at its very core. No one can read the facts about crime and not be aghast. No one can know the facts of juvenile delinquency and not gasp; statistics change each year and always for the worse. No one can face the moral filth of our generation and not hold his nose for the insufferable stench. How can cinema stars publicly flout all moral decency and still find acceptance at the box office? It is with this culture that the Church is penetrated through and through. Ministers priding themselves on being up to date wade through the obscenities of books and plays and preach piously about 'real life'.

None the less a few intelligent believers truly care from the Christian perspective. They refuse to be identified with churchianity, even while they believe in the Church. They are a remnant of reality and a fragment of the better future. The Church will change or die; we shall repent or perish. God has shifted the gears of history and we must learn to drive at his new speed. What is the nature of the true Church, the Church of the Living God, the Christ-community that will replace the old? So far I have only impressionalistically pointed out a few flaws of the institutional Church in order to stress how deeply embedded in culture it is. No one can deny all the good the Church does and stands for. No one should belittle the importance of the faithful witness and work of multitudes of ministers and people. I believe we are about to experience radical changes towards a constructive understanding and acceptance of the Church. The reason I have resorted to the negative in beginning this chapter is to make clear that I am not mostly endorsing *status quo* churchism. I believe strongly in the true Church, the people of God's universal care and wisdom for the world; but only when the actual Church is deemed inadequate in the light of that true Church and only when we compare our lack of zeal and lagging confidence with the vigour of communism do we get perspective on the proper role of the Church today.

II

In contrast to the divisiveness and faint-heartedness of the Church, communism is on the march. It has the initiative. It is alive, expectant, on the move. Let us take an objective look at communism apart from Christian orientation or motivation, while not forgetting, of course, that communism as the will of the common people for a new day has been greatly stimulated by Christian ideology and enormously motivated by centuries of Christian concern.

Communism, in spite of internal difficulties, is the fastest spreading movement of history. Perhaps the closest parallel would be the spread of Islam as it quickly caught fire and fanned out like an uncontrolled blaze, reaching out from its native Arabia to conquer the Near East. Its tongues of flame encircled northern Africa; it singed the East towards India; it lusted for south-eastern Europe and even after its quick first burning was spent, lay smouldering like fire in a pile of leaves too wet to burn after the topmost dry ones have exploded into lively conflagration. It took the smashing force of Charles Martel, the Christian 'Hammer', to stamp out this fire in Spain.

The fire of communism, however, has spread even more remarkably. The least likely instrument, unindustrialized Russia, took over the movement that was focused by one man's technological analysis of human ills. The mystical Russians listened to the cold, scientific analysis of economic history. The masses, workers and serfs, were readying for freedom. Earlier there had already been desperate attempts in this direction, as when, for example, in 1905 the crew of the *Potemkin* had risked their lives for freedom in their mutiny against impossible living conditions. The Czar, Orthodoxy and Aristocracy were already despicable words, especially in combination. Oppressive privilege and murderous oppression hung over the land. Time was ripe for the revolt of the masses.

The eschatological idealism, the high expectations engendered by communism spoke so directly to the situation that the movement, once started, could not be stopped nor even contained. The communist movement was not mostly theory nor political machination, but a general, restless, inchoate urge of the people for a new and better day. Neither capitalist armies nor economic strangulation could daunt the new standard-bearers of the world's hope. The flame of the new day could not be quenched nor could it be kept from leaping beyond the walls of confinement.

To be sure, the drive towards the day of the people presented no pretty picture. The stubborn individualism of the kulaks had to be ruthlessly suppressed. The harsh power movement could not appropriate or incorporate the authentic longing for freedom on the part of the people of the land, those who worked the soil long and laboriously. To the movement of the people they appeared merely as opponents of the communal good.

Demonic power pulverized opposition, often with what seems to us gross injustice. But for the nation as a whole, communism met the need for a new day radically different from the former day of the privileged few. The masses would no longer exist for the few. The masses knew themselves to be people. This knowledge, this deep drive, kept pushing them on.

Communism called itself scientific, and with the prestige of science such a label helped. It was not science that conquered, however, but the will of the people to a new day. Science was a magic word. The people felt, deep down, the inevitability of truth in the movement. Marx's book, *Das Kapital*, was so learned as to bring the complaint at first that it was unreadable. Only after some time did the first small edition sell out, a handful of books in the midst of a huge world. Many languages were in it and much economic erudition. Marx was one of the first to grasp in depth the meaning of the sociology of knowledge. He also saw clearly the meaning and power of socialism in its broadest sense of economic necessity with the spiralling of economic production and the incoming of the universal technological age. To be sure, it was partly truth and partly faith in science, however naïve, that contributed to the advance of communism, but the real explosive in this fastest spreading movement of history was the will of the people for a new day. When we speak of communism as an ideology we often fail to feel the restless depths of the irrational will to a new day, the often fanatical faith of the people.

The leaders of the people committed totalitarianism. The new order had to be held together with whip and spur. The reins directing it cut deeply and painfully into the steed that pranced under the ruthless rider. Imposed loyalty tests kept most people out of the Party. The masses moved, but only the few were trusted to lead. Ugly is the history of oppression that preceded the new day. Ugly was the breaking of the yoke of oppression. Threatened both from within and from without, communism lacerated itself. But it spread, and it is still spreading.

The old order prophesied and promised the death of the new; communism would soon collapse from its own structural weaknesses; Russia could not last. Nevertheless the will of the people for a new day could not and cannot be stopped. Communism in the widest sense of the people's world, the day of all the people, is here to stay, just as democracy and general education are here to stay. All of these have their problems, but the faith of the people in them is power for survival.

The old order once also fought this dreaded movement of democracy, the egalitarian levelling movement of the masses that surely would have neither financial responsibility nor ruling wisdom. Only harm could come of it; only collapse of order and progress could come of it; only debasement of all values could come of it. Yet political democracy is here to stay and to grow because the people demand it. They cannot yet take full advantage of it; they keep abusing it. But it is here to stay in some form until it can become a reality. Democracy is like an infant born prematurely, not just here and there throughout the world but practically everywhere, an infant destined to live and mature. If I believe in God, if I believe in his people, I cannot but believe in democracy.

Live and mature, too, will economic democracy. People no longer will tolerate production basically for the few. People will not forever dread peace and plenty as meaning unemployment consequent to curtailed production of war goods and overproduction with its frustrations of marketing and storage. Theories, politics, even ideologies are unimportant in comparison to the facts of the situation and the rising worldwide unrest. People as yet cannot entirely see what is wrong, but they know something is amiss. Feelings are vague but they cannot be suppressed. People cannot be deluded much longer. The day of reckoning is here. The masses are rising; they cannot be kept forever from the promised land.

The people's movement in Russia leaped to the East. Through wars, to be sure; but it leaped and caught. It leaped into the most populous nation in the world and the most patient. There ready tinder burst into a flame that cannot be quenched. The masses of China have gladly responded to the news of the day of the people. Their politics is secondary. The theories and experiments change. People are hurt and flee. But the fires of the people's passion for a new day burn ever higher.

For years we listened to comfortable assurances that Russia would break economically in a few years because communism 'couldn't work'. Predictions were that its atheism would demoralize the masses and undermine the system. All we had to do was to wait. We have waited; but we have seen Russia become a mighty and proud new nation of the people with power enough to reach out to help and to influence the under-privileged of the world. Similarly we were assured that back-ward China must break under the new system. Shunned by the commercial nations of the world, People's China changed so fast that even Russia drew back in fright for itself. Through drought and trouble China kept on, isolated and forsaken, but even so, steadily on her way to becoming a great industrial nation. The masses are on the move. The masses of Chinese origin outside China are seeing this fact more and more clearly. Therefore communism is on the move throughout the rest of Asia. Now the flames of the people leap in Africa and South America.

Theories and actual political situations are changeable and secondary; the means are ugly and frightening. But the people will not be kept back. They are out to win. If the Church is to side with the people it cannot afford to label all this longing for which people are dying throughout the world as mere 'radical-ism', as 'atheistic communism', or as inimical to our established order. The ground swell is too heavy. The foundations are being shaken. The people, like sleeping giants, are rising to power against the arms and wealth of the few who have lived on them and kept oppressing them. The Christian believer should offer the people faith and guidance. Communism as the will of the people for a new day and the Christian faith as God's will for a new day must walk together. Otherwise com-munism will mean destruction; and Christianity, sterility. Christianity and communism come together in authentic social democracy, in a union of political and economic democracy built under God on the faith of the people in responsible freedom for all.

Communism in this sense is a worldwide movement of hope. The old order sends out its armies, but the war of the people demands new strategies. The old order tries bribing the nations of the world. 'Hold back the fire,' they cry. 'Join our fire brigade. Scorch the earth or build up walls, but hold back the movement of the people!' But the people march and march. The people will not be stopped. The beasts that tore apart the Christian martyrs were as nothing to today's bombs, but in both cases lives were and are freely given to causes worth dying for.

Let us remember, at this point, once more carefully to distinguish between Marxism and communism as a whole. Marxism is only a part of the communist ideology; one form in which it comes. Marxism is an intellectualism full of both important truths and dependable directives and falsehoods and faults. It is not Marxism that is winning the world. It is not atheism that is winning the world. It is not class conflict nor economic prescription that is winning the world. The people of the world move on faith, for faith is ultimate. The people move with hope, for hope is ultimate. Even the fullest ultimate, love, is not really lacking, for here is expressed concern for all people. Here is caring beyond individualism. Here is involvement in its total dimension. The people's march is the movement of hope because it is the movement of faith, because, in turn, it is the movement of total concern for mankind.

This faith is mixed, often hideously distorted, and generally partial even in its drive for all the masses. But it is a faith that history can change, that man need not be slave either to others or to the machine, that history is made for eventual full freedom and material plenty. The Christian forces cannot afford to stand athwart such faith. This faith also turns to hatred, hard repressions, cruel violence, prolonged totalitarianism in the name of eventual freedom. The Christian forces cannot afford to ally themselves with those evils, but must know how to direct the dynamism of this faith of the people to a constructive and cooperative building of a true democracy in line with history and centred in faith in God as the Ultimate Concern for all and for all conditions under which men must live.

The people of the world are on the move. Tramp, tramp, we hear their feet. Awakened from their nightmare of existence, the masses are moving. They cannot be stopped because they have seen the promised land. Too long have they suffered in the wilderness. Now they, too, are about to inherit the land of abundance, of general education and full culture. Machines can shorten their long working hours and give them a chance for life. Production can be plentiful out of resources of atom, of sun, of marine life, perhaps out of yet unheard-of resources. The people will not be denied. Theories, practices come and go, but the people march on.

Our own old order in self-defence tries to keep pace. No longer do butlers and dinner jackets stand as the symbols of real life. Culture is no longer so sharply built on invidious comparison and conspicuous display. To smoke cigars wrapped in hundred-dollar bills or to release thousands of live butterflies at costly coming-out parties are no longer signs of distinction. Rather, the old order hastens the attempt to provide government help for general education. The yeast is working. The rich and mighty see the handwriting on the wall and bend their efforts both sincerely and prudentially to satisfy the wants of our underprivileged. Who can know how much the peace of change in this direction has been quickened by the swift advance of communism all over the world?

The people's movement spreads into Negro life. The slaves of yesterday and the untouchables of today demand full freedom in the land of the free. They go to prison, they are shot, or they simply sit quietly to be spat upon and to be heaped with abuse. For the call of the people is the call of all races, a worldwide movement of hope that has reached every shore. Every continent now resounds with the marching feet of the people. Begun in Europe, spreading to Asia, now the movement surges with power in Africa and South America. Let it not be said that the people's movement will come last to the Anglo-American countries, that ours are the last bastions of privilege, the last homes of colonialism. Thank God the Christian forces have in part at least already joined vigorously in reappraising the racial situation and in opposing war and economic manipulation.

At the time of writing, we must hold the line in South-East Asia, we are told. We may destroy the people but we must hold the land, for 'freedom', our markets and privileged way of life are at stake. Our 'way of life' is threatened in Asia and in the last analysis throughout the world by the Asian hordes that march for freedom. Television newscasts show us these people of South-East Asia dying gallantly for their movement, for communism. Dying, they die for the new day. The people march and we pit arms and money against them. But the people's movement is not to be stopped. In the Western hemisphere, Cuba, isolated and cut off from her normal past, is persevering and unless crushed by the arms of reaction may become a demonstration of what a people can accomplish if allowed to be themselves. But if isolation and economic bleeding is not enough to halt the people's march, some of our old order would like to block it with bombs, threatening even nuclear war. Who knows how any solution will ever come? We may have to pass through an age of universal fascism, if the old order tries to control the world against the new day. We may have to wait long for the new day. No writer is wise to try to out-guess history, but my conviction is that eventually the people cannot be kept back. If the world stands, in some way the common people will find ways to attain the fuller and better life.

The people of America, the land of the people, the land of the free, will surely awaken to claim their own heritage. The American people are a great and a humane people, God's people. They will respect God's creation, receive it and use it creatively. And they, too, will march to freedom and to a new day. The reactionary cry, 'Better dead than Red' will give way to 'Better give and live'. Let us remember that the common man has had an honourable history in America. Freedom for the people was more than a slogan for the founding fathers. Democracy, the political power of the people, has grown here, has been cherished here. The Statue of Liberty represents our proud heritage: 'Give me your poor . . .'. Through most of our history we have traditionally sympathized with and supported the struggles for freedom of the peoples of the world against their oppressors. What generosity is in the American heart for the peoples of the world! Hoover's food for Europe during the First World War, the Marshall Plan, the Peace Corps, wheat for India—these have been often cynically dismissed as mere weapons in the cold war, but they were also prompted in large part by higher motives. Our love for America is all the deeper for its call for freedom, past and present. Even though vast numbers of our citizens, the misguided victims of power politics, press and pulpit, earnestly subscribe to a narrow, nationalistic loyalty that they confuse with patriotism, they generally do so sincerely in the very name of freedom.

Nor can we say that Franklin D. Roosevelt's New Deal, the graduated income tax, Social Security and its companion Medicare, are merely results of our fear of communism. The people here, too, experience the economic realities of history and long for a better day. We are, thank God, at least a mixed economy with important socialist aspects to our government. Not even a super-right radical like Goldwater dared repudiate in actual political action such products of socialism as Social Security.

The people of Britain, both by conviction and by circumstance are far ahead of us. So long as they are tied inextricably into the economic and political network of our conservative capitalist power-structure, however, the British people lack much freedom of choice. Britain also has the problem of a colonial heritage. But by God's help we can change our systems constructively and progressively from within, not bringing on a communist revolution by our reactionary fears and policies but rather evolving increasingly into the kind of democratic socialism that combines faith with freedom and creativity with responsibility. For the Christian faith to become conqueringly vital for our day is our deepest need. In the United States at the time of writing, our internal policy, the 'Great Society', motivated by whatever mixtures of incentives, seems generally strongly in line with the drive of the people and if early enough and strong enough can prevent radically destructive revolution even though a militarily dominated foreign policy seems sharply and bitterly to oppose that drive. History is ever open to change.

We cannot tell, of course, how much our history has been changed because it has been prodded by fear of communism; nor can we deny that 'socialism' and 'communism' to most Americans are swear words rather than words of hope. Certainly we cannot deny our government's heavy involvement with the reactionary forces of the world, trying to hold back communism. Instead of accepting the drive of the people and touching it all we can with freedom and faith, with personal dignity and responsibility, we have chosen to fight communism. But we ought to discriminate carefully who our real foe is. Communism as the drive of the people cannot be stopped. Atheistic, totalitarian Marxism *can* be stopped if we change our weapons. Why not fight totalitarianism and fear with freedom and concern for all? Why not challenge the drive of the people with Christ-community?

It should not be difficult to understand that rightist repression breeds leftist destruction. We can take the heart out of

Marxism by accepting the heart of the people's drive for a new day. The Christian West has far more and better to offer the people than has Marxism—full freedom under God, a democratic economic order under political democracy made vital and meaningful through extensive and intensive general education. We must have a committed education of revolutionary strength and depth to match the longing of the people for fulfilment and to relieve their dread of our technological Frankenstein monster.

Communism as the movement of the people for a better day has the initiative and will not to give up. Neither force nor finance can stop the people of the world. They will march past the proffered bribes and into the line of fire and die, but they will march, march, march. Communism offers the world hope and the people will march towards hope. Hope leads them to die for their cause by the hundreds and thousands. In vain would we draft our boys and sacrifice them to stop the people's march, for they will march until they win. Nothing short of the end of the world can stop the march of the people. It is conceivable that the beleaguered old order may commit universal homicide, total murder and suicide. In its pathological fear of the new day of the people it may help bring about the war of annihilation, whoever starts it, that cannot be ended; certainly our policy of exclusion and antagonism could drive China to frenzied action. Time is short. The people must win and save the world. It is our obligation to win the world at once for the people, for worldwide order, for peace, for plenty for all.

What will the Church do about all this? What will the Church do with what may be its final chance either for destruction or for a radically reoriented new age? How will Christianity act in this critical hour? How, in turn, will the people respond to Christianity if it fails its last chance to be human, to be concerned, to march with them? The Church has only one option, I believe, to identify itself with the people's movement as Christ-community in total concern for the world.

III

I propose that the Christian faith, in the sense of God's will for the total good of all and for the full, free and democratic use of all resources of the created world, expresses true communism.

Why give away this highly-charged, idealistic word to the Marxists? If the Church accept its own authentic faith it may yet be reborn to new strength and importance. If the Church deny its faith, it is no longer Christian and may have to die as an institution. Christianity can either live authentically as Christ-community or die a traitor to the people.

'Christ-community' must not be limited to an ingroup cliché, a pious term. Christ-community, on the contrary, is the conviction that since we all belong together as human beings under God we ought therefore to accept all things together and to use them for the common good. Christ-community cannot be atheistic because if the human is the most important in the creation we know, God, or the ultimate nature of reality, cannot be less than 'human' and must be *for* all that is truly human. God the creator is known by his best creation, the direction of its purpose. The highest in creation is the most fully human. The most fully human we see in the kind of inclusive, unconditional, creative concern which we encounter in Jesus as the Christ. Man is most fully and maturely human when he is most fully and rightly related to God. God is the eternal prototype, however much more and other he surely is, of humanity at its highest. Therefore Christ-community (true communism) is Christian in the full and real sense of that term. Marxism and Christianity as metaphysics, as ultimate faiths, are mortal enemies, but communism as the total common good and Christianity belong together. When such communism and true Christian faith come together we have Christ-community.

The Christian faith offers a radical standard of judgement. It points up with utmost clarity what is wrong with the individual, with society, with every arrangement of human life. Christ-community gives the fullest possible scope to the personal. Humanity as it should be consists of persons, persons who are rightly aligned with God, with nature, with each other and with themselves. Each person needs room for development. Each person needs freedom. Each person needs responsbiility. Each person needs creative adventure. Whatever is needed for such development Christ-community provides. If the need be private property for the fostering of initiative and responsibility, Christ-community must provide it without stint. Christ-community abhors totalitarian regimentation and rejects resolutely all 'statisms' or collectivisms that run rough-shod over individual liberties in their proper place. Or the need may be for privacy. The herd is not for true humanity. The personal flourishes not in tight rows of togetherness but as individual plants creatively placed, often in highly irregular patterns. Growth in intellectual and artistic realms, where ability and desire permit, demands freedom of place, freedom of time and freedom of material means.

The Christian faith as true communism places as much emphasis on each as on all. No person is ever a means to an end. No person is expendable for the general good. Christ-community is the guardian and releaser of what is most authentically personal, even in the individual sense. Denial of such opportunity of whatever kind is the denial and forfeiting of the universal faith, the forsaking of God the Creator and Ultimate Concern. Christ-community lights up the problems of the personal. Without this light, man either becomes selfish, pushing himself, grasping for himself, or he becomes selfless, running from self, refusing responsibility for decisions and events. Christ-community is freedom and faithfulness in fellowship based on the kind of love first fully revealed and made effective as life and light in Jesus Christ.

In the same way, Christ-community guards and promotes all creative minorities. The Spirit, deepest down, is our final unity; none the less the creative Spirit of Concern always differentiates. Spirit makes for unity with distinction. Therefore man lives in groups, in communities which differ from other groups. Difference is what makes life zestful. Distinctions are interesting; variations are exciting. In no field of human endeavour will there ever be plain sameness. Sameness wearies, sameness degrades, sameness by itself is the touch of death. Christ-community is the search for creative difference, the promotion of satisfying variation. What exciting use we could make of God's highly varied creation and of all the historic developments of difference if we genuinely lived Christ-community! Pluralism is a necessary ingredient of every good recipe for the life of humanity. No aspect of life can be excluded. Pluralism and relativism are part and parcel of life itself.

The Church's failure, however, has not been basically in

these respects. The Church has fallen conspicuously short of Christ-community not only in religion but with regard to its proper responsibility for nation and the economic order as well. Let us examine Christ-community's mandate to the Church in all these respects.

With regard to religion the traditionalistic Church is far from Christ-community. It falls short because it fails to be universal in nature. The Church of official Christianity is an esoteric, invidious ingroup. At heart the Church says, Let all people become Christians, and then we shall all have the same faith. It is imperialistic, arbitrarily at war with the rest of mankind. Often the ingroup use of Jesus Christ is downright embarrassing to a person of universal faith and concerns. Much missionary strategy, to be sure, is no longer a matter of proselytizing. Many Christian leaders now advocate encounter rather than conversion, or conversation rather than surrender. But the main cry is still some arbitrary confessional, 'Jesus is Lord'. The silent assumption is all too much, Let every knee bow to him. As we saw in chapter two, Jesus is made the one unique Son instead of the Son of God among all sons to be. If the fault is not in the Church, if not in official, dogmatic, culture-mired Christianity, then it is in the Christ of the Grand Myth rather than the Christ of the full Gospel. The universal God who is Creator and who wants to be 'saviour of all men' is left out of account.

The Church will gain a right to live authentically only if it becomes a truly universal faith. Then Christ will be final in the sense of living truth, the truth of life. In other words, the Christian faith has a right to propagate itself only in so far as it is genuinely human in the universal sense. It can be no arbitrary faith of an esoteric ingroup. Christianity as the true Church, Christianity as Christ-community, must obviously be faith, and a faith unashamed. Man must live by faith because of his finiteness, having to have an unprovable presupposition even to live; because of his sinfulness, needing forgiveness of sin in order not to rationalize; and because of his having to live in an unfinished cosmic process with the evidence now mixed and ambiguous and, above all, not yet in. Faith we must have and faith we shall need as long as this world lasts.

Faith can be universal in scope whenever it chooses to become the expression of universal truth. The basis for universal discussion cannot be ingroup assumptions. All men are part of creation. All men at their deepest level of humanity have common needs. All men are in a common situation of life and death. Our cultural anthropologists often fail to recognize and to stress what is obviously common to human life the world over and for all times. Basic circumstantial needs remain the same. Whatever most fully answers those needs constitutes the object of true faith. Creation reflects the work of the Creator. God himself is the Source of Significance and the Wellspring of Satisfaction. Man's needs can be known: the need to be one's true self and to develop in maturity, the need for meaning, for standards of right and wrong, for forgiveness, and for help in the fullest possible attainment of the purpose of life.

All religions must somehow deal with these needs. The Christian faith, as we saw in chapter one, offers Love, Spirit and the Personal as the ultimate answer to human needs. This offer must be made to other religions with full openness to their questions and their looking at the meanings and problems of life. Experience with non-Christian religious leaders throughout the world has taught me that Integrity and Concern are categories that can constitute the basis for ultimate inquiry. Integrity and Concern are also basic to true Christian faith. Therefore the Christian faith at its depth offers true candidates for a universal, objective inquiry into human needs and how to meet them within a configuration of faith. It offers them mostly, however, as a context for inquiry and for creative formulation rather than as the final dogmatic theology. The Christian faith can no longer take for granted either its primitive historic basis or its obviously crude and sometimes even immoral doctrinal development. Its Grand Myth and its demonic eschatologies must go. What remains is no minimum deposit but the courageous centre of life itself. Christianity must plunge into a thorough house-cleaning, boldly discarding the outmoded furniture of Jewish and Oriental myths and the shabby trappings of Greek and other philosophies that vitiate and distort the truth. Traditionalistic Christianity ought to be a forbidden export, for it sins against both truth and human dignity.

The Christian ultimates of Integrity and Concern, of Truth

and Love, of Holy, Creative Concern, however, will stand the most critical tests as context for ever fresh formulation of a universal faith. This faith may continue to be called Christian or it may receive a new, unprejudiced name. Christ never fights for his own name when it becomes a barrier to salvation. Perhaps if the Church gets another chance at life it may truly find itself by losing itself. In so doing it will both emulate and honour Christ. Christ-community demands a universal faith built on truth, the truth of genuine, basic human needs and the authentic answers reality holds for these needs.

The formulation of this universal faith cannot even be outlined here; it must, for that matter, be worked on by people of all faiths, not only by scholars, but by seers and saints as well as by all those who in full trust, at least in aim and inception, will rise to universal Concern wherein history itself becomes creative. The Eternal Spirit will visit his people with the gift of the truly needed faith when the world, as one, opens the main arteries of its heart and the main nerves to its brain to the seeking and the accepting of the genuine answers which even now are here if we want them. Only the whole world seeking can be the whole world finding. God is greater than the world, and his messengers stand ready to begin formulating together in Integrity and Concern the theology of the universal faith that will surely be as open-ended as it is reliably directive. We need and can have religion for one world, a body of faith with one head and one heart but with many members.

With regard to the nations of the world, Christ-community similarly involves one world of common responsibility with all needed regional and local distinctiveness and freedom. Christ-community means, in short, that one humanity must have world law and world government, the national sovereignty is not only outmoded but suicidal. People are now conscious of the need for one world in international and supranational relations if we are not to perish by our own hand, and loyalty to humanity requires implementing the answer to this need. Some say we are not ready for one world; the fact is that it is almost too late to make ready. Many of us have known that the United Nations is in need of overhauling. We were deeply grieved that no basic revision was made in 1955 when it was called for by our original agreement. We cannot afford merely to let the

United Nations go. We must not block nor undermine its effectiveness by tactical manœuvres that prevent its usefulness both as a sounding-board and as an agent of responsible action. We must, rather, work out a representative power structure with real power for the many nations to curb the giants.

For years Russia, with remarkable patience, watched the West use the United Nations for its purposes. We of the West must now be mature enough to be willing to live in a world of discussion and divided power rather than depend on mere armed force to impose our will. The Christian Church should act as a creative critic to this end by example, instruction and responsible shaping of public opinion. The ways to achieving genuine world government with effective control of all major sanctions under world law may be many, long and winding, but our urgency and creative response should match our cataclysmic danger.

The Church must furthermore choose between a culture-loaded 'Christianity' and a Christ-community that becomes its true, effective self. Too many churches, if not determinedly nationalistic rather than Christian, at least equate Christianity with nationalism. The Church supports the *status quo*. Most church people in the United States, at least, take for granted that God is on the side of America and free enterprise. In their heart of hearts many churchmen know that they are churchmen largely in order to support the *status quo*. The Church, then, reflects the life of the nation. To choose between church-Christianity and Christ-community is almost to choose between nationalism and the reality of one world. Such choice has high priority on our immediate agenda.

'Christianity' on this issue is already almost entirely dead, at least as far as vision and power to change the world radically are concerned. Its periodicals discuss world issues as though brainwashed by the Department of State. There is little prophecy in the land; therefore 'the people perish'. But can the church people be blamed when many of their leading theologians have been false prophets peddling the poison of secular social science? The world is already on the brink of destruction, helped along by the demonic rationalization of many a theological leader of 'Christianity'. Some Church leaders have even endorsed the annihilating use of the bomb. Genuine

Christian prophecy, rather, stands for love's freedom and faithfulness in fellowship under God which alone is Christ-community—God's will for all for the common good. Christian prophecy demands an immediate end of the cold war in its totality. We must trust God for the wisdom and power for a new start.

If the Christian Church is to keep its name in truth and be reborn rather than replaced altogether, it must trust God and his people, believing that we can attain responsible world government in such areas of the life of humanity and at such a pace as is now necessary. God never makes impossible demands. His message now, in summary, is quite clear for full conviction: Do away with the cold war attitude. Disarm with all possible dispatch. Effect such world government as can be had in terms of the enactment of requisite law and organs for needed sanction. Recognize all nations, from the People's Republic of China to the Republic of South Africa, and take them into and keep them within the framework of the United Nations. Revise that body drastically to make it both more pliable and more effective. Let the Assembly of all nations become the real power for world law and world government. Ensure that all power for world suicide be internationally owned, controlled and protected.

Christ-community stands for the right of all to live, to develop and to find maximum satisfaction. Rights and responsibilities can be enacted and progressively enforced. But even more important in the long run and prerequisite for effective world law are education and religion on a world scale and with world orientation and world motivation. Here is where the Church ought to come in. The Church should be the organ preparing for a united and co-operative humanity. The Church should be a universal leaven for a cooperative new day. In both education and worship the Church should promote the unity-with-diversity that is inherent in the Spirit of Concern, in Integrity and Love. The worship of the Church must be of the Eternal Creator and Compassion, or the World Judge and Transformer. Such worship always embraces worldship. Right action now calls for some effective measure of world law and world government, but the right action needs the effective disposition and carry-through of the good will. Power and wisdom to this end come from the worship of God, and worship of God can no longer be congruent with less concern for the world than that evinced by communism. The Church must rather join forces with the people's drive for a new day against Marxism, against capitalism and against reactionary Christianity.

Christianity deserves to live only if it can be born again into Christ-community, recognizing and embodying the realities and rights, the privileges and satisfactions of the one world which God is even now creating. For the Church to fail at this point would be suicidal, with the double shame of helping to hold the rope of disaster for the world itself. The time for debate has passed; the question has been called. The Church must now vote for its own death or life, casting its ballot for culture-Christianity or for Christ-community. If the Church sincerely chooses rebirth, let it carry on its religion and its education on a worldwide scale and with world orientation and world motivation.

Alas, small, defensive views of property stand in the way. We have too far divorced our faith from our economic order. The World Council of Churches has done creative work in this realm, but much more needs to be done concretely. Perhaps in this regard we in the United States are the least reconstructed. On this score we can easily be the blindest and hence the most dangerous nation in the world. What is the private or free enterprise of which we speak? Surely it is not *laissez-faire* capitalism. If ever such a thing existed in a defined nation, at least it does so no longer. Rather is our government up to its eyebrows in economics with distributive income tax, control of interest rates, tariff regulation, social security, federal housing, aid to education and Medicare. Nor do we merely have monopolistic corporation capitalism, as some like to think. We have this in a real measure, free enterprise in part and, surely, socialism in part.

By communism in the technical sense I mean complete common ownership of property in the sense of the means of production and full control of all processes of distribution. By socialism I mean the most effective regulation of all property, public and private, for the common good. Neither system can do without private control and responsibility in some sectors of life. Democratic socialism stands for the use of property for the common good, controlled by a genuinely elected civilian government under a constitution enunciating the rules for such common control with full and equal concern for individual persons and for all people in their collective capacity. Control can be delegated and relaxed in so far as the common good is genuinely served, in production, distribution or the processes of consumption by a creative opportunity for personal or group pioneering. As far as possible, all private power structures of whatever kind and in whatever guise should be done away. Britain and the United States have a mixed and indeed a mixed-up economy that finds the possibility of peace worrisome because of the heavy stake that private enterprise and corporation capitalism have in war production. In the United States even the farm economy has to be controlled and aided at heavy cost.

A look at Sweden reveals a mixed economy, too, with its blend of state capitalism or socialism, its co-operatives and its free enterprise. Whether we term its highly successful system socialism or regulated capitalism, for our purposes it serves as an illustration of something in the socio-political realm that approaches Christ-community as far as it can in an almost entirely secular way. The total Swedish community is involved. Labour and capital, managers and Church leaders, consumers and statesmen—all work together for the common good. Of course there is tension. There must be tension where there is creative diversity of interest. But the tension is generally productive of progressive government and economic welfare. Sweden stands out as a land that we could call Christ-community if only it had faith. With a vibrant faith Sweden's political freedom and maturity would not only have more meaning but would surely bring about sharp decline in its all too prevalent problems of alcoholism, juvenile delinquency, sex, divorce and suicide. Sweden's lack is a total meaning and motivation to enliven culture and to invigorate life.

Here, then, is the rub. Sweden knows no faith adequate to support its advanced educational, social and political attainment. Sweden has outgrown its Church life. Traditional Christianity there has indeed proved to be the opiate of the people. Where the Welfare State succeeds (at least so suggest the results in Britain and Sweden) religion takes to its death-bed. Sweden has exorcized the spectres of slums, poverty and the economic anxieties of illness and old age. In these respects it is far ahead of most of the rest of the world. But to work out a religion of universal faith based on universal human needs and the realities which can meet those needs yet remains a task undone. To match Sweden's social, political and educational achievements only a positive religion built not on ignorance or failure, but on enlightenment and attainment will do. The whole world potentially faces the same problem. How can we work it out? Faith, to have power, must be concrete; meaning, to be adequate for the common good, and motivation for action must have a universal basis in reality and truth. Somehow faith and truth must again court and wed.

Sweden, however, is a small country with a homogeneous culture, a far cry from the vast, amorphous, multi-cultured United States. Its situation is hardly directly relevant even for Britain. A socialistic system in larger countries, many say, 'would never work'. Yet Russia and China are still larger, both with their own problems of diversification of geography and culture. Communism, or even its precursory socialism, has worked amazingly for them; not only are these nations surviving and becoming increasingly industrialized in spite of having been shut off in large measure from the developed capitalist countries, but they are even reaching out to Egypt and India and to the far corners of the world. For that matter, in France and Germany and even in Britain the lines between socialism and capitalism have become heavily blurred. There is increasing recognition even on the part of British Conservatives that socialist features are not only necessary but here to stay.

Still, in the name of freedom, at the time of writing we are devastating South-East Asia for capitalism and many resent seeing Cuba succeed not only economically but also intellectually and morally, and against every possible obstacle placed in her way. What does the Church say! What does the Church do? But for a few rejected voices like that of Dr John Mackay, it is deaf and dumb, naïvely supine or even supportive of our own corrupt, crime-ridden status quo. We need to be ashamed of our record. Can it be that in the 'land of the free' we are in the situation of the Russian Church before the revolution: supporting the Czar, Aristocracy and Orthodoxy? Are we in the situation of the ecclesiastical backwardness and blindness of the Church at the time when the French Revolution could have become constructive? Shame on the American Church where-ever it has blindly supported our high-handed ways at home, in the Latin American countries, in South Vietnam and Cuba. Thank God for the change that seems to be coming over numerous leaders of the Church. Both on the race front and on the international front the National and the World Council of Churches, and special denominations in their top leadership, have been amazingly understanding in their analysis and astonishingly courageous in support of the movements of the people. Students, too, are now joining those who dare to stand for the fuller freedom of the people. All honour to all these leaders. Are they not hearing the people's cry for freedom? Do they not hear marching feet?

Christ-community is the march of man towards full liberty from tyranny and want. It is man's refusal to be choked and maimed by any *status quo* system. It is the spurning of colonial-ism. It is man's revolt against the upside-down fear of peace and plenty in our so-called affluent society. It is the deter-mination to release our full potential for all men. It is ending race discrimination and race hatred. It is facing the future unafraid. The Church either will accept the realities of human hope, of real faith in God, or when the new day of humanity dawns will die, and die rightly scorned and never mourned. I genuinely believe that God is bringing in his new day, and not even theologians or churches can hold back the dawn. God waits for the resolute few who dare to live, witness and work in line with his total purpose for all the people and peoples of the world.

Marxism is not the main question. Marxism is even now being superseded in many respects both in theory and in practice in several communist countries. Nor is totalitarianism the final question. We must never give in to that; but neither must we let fear of radical change prevent our working for the day of the people. The peoples of the world are marching for freedom. What change and turmoil in the nations of men; what seeking for peace and freedom! Flags of nations are secondary; so are flags of systems. What matters are the realities of concrete human communities. Perhaps some day we may even be able properly to use 'communism' as a general term to stand for our common humanity under God, with all things under him for the benefit of all, and with all possible faith and freedom. Such communism is Christ-community. Why even now surrender this word to Marxist thinking? Why dare we not claim it for faith and truth?

We are in a fluid state. Call the new whatever you will: regulated capitalism, democratic socialism, Christ-community. Work out whatever system (or most likely, systems) will best serve the varied cultural, geographic and historic backgrounds; but work out each system according to whatever way provides the maximum faith, the maximum freedom, the maximum initiative, the maximum security and the maximum openness to further growth. The final guide lines will have to be God's ultimate concern, the kind of world he has made, and a co-operative, creative, intelligent approach to all concrete possibilities of human life and for human use of nature. There will have to be great flexibility and willingness not to be doctrinaire in working out together the future of the world.

What of the Church? Let it renounce dogmatic Christianity and accept its true nature as the community of creative concern within the holy Love of God. High Hinduism in some respects is today closer to that community than is traditionalistic Christianity. For that matter, even historically, consider the same point of view in Ramanuja's *Vedarthasamgraha* or the position of Caiva Siddhanta. Read with care Kulandran's *Grace in Hinduism and Christianity*. How much in Vishnuite faith, too, can come into creative play! Even Sankara, India's crown of religious brilliance, according to Dean Murti of Benares University, held a transpersonal view of God that takes creation and history more seriously than most Western scholars have allowed.

How far we ourselves have to go who are brought up on a Jewish myth of creation, however beautiful. High Vedanta, as some of Radhakrishna's latest writings show, can join powerfully in the understanding and development of the meaning of the Ultimate Concern when all of us are willing to meet in the Spirit of the Ultimate Integrity. I have discussed these questions deeply with Mahayana Buddhists in Japan, and know how near we all can be to a new, creative day in religion if we care and dare. Let us not underestimate the Holy Spirit or make Christ into a wall instead of a door. Some of the new religions in Japan have so many common features with the great drives of need and practice in the West that in many respects we are walking down the same road. Need I mention new attitudes in Islam and a fuller understanding of its great history and its own modern problems? And is not Judaism a common forebear of many of us, rich at the very centre of our faith? Many modern Jewish leaders stand ready for the universal faith of love and truth. I do not foresee, nor do I wish to see, any one fully fashioned religion sweeping the world, nor any effective eclecticism, nor any livable pluralism based on mere relativism or negativity. Of course, no one can predict concrete history. But I believe that common to all religions are Ultimate Concern and a universal will to co-operate creatively in the finding, the living and the formulating of the faith of universal man.

There can be and must be main stress on the theology of the universal faith in this free, full and flexible sense. The living God of nowhere and nothing is great enough for any and all approaches to reality that are consistent with Integrity and Concern. God is faithful and the world must learn to trust his creative Love. Once it became effectively Incarnate in Jesus. God now wants to communize that love, to make it effective not only for persons but for communities, and not only for peoples but for the whole world. God the Son in Jesus longs to become God the people in Christ-community. God is the constituent reality of both Son and Church. Then let history not only decide but produce its own effective answer. Even Theravada Buddhism can see and come to accept that Concern which motivated the Buddha for the enlightenment of all mankind and which can pass from mere psychological meaningfulness into the fabric of reality where it belongs. This Concern alone explains adequately that great compassion of Gautama. In Christ-community we obtain the real Nirvana as true 'suchness', reality now with power intrinsically to change the world.

China, too, can rise with its great classics and with its

monotheism of love as taught by its great pre-Christian prophet, Mo Ti, to produce the fuller and freer, all-embracing faith of the one world of Christ-community. History can create a meaningful Christ who is *jen*, humanheartedness, in new dimensions of meaning and motivation. A study of the development of such words as the Chinese *jen* will show how creative history can be. We may be ready for the religion of one world of a height, depth and breadth as yet undreamed of, with sterling intellectual integrity and full relevance for all of life. Then let it come, by whatever name. The living God of nowhere and nothing is greater than all objectified names, and his Love cannot be contained nor confined within any concrete religion. God always outruns all his followers. We never can complain that we have nowhere to go in worshipping the God who creates ever new where's.

If the Christian Church is to be relevant for the future it must become fully open not only to creative faith but also to critical reason and to social relevance. Christ-community may be its form. Let the Church embrace it wholeheartedly and live. Let it stand for the universal Faith and the universal Truth because it lives within the unconditional Integrity and the Ultimate Concern. When it does so the Church will cast off its dead past in so far as it has been identified with corrupt cultures and confining economic systems or attitudes, to reach out instead for the full Gospel of God's overflowing goodness for a new world of creative leisure as well as meaningful work; for abundance of material means with a planned population; for automation for drudgery but ever sharpened intelligence for creative life; for freedom of full personal and social expression for all within an ever open-ended but reliably directive faith.

My aim in this book has been to present the central tenets of the Christian faith in terms of the greatest possible view of God, the open-ended faithfulness, the creative concern, who is ultimate and unconditional, far beyond all human imagination and incomprehensibly beyond earthly existence, who from our point of view must surely be called the God of nowhere and nothing, beyond all objectification of substance and process, yet who is the living Spirit of Love who penetrates all and can be trusted now and forever. This God cannot be confined to any self-disclosure in human history, whether of nature or purpose, for all earthly life and all human words fall forever short of correspondence; yet I believe that in the kind of universal love which Jesus lived and taught, and for which he died, we have a model, a pattern, a reliable direction which is itself capable of continuing expansion with all growth of human experience and knowledge.

We do not, then, worship the human or the historic, but *through* the human and the historic we find a way of walking for all men. God did not reveal himself for himself, but for us, in order that within our conditions and within our circumstances we might find a relevant way of relating ourselves to him according to a common pattern that must nevertheless be appropriated uniquely by every person. Thus God the Father, the eternal Spirit who is Love, became conclusively the Incarnate Love, the Word made flesh, that all men might according to the same pattern and the same power find their right relation to God and thereby discover both their true selves and their consummating yet ever creative relationship to their fellow men.

This pattern reveals a continuing deposit in the Bible, not woodenly for explicit doctrines or for external rules for conduct, but livingly for faith, as the believer, in line with the proper pattern for interpretation in Christ, and within the power of the Holy Spirit, appropriates for himself the meaning and motivation of the Bible, God's total love for the world. The Bible, then, is no defensive fixing of literal truths, no textbook for doctrines, but rather the ever fresh sourcebook for finding human experience illuminated by the universal Word. The finding is for faith in concern for the world. Thus use of the Bible gives reliable directives for the creative appropriation of the truth itself which is always in life for life. The Bible can therefore be regulative of all open-ended truth, of all creative finding.

God's total living speech to man must forever be written in the Book of God. The Bible never forecloses truth; it engenders, awakens and stimulates ever new truth in man's continued walking with God throughout ever new stretches of human history. But the pattern of God's universal Love, the Ultimate Concern, forever precedes man as he continues his weary march through the wilderness of his existence or his happier approach to and arrival at the promised land. The Bible is more than a book of the past for the present; it is the reliable roadsign, when rightly read, towards ever fresh adventures in the land of truth. God, the living reality, still speaks. The Bible as definitive truth in this creative sense thus becomes man's releasing reality. The Bible becomes Gospel.

In the same way man's morality needs the Gospel. Man is free only when he is fulfilled according to his nature in creation. Freedom of choice therefore cannot attain satisfaction apart from freedom of life. To become genuine man must go his own way until he discovers that God's way is best for him. God's way with man, however, makes him more, not less, free. Love sets men free. Life in the Spirit is freedom. Such a life of freedom in love, at whatever cost, produces the joy and peace which nothing else can give. Our age is revolting against external repression of life, against the choking of life's creative abundance. But it is running away from life to find it. To be sure, there is more life in libertinism than in Pharisaism, in fulsome sinning than in suffocating moralism. Jesus knew that and took account of the fact. But there is morality beyond moralism where concern is responsible and creative.

We have a pattern in the life of Christ, a corresponding image of God for each and all, and a community of common quest; we have the Holy Spirit, the active agent working in human history, prompting us to free action and providing the requisite power for it, and as human beings we have the privilege of prayer, the creative adventure of study and the stimulus of creative choice. These realities are ours for the putting them into practice. The world will be moved by incarnational reality, not by thought detached from life; for final truth is a matter of personal relations that can be consummated only by and in love. Never before in human history, I believe, was there such a strong chance for a creative morality of freedom if we dare pass beyond mores and moralism, both external and internal, into doing the will of God from the heart, which is more than obedience. We need a morality, not first of all of servanthood, but of sonship. With such freedom Christ can set us free.

Finally, we looked at our world in the light of the nature of the Church. The true nature of the Church is to be the universal, open, creative community of Ultimate Concern. Man was created to be fulfilled in such community. All discussion of the

Church in lesser terms has need and value, but the final questions are settled only in terms of the Church as expressing at inmost man's full nature according to God's purpose in creation. We need now to trust God for the realization of that community. The Church has its own indispensable place; the Church as the worshipping community is irreplaceable. But the nature of love is to be completely and continually concerned everywhere. Therefore the Church must seek to witness and work for the whole world, that it find such fulfilment in community. We have rejected both Marxism and capitalism, furthermore, believing that Christ-community through faith in God calls for its governmental correspondence in democratic socialism.

All systems, however, are only partial and will fail to satisfy. They are all subject to corruption and there is no health in any of them as such. We need a universal faith to sustain a one world ethos. We need a universal meaning and motivation, the religion for one world. Universal Love as Ultimate Reality, the Ultimate Concern, that respects all integrity of thought and seeking, that can provide identity of reality and motivation, with the ever enriching varieties of love's creation in nature and history, constitutes the unity that releases creativity, the identity that promotes variety. Such an Ultimate, too, is no stop-gap for knowledge and no palliative for human ills. We need faith for a positive new day that becomes more real even as men solve external problems by peace and plenty. Thus we have suggested that the God of nowhere and nothing, shown as universal love in the life and spirit of Jesus, the living God beyond substance and process, can still write his Book of Life in human history, setting us free for personal and communal life within the truth that calls continually for creative adventure.

Appendix

The Given for Christian Theology

THE topic of the given for Christian theology should be treated with utmost seriousness. It concerns the heart of our faith. More than that, since theology is involved, the topic is a matter of the reality and relevance of that faith. We have before us, then, no mere historical question in the factual sense, but the decision concerning both the meaning and the significance of our faith. In a world perplexed over the very question of meaning, have we a faith to offer that is both reliable for truth and effective for life?

Christian theology, dealing with faith, is by nature more decisional than informational. Faith is for commitment, not for speculation, and the theologian who ignores this fact is unworthy of his calling. Today, especially, mere academic shoptalk is treason to humanity. Such theological responsibility, however, does not entail the theologian's turning preacher. He may not neglect the scholarly aspect of his investigation for the sake of mission. Our topic accordingly calls for both an historical investigation and for an appraisal of the significance of what is given.

Is there, then, in the first place, anything given in the Christian faith? Does the Christian faith contain a definable body of truth for all times? Is there an ascertainable Christian core? Or is the Christian faith merely one movement in history among others? Can it change beyond all establishable continuity? Some theologians indeed write as though there were varieties of the Christian faith with no objective standard given for choice between them. Some find it difficult to say unequivocally that any position that claims to be Christian is not so in fact. They label as neo-fundamentalist any attempt to understand what is given in the faith.

To the question whether the Christian faith is merely a relative movement of human history the faith itself, at least, answers a resounding 'No.' The Hindu faith affirms

223

appropriately that whatever is born in history dies in history. All religions, it claims, are relative and subject to this invariable law of history. The Christian faith, quite oppositely, affirms that it is the revelation of God himself and of his eternal purpose. To be sure this revelation comes in 'the flesh' or in 'earthern vessels' but 'the exceeding glory' of it is its disclosure of the eternal Word of God. There can be no question at all as to the uncompromising denial by the Christian faith of the merely relative. At the centre of its own testimony it affirms that it is more than human history. For the Christian theologian to ignore this fact is tantamount to putting himself outside the Christian circle of faith.

The counter-claim may be made, of course, that the Christian faith is not true in fact and that, therefore, what is given in it is as much subject to reduction to human history as the distinctive content of any other movement. If such a counter-claim is accepted the Christian faith, of course, can be interpreted in terms of psychology, sociology, anthropology, or any other relevant branch of human learning. If the counter-claim could be proved true, however, we should no longer be dealing with our topic, the given for Christian theology, but rather with an investigation within general knowledge as to whether there is any necessary ideological continuity within the historic movement called the Christian faith. We should, in such a case, inquire into the given in the Christian faith much along the same line as we should do if we tried to ascertain whether Freudianism stands or falls with some relation to man's unconscious or whether Marxism remains itself with no reference to the means of production, the revolt of the proletariat or dialectical materialism. My own life-long investigation of the reality claim of the Christian faith has led me to the conclusion that as a faith (and some faith man chooses inescapably) the Christian claim to be true is the most adequate and valid I know. Both from within the Christian claim, therefore, and from within my own conviction and seeing, I accept today's topic as legitimately theological.

The Christian faith, then, by its very nature, must be theologically understood. It deals necessarily with ultimates, with the eternal, with the no matter what, with *theos*, with God. At its centre it is revelation, God's self-disclosure in Christ. It nevertheless cannot be understood apart from its Old Testament heritage, which deals insistently with God's will or purpose in creating. In the Old Testament the Creator who is also the living God of history calls a people and gives them his *torah*. Apart from the mighty acts of such a personal God of human history calling, disciplining and delivering his people there is no Christian faith. At this point there is no open choice, no option!

The Christian faith may originally have called mainly for a decision for or against the Kingdom of God at the behest of the prophetic teachings of Jesus; and such a decision may still be called for, as the given for Christian theology, in whatever way the Christian faith is then interpreted. Thus Rudolf Bultmann may feel that the whole supernatural world of the original Christian faith is mythological and as such impossible for modern man, and still maintain that the Christian faith is an ultimate calling for decision. He and those who generally follow his line of thought may then differ as to in what way the Kingdom is known or available with regard to Jesus' teaching or exemplifying it.

Such positions I take to exhibit a given for Christian theology in that they deal with ultimates in terms of Jesus Christ. At the same time they introduce a problematic or ambiguous element at whatever point the living God, the Creator God of human history, is existentialized to the effect that the personal God and the Father of Jesus, his special providence, and life after death are no longer taken in their main original meaning. The answer as to whether such positions contain an authentic given for Christian theology is not simple because the positions are theological and deal with the origin of the faith itself in the life and teaching of Jesus himself; they are then not merely psychological in general, or sociological, or merely relative in the sense of general movements in human history, but offer, rather, an ultimate for faith. At the same time the ultimate they offer may be so radically different from the original faith-claims as, in effect, almost directly to deny it. Are modern science and existentialist philosophy the real directors of such so-called Christian faith, which then while excising from the original material what was central to it, extrapolate from it and indeed make central to it an anthropological base which obviously must be ascertainable in any movement of human history.

Those who genuinely have given up the classical view of 'the more and other' of a God-centred faith, wherein nature and human history are distinguishable as creation from the creator, or our space-time world from God's eternity, have a right nevertheless to continue to call themselves Christians, not only legally but morally, since they deal with ultimates in terms of Jesus Christ, whether through what he exemplified or through what he taught. On the other hand, those who are convinced that the Christian faith stands or falls with the living God who actually, in whatever way, has created or does create, who works personally as providence in human history, and whose love and power remain through resurrection beyond human death, have also both the right and indeed the sacred obligation to deny the name of Christian to those who change the essential nature of the faith. With a change of ultimates the basic nature of what is given also alters. Even such a way out is not entirely satisfactory, however, since no clean line of demarcation between these two positions is generally available. Many interpreters, for instance, discard merely certain features of the original faith while keeping some core that is supposed not to be violated without destruction or denial of the original faith. Thus the charge of obscurantism can be made from various positions of a reconstituted faith while the charge of needless unbelief can also be hurled from differing theological contents. Unless there is, then, some way that we can establish fairly objectively a Christian given (whether or not it can then be accepted by modern man) we are always courting the temptation of the preacher who declared that if anyone believed more than he did he was superstitious, whereas if he believed less, he was an atheist!

The Christian faith, to continue, may deal with some new, final covenant, fulfilling the Old; even though the New Testament never explicitly mentions the New Israel, the Church may be conceived of as just that. In Christ came a new dispensation, 'a covenant based on better promises'. Or a new man replacing the old, the man of the Gospel rather than the man under law, may seem a way to differentiate the Christian faith from what was true before it and to delineate what is characteristic of it, the 'given' in the Christian faith. To be theological the stress must fall, of course, not on some new historic entity, or even on some new creature, but on what God has done, on God's new creation. There is no easy way to distinguish the many positions within the general category because they cross and overlap, albeit with differing presuppositions or theological content. Even Bultmann's 'authentic existence' as exemplified and made available in Jesus Christ falls in some ways under the present heading, but it will also fit under coming divisions of our analysis. There can be no question that in some sense there is a New Testament, according to the Christian faith, replacing the Old. The real question is as to the nature of the new and its relation, yes, even its continuity with the Old Testament.

Or the 'given' for Christian theology may be thought of as some new essence. Thus, for instance, Nygren's understanding of the Christian *Grundmotiv* as Agape constitutes an isolation, a *diastasis*, of the characteristically Christian. According to this view each religion depends upon a basic motif: Judaism on *nomos*; Greek religions, on *sophia*; the Hindu faith, on *karma*. Jesus, then, taught and lived Agape for the first time in human history, the God-centred, Christ-centred love of the New Testament that is completely and unconditionally outgoing, in creation and redemption, the heart of the Christian doctrines of the atonement and of justification by faith. To be sure, if Agape is defined closely enough in terms of its Hebrew background of transcendence and creation, from this point of view a strong case can be made for Nygren's claim that Agape is the distinctive and determinative motif of the Christian faith, distinguishing it from all other religions, as I discovered after several years of fighting Nygren's position. But if a more general understanding of the ultimacy of grace for salvation is allowed, one need read only Kulandran's *Grace in Christianity and Hinduism* to become aware of the limited nature of the claim. Further pursuit of the topic in the case of Amida Buddhism and of the religion of Mo Ti illustrates abundantly that what is particularly distinctive is the historic framework.

Nevertheless the total carrying out of the meaning of outgoing love that is in no way motivated by the object but solely by the nature of love itself, so that the object of love becomes merely a conditioning element for the application of love, is, to the best of my knowledge, distinctively Christian. If such a

227

distinctive motif in its wholeness is also determinative of the
Christian faith, we face a far more complex problem of relationships than as if it were cleanly and neatly a separate and
exclusive offering of the Christian faith. The question then
becomes not of a 'given' which finds close approximation in
other faiths, and which indeed for that matter, has no clear face
in any faith at all, including the Christian. What is then given
in the Christian faith becomes a profound problem, not only
of history but of human experience and understanding, seen in
their ultimate theological significance. We shall return to this
question, for it both supports and undermines the entire
approach to religion as having essences. Perhaps motifs are not
found by mere *Auseinandersetzung* but also by *Zusammensetzung*,
not only by diastasis by also by synthesis. Faith ever seems to
escape neat schematization!

Or the Christian faith may centre in God's actual presence in
the life of Christ. The given for the Christian faith, then,
strictly speaking, is Christ. To be sure, even to name such a
category is to encourage superficiality. The essence of the faith,
say, Agape, could have come both by the teaching of Jesus and
through his life. He who was the 'Son of God's love' naturally
also taught God's love. Thus there need be no genuine contradiction between the Gospel of Jesus and the Gospel about Jesus.
They are not contradictory but contrapletal. Or to go on, Paul
Tillich insists that Jesus is the 'unique, non-recurring *kairos*'
and in this sense irreplaceable. In the life of Jesus we find the
final synthesis of essence and existence. In Jesus we encounter a
life transparent to the Ground of Being, to the God of our lives.
And yet Tillich dismisses as nonsense and blasphemy the claim
of Incarnation as God's literal presence in the life of Jesus. We
have, then, in this instance an ascription of finality to Christ
which is clearly theological without, all the same, any acceptance of the classical content of the doctrine itself.

As in the case of Bultmann, so here; Tillich has the right to
call himself Christian and to feel that he offers us the truly
Christian 'given'. He approaches the ultimate in terms of
Christ and therefore clearly establishes a legitimate theological
position regarding the nature of the Christian faith. From the
point of view of his theological method, arising from an analysis
of what it means to be, or of being itself, Tillich arrives at an

amazingly Christian position which surely is based more on faith as heritage than on actual historical analysis. Therefore, not surprisingly, he can be both insistent on the centrality of Christ and free as to the specific historic life of Jesus.

On the other hand, those who begin with Incarnation as an authentic fact in history and find also the fullest general explanatory adequacy theologically, and that perhaps even in terms of truths in general, would have not only the right but the solemn duty to insist that Tillich has surrendered and forfeited the theologically 'given' for the Christian faith. There seems to me no escape from this dilemma apart from some objective establishing both what is given in the Christian faith historically and what can be considered generally true; for we can agree, perhaps on much of the content of the original faith as it was held by the disciples and still differ essentially as to what was the deeper significance of their faith in the light of what we now understand to be true.

There is, then, double danger in the approach to God through the life of Christ unless, in the first place, we avoid separating life and teaching, and unless also we acknowledge that the life of Christ can be used as a basis for our fullest knowledge of God without belief in literal Incarnation. Edgar Brightman, for instance, was wont and willing to say that in Jesus we have no metaphysical Incarnation but as much of the will and purpose of God as we can see in a human personality. Another instance of the same approach would be the treating of Christ as the new man in whose life we must share. Bultmann's authentic existence would to some extent come under this heading. Tillich's ultimacy of Jesus as the finite life that claimed no ultimacy but made the Cross become its intrinsic symbol also offers us from his basic assumptions life's deepest dimension of depth or its highest eschatological transcendence.

Many features of Lionel Thornton's use of Whitehead's process philosophy as background for his Christology put his position under this rubric. The finality of the Christ novelty, the fullness of time in this conclusive ingression into the process of human history, opens up for mankind a new relation to God which constitutes the 'given' theologically in the Christian faith. The fixed substantive categories for interpreting reality have in this instance been left behind, and God and man are conceived of as related to a cosmic process wherein God is continually a participant. Such an analysis breaks the old forms of classical approach and, so to speak, arrives at a semi-incarnation. The Christian faith, in any case, has a definite 'given' to offer that is final and saving, even though a new stress is now put on the creatively fulfilling. The historic uniqueness of Christ's Incarnation is kept inviolate, in one sense, while Incarnation becomes also God's generally intended relation to all men. Christ is both mediator and representative. In all these instances we have a claimed 'given' for Christian theology which while overlapping other positions puts the primary stress on Christ, but mostly as an example, as a unique human representative of man in his relation to God in some sense, but not on Incarnation in the full classical understanding of the term.

The 'given' for Christian theology, moreover, may be Christ as the Godman who brings into the world the eternal Logos. The Logos may be considered God's purpose embodied in human history as the fullness of time (involving an obvious overlapping with other positions). The Logos is what God meant and means with the world. The life of Jesus is the light of the world. The event of revelation affords God's fullest meaning with and for man. That same purpose God expressed in creation and in human history. That personal purpose alone focuses God's light for every creature who comes into the world. To all who receive him the Logos gives power to become sons of God, born not of blood, flesh or the will of man, but directly from God. The Logos in this sense is not full deity walking in a human form but the eternal and divine purpose for the world in which man may participate, and in which he must in order to be rightly and savingly related to God. Of that fullness we may all partake grace for grace.

Or the Logos may be exclusively identified with Jesus. Jesus is no general purpose, however divine, no general divinity of nature of which we, too, may partake, but a particular human personality whose ego was really eternally the pre-existent Jesus of Nazareth. Thus, at least in some moods, does Karl Barth severely limit Incarnation to the historic Christ, whatever be the details of the life of the historic Jesus. In this way the believers have their election, their sanctification and their eternal life 'in Christ'. What is given for Christian theology in this case is Christ as the revelation of God, who is his own method and message. Many interpreters, at least, skirt making the second person of the Trinity the ego of Jesus, with whatever secondary distinctions between person and personality. Some say outright that Jesus is God, with little concern for his human nature except as a mode of communication, in which case what is theologically given for the Christian faith is rather unambiguous, Jesus as God. He alone, as the Incarnate Son, is the meaning of the Christian faith. He is found in no other religion. The Christian faith is thus clearly and cleanly unique and final in its possession of a definitive 'given'.

There is no room here for appraisal of these positions except to own that they have much biblical and historical material on their side. The former, the general divinity of the Logos, is easier to establish biblically, especially with respect to the Johannine literature, while the second finds some real support in the Pauline corpus. Neither of them finds much support in the Synoptic Gospels. I personally cannot accept any one position as exclusively true to the New Testament. I cannot find for myself any option at all that can be nailed down and kept steady as the only 'given' in the Christian faith. Naturally to give my full reasons would require both extensive and intensive clarification and vindication of my claim. I want, instead, simply to propose as succinctly as I can my own understanding of what is 'given' in the Christian faith and in what way and in what measure it is so given.

The Christian faith must be seen against the background of the Old Testament, as having intrinsic to its very meaning, the living, personal God who is Creator of the world and who ultimately controls human history and destiny. The whole meaning of Jesus' life was to please the Father and to announce the coming of his Kingdom. But there are two more keys to his life and teachings in addition to God as personal. This God was love for both the just and the unjust, who gave to even the least deserving according to need, who sought the one lost sheep though the rest were safe, who broke through barriers of nation and of station, and who would judge all men according to their love for the least of human beings. A third component of Jesus' life and teaching was that God was Spirit, not to be worshipped in temples and mountains, or to be understood basically in terms of human wisdom, but to be worshipped rather in Spirit and in truth. The stress on Spirit may have come from Eastern sources into the Palestinian intellectual climate. Its origin may have been at one historically with whatever influenced Heraclitus and later Philo. Thus Western, especially Jewish, transcendence became complemented or even more contrapleted by Eastern immanence, 'the above' with 'the within'. These three categories, the personal, love and spirit, are original foundational aspects of the Christian faith that, whatever their origin, cannot be separated from the faith without a basic alteration of its nature.

Christian faith, of course, was founded not on categories but on a life which lived these truths into history. Jesus, I believe, became the Christ because within the finitudes and fallibilities of human life and history he actually came to know and to live the life of God. God is the personal Spirit who is Love. By his own sovereign initiative which yet respects human freedom God indwelt and clothed the life of Jesus, affording the fullest view of himself through this life and the truest meaning for all life and creation through the teachings of Jesus. Both this life as such and these three categories (the personal, love and spirit) became accepted as the apostolic witness in the Christian Scriptures. These categories, indeed, formed a trinity of understanding: God the eternal Father, the personal purpose, became centrally known in history through the Incarnate Son, God's love in and through Jesus, and can be known to the human community in its fullness only as the Holy Spirit. The ultimate love of God the Father, the Incarnate grace of our Lord Jesus Christ, and the fellowship of the Holy Spirit is a formula that approximates the needful understanding of God through all three of these categories: the personal, love and spirit.

God the Father is Creator. This personal category stands for the ultimate truth of personal Purpose; no process as organism or as cosmology can constitute the final category of transcendence. (Gordon Kaufman is currently working out theological distinctions along these lines.) The model may be deep or shallow, more or less opaque or transparent, but in the end there are no ultimate explanations that fall short of personal Purpose.

The 'how' is merely descriptive and not explanatory; only the 'why' will do for an ultimate. That may be the reason that mythology, as Mircea Eliade has shown, has always turned for the ultimate explanation of things that are to terms of the supernatural or to some miraculous understanding of original becomings. In this sense the true myth is not dead; it guards the reality of the sacred, or the ultimate mystery which underlies and sustains meaning. Original hydrogen molecules, astronomical cycles, or constant re-creation are attempts at explanation that aim at hiding from man his having to face the ultimate in terms of some faith judgement. They are as mythical as Hindu *kalpas* or Hebrew special creation. As a matter of fact they are pseudo-mythical because they attempt to couch the question of ultimates in terms of how's rather than why's. Man then fancies himself as having control of ultimates in terms of meaning that destroys the reverence for the sacred and undermines the ultimate power for meaning and morality. Faith in God the Creator can allow for the kind of secularism which results from God's having granted man and the world, for pedagogical purposes, freedom from himself in important areas of life. But the secularism that revolts against God the Creator in the final sense of power for becoming and of ultimate control denies the Christian faith at its heart.

The first and foundational category which is given for Christian theology, then, is God not as spiritual Personality but as personal Spirit, with the personal, or personal purpose not as the ultimate category but only as the transcendent reality of Spirit. God the Son is Incarnate Love. Jesus is Son of God, 'the Son of his love', because the personal purpose, the transcendent or ultimate meaning of Spirit, became received and lived in the life of Jesus to the conclusive climax that makes him the central way to God and the centre of human life and history. The Christian 'given', I believe, stands or falls with the testimony and the understanding that in the life and teachings of Jesus we meet the reality and meaning of God. God is Love but love is not God. God is the personal Spirit, not primarily ultimate meaning. He is not being but Love. He is not process but Love. Ernst Fuchs is right that love has the widest radius that being can have, but love also encompasses becoming and non-being. The cosmos, human history and human life are processes, but they are processes ultimately to be understood and to be under the control of Purpose, and a purpose that is Love.

God is Love then, but love is not God, the God is the personal Spirit who is Love. To make love alone ultimate is to detract from the fullness of the Christian understanding not only of reality but of personal relations. Nor is love a philosophy, except as the generator of one secondarily, but love is personal life and can therefore be seen primarily for what it is in a concrete life and only secondarily in teachings as directive to the life of love. Human language is deficient, but the Son of God as Incarnate Love is the best formula I know for the second Christian category. In this sense both summarily and suggestively Jesus is the Christ, our 'given' for Christian theology.

The 'given' for Christian theology, furthermore, includes God as Spirit. Whatever the origin of the understanding of this term and whatever its exact use in New Testament times, the Spirit stands for the ultimate unity which underlies all distinctions whether of the personal, of being, of becoming or of non-being. All identity ultimately roots back in the reality of God as Spirit. God is personal, God is love, God is spirit. God the Father is known through the Incarnate Love within the reality and power of the Holy Spirit. This trinity of ultimate reality became known and creative of a new age in Jesus as the Christ, through his life and his teachings and through the way his life and teachings became understood and used by the early Community. The Creator is thus Spirit, ever beyond all objectification as being. Tillich rightly refers to God as 'the Ground of Being'. But God, the Ground of Being, the Spirit Creator of all being, creates because he is love. Therefore he creates finite persons who *are* spirits, but *have* being, that they might learn love. To learn love man needs genuine self-being, genuine freedom; therefore man is put in an indirect relation to God within a pedagogical process where he can go his own partial, rebellious and faithless way until he discovers, through fear and frustration, indeed through all the opposite experiences from Love, that God's way, the way of love, is alone in accordance with man's deepest nature and alone can satisfy his deepest needs. God as Spirit thus creates what is not himself, giving it authentic self-being and genuine choice, while still remaining the underlying reality and inmost identity of all there is. God thus remains selfsame as Creator Spirit and yet also available for man in creation.

God also communicates as Spirit. He communicates by creating, as we have just indicated. He also communicates by working his mighty deeds in creation and history, by speaking to prophets and seers and by himself coming into the world as Son. God as Spirit remains selfsame in his aseity of purpose but communicates in different ways as Spirit. He communicates by maintaining creation in being without being personally present. He communicates on the level of general providence by working through man's conscience and through acts in history where there is power of purpose, as Spirit working towards ends preparing for his fuller communication. And he communicates as Spirit, in open Love, when the Son is disclosed and when the Spirit is received, wherein the ultimate distinction of person and community are established from within the eternal reality of God himself. Thus God as Spirit is the ultimate ground of the identity which as Love creates genuine distinctiveness in creation and in persons.

Such a view of the giveness of the Christian faith gives us a doctrinal basis which offers creative and vibrant solutions to the age-old problems of the relations of God to the world; of being, becoming, non-being and the need for all of these categories in their proper places; of change and suffering in God the changeless and the eternally victorious; of a transcendence which is no withdrawal from the world but which unconditionally generates concern unto the least and the last; of a love that produces the fruit of the Spirit in human conduct without moralism and legalism; of a permanent source of the kind of principles for conduct which are always subject to the concrete relativities of concrete contexts; of the relation to the world that is all for it and with it while also having both transcendent directives and motivation to offer it. All three New Testament categories are needed for the new day of theology and for the new understanding of God and the world which yet roots decisively in the givenness of the Christian faith itself. In this total sense, the meaning of Christ is final for faith while ever open to all new knowledge consistent with it.

More than that, therefore, such a given for Christian theology must remain faith, for it centres in what is more and other than our ordinary world. Its authority is unexceptionally revelation, requiring the acceptance of God's grace in committed and receiving faith. Nevertheless it is also truth, a truth of God, a hayatology, which has to be worked out not only over the ages but with and for all new knowledge and with and for every generation. Last year in the American Theological Society John Smith submitted a brilliant and searching paper on the relation between theology and philosophy. He gave us the option of accepting one dominant philosophy as do our Roman Catholic brethren in the case of St Thomas, of trying to get along without any as does Karl Barth, or of carrying on a vital dialogue with the best of contemporary theology. He appraised the strength and weaknesses of these positions. As a critic of his paper I then proposed a fourth approach, the developing a Christian philosophy out of the given in the Christian faith itself, namely out of the three basic categories of the New Testament which underlie the Christian doctrine of the Trinity. At this time I suggest once again that we cannot reduce the Christian faith to philosophy. Christian theology stands or falls with revelation. But the revelation of the nature of God is also the only proper categorical base for ultimate truth. Otherwise the Christian faith is itself a contradiction. A full doctrine of revelation invites our development of the New Testament categories.

To my surprise I found in non-Christian lands that some of their keen scholars are quick and ready to discuss ultimates in terms of such philosophical categories. When we offer our faith in a take-it-or-leave-it spirit on the basis of an authoritative revelation we generally meet neither understanding nor willingness to discuss. If we are now ourselves ready for what the Pope has called 'the wider ecumenism' we must surely be willing to speak in terms of categories that can awaken faith through understanding. If Christ is the truth, as I cannot help believing, we should find how best to commend him to non-Christians. St Paul well spoke of using all means to win outsiders and advocated appealing to them through their understanding. The Christian categories are wide and deep enough, as Calvin eloquently maintained, to accept humbly and enrichingly all truth from all quarters. The Christian faith does not need to be untrue to itself nor to propose syncretism in order to commend itself to the whole world. It need only learn to understand itself at its own inmost truth. But then it must be willing drastically to reformulate its entire theological heritage, doing away with false philosophical frameworks, especially those of being and more recently of process, to develop instead its own creative and consistent understanding of the personal, love and spirit as ultimate categories of truth. As this understanding is carried through a doctrinal revolution is sure to result! When we are ready for a biblical base in this deepest sense of what is consistently Christian the Christian faith will present its own case both for its own need and for all the religions of the world.

More than that, we need patiently to begin to create the categories for faith that relate the ultimate to science and to the social sciences. We must fulfil the how's of description by the meaningful why's of faith. Only thus shall we find, once again, a unified world view and a universal discourse for both knowledge and conduct. Surely the task is staggering and the workers are both few and far from adequate to the full task. Our hope, however, is in the Holy Spirit who once delivered what is given in Christ and who has been promised as our guide into all truth. Christian theology can be true to itself only by the discovery and acceptance of its own nature, but it cannot remain true to itself without being also the son who is servant to all the needs of the world. The fields, indeed, are white for the harvest. We pray now that the Lord of the harvest send effective labourers.